The
Economics
of the
Stock Market

New Directions in Management and Economics

... a series of authoritative books for more effective decision-making ...

The Economics
of the
Stock Market

RICHARD R. WEST
and
SEHA M. TINIÇ

PRAEGER PUBLISHERS
New York · Washington · London

PRAEGER PUBLISHERS
111 Fourth Avenue, New York, N.Y. 10003, U.S.A.
5, Cromwell Place, London SW7 2JL, England

Published in the United States of America in 1971
by Praeger Publishers, Inc.

© 1971 by Praeger Publishers, Inc.

Library of Congress Catalog Card Number: 78-149284

Printed in the United States of America

Contents

Preface

Books about the stock market are written for a variety of reasons, not the least of which is the expectation that their authors will garner income or fame. Harboring relatively few illusions, we doubt that the present volume will yield us much of either — although we would gladly accept both. We do hope, however, that it will prove useful to persons seeking a better understanding of the process of exchange in the stock market.

We have attempted to present an analysis that is readable yet sufficiently comprehensive to be of interest both to professionals engaged in various aspects of securities markets and to relative neophytes. Believing that it is important to concentrate on underlying economic functions and relationships rather than present institutional arrangements, we have generally eschewed mere description. Readers who desire a fuller discussion of these arrangements are referred to any of a large number of existing texts.

An attempt on our part to identify the sources of all or even most of the ideas in this book would be futile. However, we must acknowledge our gratitude to Harold Demsetz, George Stigler, Michael Mann, Eugene Fama, Seymour Smidt, Robert Doede, Victor Neiderhoffer, M. F. S. Osborne, and William Baxter, from whose thoughts and ideas we have drawn in abundance. We also thank William F. Sharpe for his review of the manuscript and suggestions for revisions. Our gratitude is extended to the Graduate School of Business and Public Administration, Cornell University, for providing a stimulating environment within which to work. Finally, we acknowledge a debt to Marjorie Markell for her patience and skill in typing numerous drafts of the manuscript.

The
Economics
of the
Stock Market

1 Introduction and Overview

This is a book about the market for corporate common stock. Unlike most books on the stock market, however, this one does not focus primarily on the forces influencing the supply of common shares or their demand by various investor groups. Nor is it particularly concerned with the analytical tools and techniques buyers and sellers of stocks use to evaluate the worth of individual securities or the composition of their portfolios. Rather, taking these various factors as given, the book focuses directly on the processes and institutions that are used to bring buyers and sellers of stock together to engage in exchange. In other words, it focuses on the *market* itself, seeking answers to questions such as the following:

What economic functions do brokers and dealers perform?
Why do some stocks trade on an exchange while others trade over the counter?
Why are there only two major stock exchanges?
What factors influence the size of the spread between bid and ask prices for a stock?
How do institutional investors influence the structure of the stock market?

This chapter presents some background materials and sets the stage for what follows. It begins with a brief discussion of the general role of markets in the enterprise system, followed by an equally brief examination of the functions performed by

1

securities markets in the enterprise system. Against this background some observations are made about the economic role
of the stock market. Finally, after discussing the tenor of recent
economic analysis of the equities market, the chapter summarizes this book's approach and scope.

The Primacy of Markets in the Enterprise System

One dictionary says that economics is the "science that deals
with the production, distribution, and consumption of wealth,
and with the various related problems of labor, finance, taxation, etc."[1] As a dictionary definition, this probably serves well
enough. We, however, prefer a simpler, more operational
definition of economics: the study — scientific or otherwise — of
the processes men use to determine how their limited resources
will be allocated among competing uses. This definition appeals
to us for a variety of reasons, but primarily because it puts the
emphasis squarely on the fundamental relationship between
economics and scarcity. In a world without scarcity there would
be no real need to make choices or "economize," and economics — not to mention economists — would lose much of its
raison d'être. Scarcity, unfortunately, appears to be one of the
few truly universal symptoms of human existence. It knows
no geographical boundaries and transcends the most fundamental differences in political and economic philosophies. It
is equally important to the East and the West, the democracies
and the dictatorships, and the haves and the have-nots. In the
final analysis, even the most affluent societies (to use Mr.
Galbraith's phrase) recognize that their resources, however
extensive, cannot meet all the demands that are made upon
them, that doing some things necessarily means not doing
others. Indeed, it sometimes appears that the affluent have a
greater appreciation for this basic fact of life than their poorer
neighbors.

The institutional arrangements that a society devises to cope
with the problems created by scarcity form the basis of its economic system. Much has been written about the functions of
economic systems, and, in practice, even more is asked of them.
A recent president of the American Economic Association
observed, for example, that "the list of things that one can
'demand' of an economic system is limited only by the human
imagination, itself a fairly outrageous thing."[2] Although this

statement clearly contains a good measure of hyperbole, the fact remains that a viable economic system must be able to perform simultaneously the complex tasks of ordering the society's priorities, organizing its production, and distributing its output. That is to say, it must be able to provide answers to the three basic questions posed by the problem of scarcity: (1) What goods will be produced? (2) How will they be produced? (3) For whom will they be produced?

Any exhaustive description of the economic systems of the world's nations would demonstrate that man has devised a plethora of particular institutional arrangements for providing answers to these questions. In a more basic sense, however, virtually all of these particular arrangements might be said to represent variations or combinations of two general types of economic systems: (1) those in which decisions about production, distribution, and consumption are made by some form of planning agency or committee and (2) those in which markets are expected to make such decisions. Ultimately, of course, both types rely on people to make decisions. The difference between them is that the "planned" economy's decisions are made by a relatively few individuals acting for the whole, while the market economy's decisions are the result of the seemingly uncoordinated efforts of individual citizens acting largely out of a desire for personal gain.

In a planned economy the principal economic decision-makers are typically government officials who have responsibility for directly establishing the economy's priorities, its production conditions, and so forth. In a market economy, on the other hand, the government's role is to establish a broad framework of legal and quasi-legal constraints and incentives within which the individual citizens make decisions about priorities and production conditions. They do so by making choices about the products they will buy, the jobs they will take, the businesses they will run, and the funds they will invest. Their choices are registered in the economy's marketplaces as demand and supply forces, which, taken together, provide the basic stimuli for economic activity.

The fact that the decisions of individual citizens are responsible for the pattern of economic activity in an enterprise economy does not always guarantee that society will be satisfied with the results of those decisions. When the private and public costs (or benefits) associated with economic activities diverge,

for example, the results that flow from the decisions of individuals primarily motivated by personal gain may be anathema to
the public at large. In such cases, it may be necessary for the
government to adjust the framework of constraints and incentives within which individuals are free to operate. Having
adjusted this framework, however, the government, which is
to say the citizens, must be prepared once again to let the rules
of the marketplace govern economic activities. For in the final
analysis it is the reliance on these rules, tempered by a framework of reasonable and evolving constraints, that distinguishes
the market-based economies from their planned counterparts.

Securities Markets in the Enterprise System

Among the decisions that an economy must make, few are
more important than those related to the allocation of its capital
resources. "Capital resources" means an economy's stock of
long-lived assets – its natural resources, plants and equipment,
houses, schools, and so forth. Because they are long-lived,
capital resources form an economic bridge between the present
and the future. If they are misallocated, an economy's growth
rate will be adversely affected and the nature of its expansion
will fail to reflect the desires of future generations of consumers.
Indeed, as William Baumol has so accurately observed, "unless
the flow of capital goods is responsive to the members of the
public, the community will only be able to exercise a very short
run and temporary control over the composition of output and
of its activities."[3]

In the final analysis, decisions concerning the allocation of
capital resources manifest themselves as supply and demand
conditions in the markets for real capital goods, i.e., the markets
for building materials, machine tools, and the like. Events in the
securities markets, however, have a profound influence on the
amount and the nature of the economy's investment in real
capital; for it is within the securities markets that the cost and
availability of investment funds are determined.

To the reader who may remember a basic economics text
with its discussion of an "agrarian soul" who engaged in
activities that simultaneously involved saving and investment,
the injection of a market for "money capital" may seem to add
unnecessary complications. On reflection, however, it should be
apparent that as the process of industrialization proceeds,

saving and investment are often (usually?) done by different individuals for different reasons.[4] Thus, if significant investment in real capital is to take place, there must be a mechanism, such as the securities markets, for collecting the money capital of savers and channeling it to the system's investors. Moreover, to insure that an efficient allocation of capital resources takes place, this mechanism must see to it that the lion's share of the economy's savings flow accrues to those industries, firms, and individuals with the most promising investment opportunities.

If we were to terminate the discussion at this point, the reader might easily conclude that the markets for outstanding securities — the secondary markets, as they are often called — have little to do with influencing the way in which an economy allocates its capital resources. Nothing, however, could be farther from the truth. For one thing, events in the secondary markets frequently provide the basis for the terms and conditions that will prevail in the new issue market. In the market for United States government securities, for example, the yields on outstanding issues typically provide a benchmark for the bidding on new issues. Beyond this, the secondary markets enhance the new issue markets in more direct ways. For example, by providing the means through which purchasers of new issues can monitor the value of their holding and, if they desire, liquidate them, the secondary markets augment the supply of funds available to purchase many new issues. More important, they make it possible for an economy to finance long-term investments in real goods with savings that are of a short-term nature. This point is perhaps best illustrated by considering what would occur if the financial claims issued by governments, firms, and individuals could not be traded in a secondary market. A firm that wanted to sell a bond issue to finance a twenty-year investment project, for example, would be forced to rely on the funds provided by individuals who wanted to make an irrevocable twenty-year commitment. Not surprisingly, such funds represent a relatively small portion of the total flow of savings at any time. If, on the other hand, there were a well-functioning secondary market in bonds, the firm in question might be able to draw on the funds of investors who intend to hold them for periods considerably shorter than twenty years. In short, the secondary markets make it possible for long-term investors to obtain the funds of savers who have no intention of committing their funds for the long term. And by so doing, they provide the economy with the opportunity to consider entirely new approaches to coping with the problems of scarcity.

By and large, the secondary securities markets in the United States are among the best in the world. Certain of the markets, however, are somewhat "thin," in the sense that not enough trading takes place to provide any real guideline for the establishment of trading conditions in the new issue market or to insure that buyers and sellers have adequate marketability of their securities. In the markets for corporate and state and local government bonds, for example, trading in outstanding securities takes place on a rather limited scale and thus price quotations are often "nominal."[5] Moreover, these quotations typically reflect the prices that can be obtained only for relatively small blocks of securities. Finally, the fact that in recent years many outstanding bonds have coupon rates significantly below prevailing market conditions means that their yields reflect variations in call protection, etc.[6]

The Corporate Sector and the Stock Market

It has been alleged that the business corporation is one of man's most significant organizational creations. Certainly, it is the central economic institution of all modern capitalistic societies. In the United States, for example, corporations account for more than half of the income originating in the private nonfarm sector of the economy.[7] They employ more than half of all workers in the private sector and own about half of the nation's plant and equipment.[8]

To finance their far-reaching activities, corporations require vast amounts of capital. Indeed, it was a desire to engage in economic activities requiring the accumulation of large sums that gave the corporate form much of its early stimulus in the United States. Mason, in his analysis of the corporation for the *International Encyclopedia of the Social Sciences*, notes that "the business area in which capital requirements first demanded the large corporate organization was railway transportation."[9] In contemporary America, of course, nearly all forms of enterprise are pursued on a scale that requires the pooling of the savings of relatively large numbers of individuals.

In most cases, the assets held by nonfinancial corporations are financed by a combination of debt and equity securities, the relative proportions of which differ greatly from firm to firm and from industry to industry. Less risky enterprises, such as public utilities, often obtain more than 50 per cent of their capital from debt sources. Manufacturing firms, in contrast, typically finance less than one-third of their assets by borrowing. As a whole, however, the nonmanufacturing corporations have for some time maintained a capital structure in which slightly less than two-thirds has been equity financing.[10] In other words, equity financing has been and continues to be the single most important source of financing for the corporate sector.

In the preceding section much was made of the fact that an economy cannot expect to remain efficient unless it allocates capital resources efficiently. Given the major role played by corporations in an enterprise economy, it follows that efficient capital allocation depends on whether corporations allocate capital efficiently; further, in view of the significant use of equity financing by corporations, a prerequisite to efficient real capital allocation would seem to be an efficient allocation of corporate equity funds.

In the United States, the primary source of information to corporations about the cost and availability of equity capital is the stock market. By establishing the terms and conditions on which firms can obtain equity capital, the stock market provides a basis for making relatively enlightened investment decisions. Firms whose stock prices are high in relation to their expected earnings are encouraged to obtain more equity capital. Those whose equity values are depressed, on the other hand, have less of an incentive to come to the market for additional funds.[11]

It is sometimes alleged that the arguments just presented, although they may hold true when companies "go to the market" to obtain equity capital, are less relevant when internally generated funds provide the primary basis for corporate investment activities. W. A. Lewis, for example, argues that the stock market's role in allocating equity capital is significantly reduced when firms acquire a large portion of their capital needs from the retention of earnings.[12] If this were true, it would have profound implications for economies like that of the United States, where internally generated funds form the single largest source of addition to the stock of equity capital.

Fortunately, however, there are several reasons to expect that this argument is not important. To begin with, there appears to be some recognition among corporate managers that decisions to reinvest earnings or pay them out to shareholders should be made primarily on the same basis as decisions to invest newly acquired equity, that is, on the grounds of whether or not the firm has profitable investment opportunities. In making this judgment, the returns from reinvestment must be compared with the cost of "retained earnings." Except for certain marginal differences related to the differential taxation of dividends and capital gains, this cost is roughly the same as that established for externally generated funds in the stock market.[13] In short, decisions concerning the reinvestment of funds, as well as decisions to obtain new, external funds, are dependent on cost factors established in the stock market.

In fairness, we should note that those who play down the importance of the stock market in the presence of the significant use of internally generated funds as a source of capital usually are aware of the arguments just presented. Lewis, for example, states that "in theory undistributed profits belong to the shareholders."[14] But he goes on to say that "there are of course considerable practical problems in maintaining adequate control of directors by shareholders."[15] There is, no doubt, some validity in this position. A recent study of capital expenditure policies of a large number of major American corporations concluded that there is a fairly systematic tendency for some firms to reinvest internally generated funds even when few really profitable investment opportunities exist.[16] By itself, this evidence would seem to support Lewis's contention; after all, why should the market be expected to influence the behavior of managers who fail to look to it for guidance when setting the terms under which internally generated funds should be reinvested? Fortunately for the enterprise system of economics, there is a relatively straightforward answer. If a corporation consistently reinvests funds when it should not, i.e., when the expected rate of return is less than the cost of the funds being reinvested, the value of its shares should fall in the market. As that occurs, the company should become increasingly attractive as a potential takeover candidate. In particular, it should become attractive to firms that have profitable investment opportunities but lack sufficient funds to pursue all of them. Somewhat paradoxically, by tendering for the shares of companies that reinvest funds unwisely, these corporate scavengers simultaneously meet their own needs for funds and help to assure that the economy's over-all capital allocation is efficient. In the absence of a market for shares they could not do this.

Thus, the stock market not only provides the information necessary for firms to make relatively enlightened investment decisions but also gives the economic system recourse against firms that fail to heed its counsel.

Earlier we stressed the importance of the role played by secondary markets in enabling long-term investment to be financed through short-term savings. Nowhere is this role better illustrated than in the stock market. The modern corporation is regarded as having a life of indefinite length. Thus, while the debt obligations of corporations normally have a term to maturity, their equity claims do not. Rather, they are viewed as a source of permanent capital for the firm. Since few if any investors truly intend to make an irrevocable commitment of their funds, the availability of a secondary market is an absolute prerequisite to the existence of a primary market in common stock.

Of course, from the vantage point of the individual investor, the primary day-to-day role of the stock market is seen in more practical terms. Gone is the concern for the economy's over-all allocation of capital and the relevance of the financing of long-term investments with short-term savings. What remains is the pragmatic concentration on the market as a vehicle for providing information about the value of investments and for making it possible to buy and sell as the urge arises.

Research on the Stock Market

Economists have long extolled the virtues of an efficiently operating stock market. Over the years, however, their interest in studying systematically the market's behavior has varied considerably. With the notable exception of Wesley Mitchell, economists rarely devoted their attention to the stock market's activities prior to the 1920's.[17] The great bull market of that era ushered in an interest in the market's behavior, which was sustained — indeed, intensified — by the ensuing crash and the Depression. As the 1930's progressed, however, the market lost much of its appeal, both as a vehicle for investing and as a subject for serious research. The advent of World War II did little to change this picture, so that by the end of the 1940's very few economists were devoting their energies to studying the stock market's activities. With the bull market of the 1950's and 1960's, economists have rediscovered the market as a fruitful area for research. How long their interest will last is a question for the future to answer, but at present there is every reason to believe that it will continue for many years to come.

During the pre–World War II period, most research on the stock market had a heavily descriptive content built around describing and documenting the conditions that create the need to issue securities, the legal and accounting attributes of various security types, and the mechanics of placing issues in the markets. Not surprisingly, the emphasis of this research closely resembled that of the so-called corporation finance field. Indeed, the following comment by Ezra Solomon concerning the "traditional" focus of the study of corporation finance applies equally to the approach of most stock market research conducted during the prewar period:

> It centers almost exclusively on the procurement of funds, widened of course to cover a discussion of the instruments, institutions, and practices through which funds are obtained and of the legal and accounting relationships between a company and its sources of funds.[18]

In retrospect, the early research on the markets seems to have lacked both comprehensiveness and rigor. Its conclusions were often, if not typically, based on the analysis of isolated examples or case studies rather than systematically assembled data. Formal hypothesis-testing was rarely incorporated into this research. In fact, the entire notion of making formal tests of theoretically sound hypotheses seems to have been unknown to many of those who studied the securities markets during these years. Professor James Lorie has argued, for example, that "rigor was frequently or even typically lacking because research was usually the product of persons familiar with the financial markets under investigation but not the canons of scientific inquiry."[19]

In the postwar period, both the focus of research and the methods of analysis have changed. With the growth of corporate internal financing and the rising importance of institutional investors, an increasing number of economists have turned their attention from investigating the rather episodic phases of new issue flotations to the study of the market for outstanding issues. In conducting research, the current generation of analysts has turned to the development of model-building and the formal testing of rigorously stated hypotheses. To avoid the casual empiricizing that characterized so much of the prewar research on the market, they have spent lavishly for the collection of data and have generally restricted their conclusions to inferences that can be drawn from the results of multivariant statistical analyses performed on high-speed computers.

All this, of course, is generally praiseworthy. In some ways, however, the postwar generation of stock market economists has been hardly more helpful than its earlier counterparts in improving our basic understanding of how the stock market operates. To be sure, they have both expanded our knowledge of the techniques of security analysis and produced a rich new literature on portfolio selection. In addition, their efforts have yielded considerable information about the behavior of stock market prices. After two decades of serious scholarship, however, we still know very little about the factors that determine how the market will be organized, how institutional investors influence the market's behavior, what role automation can play in the market's future, and so forth. Put somewhat differently, we are still rather ignorant about the processes by which buyers and sellers are brought together to engage in exchange, i.e., about the market itself.

Over the same two decades, the need to improve our understanding of the market has been growing by leaps and bounds. Today this need manifests itself in a variety of ways. On the public policy-making level, it is currently represented by the SEC's concern over the impact of institutional trading on the securities markets, its hassle with the Justice Department about the structure of commissions on New York Stock Exchange transactions, and its difficulty in dealing with such securities market innovations as the recently announced Institutional Network System. To some extent, the SEC's difficulty with these questions stems from the fact that normative and equity questions are involved, which is to say that vested interests are involved. Compounding their task, however, is the simple fact that our present understanding of the basic operations of the securities markets is insufficient to cope with many of the "positive" questions at issue.

Apart from public policy consideration, the results of research on security analysis and portfolio selection also have increased the need to improve our understanding of the market's operations. The growth in statistical analysis of securities market data, for example, has raised many questions about the nature of trading processes. In particular, the spate of research related to the random walk hypothesis of stock price changes leads one to want to know much more about those aspects of market organization that seem to enable new information and variations in liquidity demands to be so smoothly accommodated. Similarly, the research findings related to portfolio selection lead to some rather interesting questions about the aspects of market behavior and organization that may influence the determination of portfolio compositions.[20]

The Scope and Approach of the Book

If the reader were to go no further, he might well conclude that we have little in the way of a storehouse of research results on which to base the rest of the book. Such is not the case. Quite recently, a small but growing number of economists, spurred on by many of the concerns mentioned above, have begun to develop a framework for analyzing the operations of the stock market. Stigler, for example, recently developed a simple yet extremely relevant simulation approach to the stock market[21] that provides a number of interesting insights into the economics of the broker function and the behavior of prices. As expanded by West, Stigler's model also takes account of the dealer function.[22] Additional theoretical work on the organization of the dealer function on the stock exchanges has been presented by Baumol.[23] Studies recently completed by Demsetz and Tiniç provide the first systematic analysis of the determinants of the spread between bid and ask prices on the New York Stock Exchange.[24] The other major component of transactions costs, the level of exchange commissions, also has undergone considerable scrutiny. Other aspects of exchange operations, including the determinants of seat prices, have been the subject of investigation by Doede.[25] Finally, the work of Smidt and of Niederhoffer and Osborne has integrated the economics of market-making into the analysis of stock price movements.[26]

The remaining eight chapters will draw heavily on the results of these and related studies. The general approach will be to move from the "broad" to the "narrow." The next chapter, for example, will be directed toward building an understanding of the basic broker and dealer functions performed in the stock market, beginning with a brief review of the basic models of price determination in competitive and monopolistic markets. The models' limitations in providing a basis for interpreting day-to-day activities on the stock market will next be discussed. The types of simulation models built by Stigler and West will then serve as a basis for examining the economic functions of brokers and dealers, the role of the dealer in providing liquidity and servicing market orders, and the impact of dealers on the behavior of stock prices. The chapter will end with some comments on the role of price theory models in analyzing the economics of the stock market.

Chapter 3 will analyze the factors that determine how the broker and dealer functions are organized. It will focus primarily on the two major forms of organization currently extant, the stock exchange and the over-the-counter market. The discussion will also take in the impact of stock market organization on price behavior and automated trading approaches to making markets in equity securities.

The next three chapters will focus on the economics of transactions costs. Chapter 4 will present a theoretical analysis of the determinants of brokerage and dealer costs, drawing heavily on the results of the studies by Demsetz and Tiniç. In Chapters 5 and 6, brokerage and dealer costs in the New York Stock Exchange will be analyzed.

Chapter 7 will discuss the behavior of stock prices. In particular, it will consider the random walk hypothesis of stock price changes, taking into consideration the economics of transactions costs.

Chapter 8 will consider the economics of exchange operations. Drawing on the work of Doede, we will discuss the factors that have led to the dominance of the exchange business by the New York and American Stock Exchanges. The chapter also will include a discussion of the relationship between the major and regional exchanges.

The final chapter will consider the future structure of the equities market and the impact of institutional investors on the market's character.

Notes

1. *Webster's New World Dictionary* (1964), s.v. "Economics."
2. George J. Stigler, *The Theory of Price*, 3d ed. (New York: Macmillan, 1966), p. 11.

3. William J. Baumol, *The Stock Market and Economic Efficiency* (New York: Fordham University Press, 1965), p. 2.
4. See W. Arthur Lewis, *The Theory of Economic Growth* (Homewood, Ill.: R. D. Irwin, 1955), pp. 260–74.
5. See Richard West, "New Issue Concessions on Municipal Bonds: A Case of Monopoly Pricing," *Journal of Business* 38, No. 2 (1965): 135–148.
6. See also Joseph Conard, *The Behavior of Interest Rates* (New York: National Bureau of Economic Research, 1966), pp. 106–20, esp. 115–17.
7. *Economic Dimensions of America's Corporation* (New York: National Industrial Conference Board, 1962), p. 7.
8. *Ibid.*
9. Edward Mason, "The Corporation," in *International Encyclopedia of the Social Sciences* 3 (New York: Macmillan, Free Press, 1968): 399.
10. Data for the financial structure of corporations are available in "Statistics of Income," Internal Revenue Service. They have been summarized in R. W. Goldsmith, R. E. Lipsey, and M. Mendelson, *Studies in the National Balance Sheet of the United States* (Princeton, N.J.: Princeton University Press, 1963).
11. For a discussion of equity prices and capital investment decision-making, see, for example, Ezra Solomon, *The Theory of Financial Management* (New York: Columbia University Press, 1963) and James C. T. Mao, *Quantitative Analysis of Financial Decision* (New York: The Macmillan Co., 1969).
12. Lewis, *Theory of Economic Growth*, p. 267.
13. See Solomon, *Theory of Financial Management*, pp. 51–68.
14. Lewis, *Theory of Economic Growth*, p. 266.
15. *Ibid*, p. 266.
16. George A. Christy, *Capital Budgeting: Current Practices and Their Efficiency* (Eugene: University of Oregon Press, 1966), pp. 28, 82–85.
17. In this connection, it is interesting to note that the *Index of Economic Journals*, Vol. I (1886–1924) (Homewood, Ill.: R. D. Irwin, 1961), lists only twenty-eight entries under its securities markets reading, except for those pertaining to regulation. Of that number, Professor Mitchell wrote six.
18. Solomon, *Theory of Financial Management*, p. 2.
19. James Lorie, "Some Comments on Recent Quantitative and Formal Research on the Stock Market," *Journal of Business* 39, No. 1, Part 2 (January, 1966): 110.
20. In the "mean value-variance" approach to portfolio analysis presented in William F. Sharpe, "Capital Asset Prices: A Theory of Market Equilibrium Under Conditions of Risk," *Journal of Finance* 19 (September, 1964): 425–42, the prices of stocks continually change until a point is reached where every stock enters at least one of the perfectly correlated efficient portfolios. Sharpe explicitly states that investors are not all expected to hold the same efficient combination, and he justifies arbitrary selection of an efficient portfolio.

We would argue, however, that investors should not merely select any efficient combination of stocks arbitrarily, since one of the important determinants in choosing a portfolio is the liquidity of the assets included in the combination. Other things being equal, an efficient portfolio that contains relatively liquid stocks should be preferred over an efficient combination of less liquid stocks. Thus, unless the marketability aspects of stocks are explicitly accounted for in the portfolio analysis, perhaps by considering the effects of liquidity on security prices and on the resulting capital market equilibrium, the arbitrary selection of an efficient portfolio will hold up only in the special case where all portfolios are equally marketable.

21. George J. Stigler, "Public Regulation of the Securities Markets," *Journal of Business* 37 (April, 1964): 129 ff.
22. Richard R. West, "Simulating Securities Markets' Operations: Some Examples, Observations and Comments," *Journal of Financial and Quantitative Analysis* 5 (March, 1970): 115–38.
23. W. J. Baumol, *The Stock Market and Economic Efficiency* (New York: Fordham University Press, 1965).
24. H. Demsetz, "The Cost of Transacting," *Quarterly Journal of Economics* 82 (February, 1968): 33–53, and Seha M. Tiniç, "The Value of Time Preference and the Behavior of Liquidity Costs in the New York Stock Exchange" (unpublished doctoral thesis, Cornell University, 1970).
25. R. W. Doede, "The Monopoly Power of the New York Stock Exchange" (unpublished doctoral dissertation, University of Chicago, 1967).
26. S. Smidt, "A New Look at the Random Walk Hypothesis," *Journal of Financial and Quantitative Analysis* 3 (September, 1968): 235–61, and V. Niederhoffer and M. F. S. Osborne, "Market Making and Reversal on the Stock Exchange," *Journal of the American Statistical Association*, December, 1966, pp. 897–916.

2 Economic Models and the Stock Market[1]

In a well-known critique of the theory of monopolistic competition, George Stigler makes the following observations about the purpose of economic theory:

> The purpose of the study of economics is to permit us to make predictions about the behavior of economic phenomena under specified conditions. The sole test of the usefulness of an economic theory is the concordance between its predictions and the observable course of events. Often a theory is criticized or rejected because its assumptions are "unrealistic." Granting for a moment that this charge has meaning, it burdens theory with an additional function, that of description. This is a most unreasonable burden to place upon a theory: the role of description is to particularize, while the role of theory is to generalize — to disregard an infinite number of differences and capture the important element in different phenomena.[2]

Along the same lines, Kenneth E. Boulding writes as follows:

> The method of economic analysis, then, is to start with very simple assumptions concerning human behavior, then to discover what consequences would follow for the economic system as a whole if these assumptions were true.... Having mastered this simple picture, we can then proceed to bring it into closer relation to real life by introducing qualifications of our original assumptions and seeing how they affect the picture as we see it. But never do we come to "real life," however closely we may approach it, for reality is always more complex than the economist's picture of it.[3]

The point both authors make, of course, is that "good" economic models are useful precisely because they can retain that which is essential to the understanding and prediction of economic behavior, while rejecting that which is mere detail.

In this chapter we are concerned with the usefulness of economic models as tools for helping us to understand and predict behavior in the stock market. We begin with a brief review of the economist's two basic models for the analysis of markets — the theory of monopoly and the theory of competition — and discuss their relevance to the analysis of stock market economics. Concluding that these models' disregard of the actual exchange process, i.e., the process by which buyer and seller are brought together to engage in exchange, limits their usefulness in rationalizing many aspects of day-to-day economic activities in the stock market, we next discuss these activities within the context of a simple simulation model. The purpose of the discussion is twofold: first, to demonstrate simulation's power as a tool for understanding the basic economics of the exchange process and, second, to acquaint the reader with various aspects of the exchange process that will be considered in more detail in later chapters. On the basis of the simulation results, we return to the role of price theory models in the analysis of stock market operations. Our somewhat paradoxical conclusion is this: Although these models may not be very useful for rationalizing the *existence* of much of the day-to-day activity in the stock market, they nevertheless can be extremely helpful in analyzing various aspects of such activity, once its existence is understood. We recognize that this statement may be somewhat difficult for the reader to understand, let alone accept, at this point; but we are confident that he will both understand and accept it on reaching the end of the chapter.

The Basic Theory of Markets

Books on economic theory do not usually provide an explicit and comprehensive definition of the term "market"; rather, they define the term implicitly within the context of the market process, where two parties, a seller and a buyer, interchange economic goods for money. The usual implication is that the parties contact each other directly, i.e., without resorting to an intermediary institution that specializes in facilitating transactions. If we let set $S_1 = (s_{11}, s_{12}, \ldots, s_{1m})$ represent sellers, and

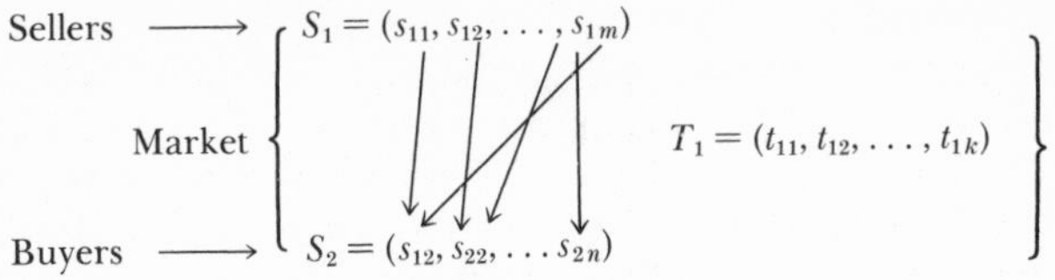

Sellers ⟶ $S_1 = (s_{11}, s_{12}, \ldots, s_{1m})$

Market

$T_1 = (t_{11}, t_{12}, \ldots, t_{1k})$

Buyers ⟶ $S_2 = (s_{12}, s_{22}, \ldots s_{2n})$

FIGURE 1　Market.

$S_2 = (s_{21}, s_{22}, \ldots, s_{2n})$ buyers, transactions among the elements of set S_1 and S_2 can be expressed in terms of a third set $T_1 = (t_{11}, t_{12}, \ldots, t_{1k})$. Taken together, these three sets (See Figure 1 above) constitute the fundamentals of a market; in other words, a market can be defined as a larger set with these three sets as its elements:

$$\text{Market} = M = \{S_1, S_2, T_1,\}$$

The analysis of markets is conveniently conceived as being of two basic types. One of them, commonly referred to as horizontal market analysis, is concerned with the study of the organizational structure of sets S_1 and S_2, as well as with the behavior patterns of their elements. Its basic aim is to identify interrelationships affecting the formation of price and equilibrium quantities of goods being exchanged in the market. The second type of analysis deals with the flow of economic goods from the raw materials stage to the consumption stage. Referred to as vertical market analysis, it focuses on the series of exchange transactions that facilitate the flow of commodities from producer to consumer. In the context of vertical analysis, a market is characterized by the presence of layers of additional sets. In Figure 2, for example, $R_1 = (r_{11}, r_{12}, \ldots, r_{1g})$ and $R_2 = (r_{21}, r_{22}, \ldots, r_{2h})$ represent additional levels in the process of bringing some economic good to the ultimate buyers, (S_2). The emphasis of this

Level I

Seller $S_1 = (s_{11}, s_{12}, \ldots, s_{1m})$

$T_1^* = (t_{11}^*, t_{12}^*, \ldots, t_{1k}^*)$

Buyer

Level II

Seller $R_1 = (r_{11}, r_{12}, \ldots, r_{1g})$

$T_2^* = (t_{21}^*, t_{22}^*, \ldots, t_{2u}^*)$

Buyer

Level III

Seller $R_2 = (r_{21}, r_{22}, \ldots, r_{2h})$

$T_3^* = (t_{31}^*, t_{32}^*, \ldots, t_{3v}^*)$

Buyer $S_2 = (s_{21}, s_{22}, \ldots, s_{2n})$

FIGURE 2　Vertical Market Structure.

type of analysis is on the over-all cost reduction (or increased profitability) of the system of exchange transactions and the allocation of incremental cost savings (profits) among the elements of these vertically differentiated (or integrated) sets.

As originally developed, both the theory of monopoly and the theory of competition involve the analysis of economic behavior within the context of horizontal market models. Each is founded on certain basic axioms concerning the number of elements in sets S_1 and S_2, as well as on postulates governing the behavioral patterns of the elements in these two sets. The two fundamental behavioral assumptions common to both models are (1) the maximization of profits on the part of sellers and (2) the maximization of utility on the part of buyers. Having stated these postulates, all the information concerning the internal organization and the modes of conduct of the elements of sets S_1 and S_2 is summarized by the relevant supply and demand schedules.[4]

The Theory of Monopoly. In terms of Figure 1, the monopoly model envisages a situation in which the set S_1 contains only one element, (s_{11}), while S_2 contains a large number of elements, $(s_{21}, \ldots, s_{2n})$. Beyond this, it assumes that there are no close substitutes for the seller's merchandise, thus giving him virtually complete control over the quantity of goods offered or the prices charged: he is, in short assumed to be a pure monopolist.[5] In the second set, S_2, each of the large number of buyers $(s_{21}, s_{22}, \ldots, s_{2n})$ is constrained by his prevailing endowment. Acting independently, each attempts to maximize his individual satisfaction by rearranging his array of assets. As long as the incremental utility derived from the addition of the item sold by the monopolist exceeds the marginal dissatisfaction of sacrificing some of his current possessions, he will enter the monopoly market.

In a closed system where the monopolist does not undertake productive activities but rather simply engages in selling his specialized holdings to a group of competing buyers, the conditions of the market can be summarized by an exchange diagram such as Figure 3. In this simple case, the monopolist, s_{11}, holds the title to all of good X, while the endowment of each of n buyers consists of Q_0 of cash. We let I_B and I_M represent the indifference curves of the buyers and the monopolist, respectively. The lines $0A$, $0B$, etc., reflect various exchange rates

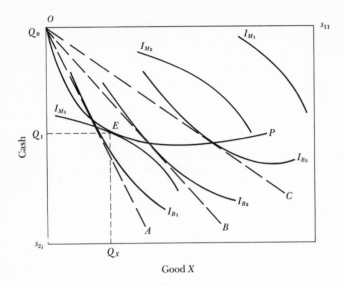

FIGURE 3   Exchange Under Monopoly.

between the good X and cash. The locus of tangencies of I_B with these lines, $0\text{–}P$, constitutes the "outlay-purchase" curve of each or all of the buyers, depending on the scale used. If we assume the above scale represents one of n identical buyers, the point E will obtain, where buyer, s_{2i}, pays $(Q_0 - Q_1)$ of cash for Q_X amount of good X. Essentially, this point is determined by the monopolist, who either adjusts the exchange rate (price) between cash and good X or the amount of good X he offers in an attempt to maximize his utility. Since the monopolist's utility is maximized at the point where his indifference curve is tangent to the anticipated outlay-purchase locus (or offer curve) of the buyer, the monopolist will offer Q_X to each buyer or a total supply of nQ_X to the market.

In a market where the monopolist engages in production of goods or services, it is more convenient to replace the exchange diagram with the demand schedule of the buyers, and work with the costs of production instead of the indifference map of the monopolist. A careful examination of the outlay-purchase curve reveals that the demand curve facing the monopolist is negatively sloped, i.e., buyers are willing to buy smaller quantities of his goods or services at higher prices. The price elasticity of demand, however, depends on the number of substitutes available, the proximity of substitutability (as measured by cross-elasticities) and the income elasticity.[6] Generally speaking, however, the demand for a good or service with imperfect substitutes and low income elasticity tends to be relatively inelastic.

Given the demand schedule and the structure of the monopolist's costs, the amount offered by the monopolist and his price can easily be determined. Let us assume that the demand for a particular good is represented by the function $p = f(q)$, where p is price per unit and q is the quantity demanded by buyers. If the monopolist's costs of producing this good are given by the function, $c = g(q)$, his profit, π, can be expressed algebraically as follows:

$$\pi = pq - g(q) \qquad (2.1)$$

To maximize his profits, the monopolist must maximize equation (2.1). The first and second order conditions for profit maximization are:

$$\frac{d\pi}{dq} = qf'(q) + f(q) - g'(q) = 0 \qquad (2.2)$$

or equivalently,

$$MR = MC$$

and

$$\frac{d^2\pi}{dq^2} = qf''(q) + 2f'(q) - g''(q) < 0 \qquad (2.3)$$

that is,

$$\frac{d(MR)}{dq} < \frac{d(MC)}{dq}$$

Hence, the optimum policy for a short-run profit–maximizing monopolist is to offer that quantity which equates his marginal costs of production to his marginal revenue. As long as the slope of his marginal cost function is larger than the slope of the marginal revenue schedule, his profits will be maximized. In essence, then, the pure monopoly model yields a determinate price–quantity solution under all forms of returns to scale as long as the marginal cost curve intersects the marginal revenue curve from below.[7]

Thus far we have been assuming that the monopolist charges all buyers the same price, i.e., does not engage in price discrimination. In real world markets, however, monopolists sometimes attempt to segment the market in order to charge more than one price. For this tactic to be profitable, the demand schedules of the segmented groups must have different elasticities.[8] In addition, it must be impossible for the segmented groups to trade with each other. Given both of these conditions a monopolist can increase his profits by equating each of his segmented marginal revenue functions with his marginal cost of production. In the case where there are only two submarkets, the monopolist's optimal policy is given as follows, where MR_1 and MR_2 are the two marginal revenues and $g'(q)$ is marginal cost.

$$MR_1 = g'(q) \text{ and } MR_2 = g'(q) \qquad (2.4)$$

In the two-submarket case, the monopolist's policies result in the following relationship between the prices charged.

$$\frac{P_1}{P_2} = \frac{(1 - 1/e_2)}{(1 - 1/e_1)} \qquad (2.5)$$

The equality of the two ratios implies that the monopolist charges a higher price in the submarket with the relatively inelastic demand.

The Theory of Competition. In contrast to the monopoly model, the competitive model assumes that set S_1 includes a large number (m) of elements, each possessing control over an amount of resources and goods that is small relative to the aggregate size of the market. Since it also assumes the existence of a large number of buyers, this model asserts that prices are determined by the impersonal forces of the market, with both sellers and buyers acting as price-takers.

If we let the total endowments of the elements of set S_1 and set S_2 consist of cash and good X, respectively, we can again represent the conditions of transactions in an Edgeworth box diagram (Figure 4). Given the indifference maps of S_1 and S_2 and the various exchange rates $0A$, $0B$, etc., between cash and good X, the outlay-purchase curves, 0_{S_1} and 0_{S_2}, can be determined for both groups of traders. The intersection point of these offer curves, E, yields the equilibrium, where buyers $(s_{21}, \ldots, s_{2n})$ with an original endowment of Q_0 of cash, exchange $(Q_0 - Q_1)$. Note that the exchange equilibrium, E, occurs at a point where the indifference curves of buyers and endowments among the agents of the system. Since the prices are equal to the marginal costs to the society, the model provides a normative criterion by which the efficiency of real-world markets can be compared and evaluated. To the extent actual markets come close to approximating the perfect competition equilibrium solutions, they will be recognized as efficient systems.

Price Theory Models and the Stock Market

For the analysis of a wide variety of microeconomic problems, such as tax policies and subsidies, few of the economist's tools are more powerful than the basic price theory models summarized above. As tools for rationalizing much of the day-to-day activity of the stock market, however, these models leave much to be desired. The reason for this seemingly paradoxical state of affairs is really quite simple: The ongoing operations of the stock market are primarily concerned with the processes by which buyers and sellers are brought together to engage in exchange, while the price theory models explicitly assume there are no transaction costs and say virtually nothing about the way in which buyers and sellers get together to do business. As William Baumol notes:

> On a real [securities] market in the real world, one encounters no supply and demand graphs and no one reads off the coordinates of their intersection points. In setting the price then, one [who understands the economic theory of markets] may well ask exactly who does what to whom—what mechanism translates the disorderly parade of data which serve as a substitute for our neat mathematical functions, into a unique determinate price figure.[10]

Economists have long recognized this deficiency in the price theory models. Yet, for a variety of reasons, they have tended to be preoccupied with considering whether real markets could *in theory* organize supply and demand in such a way that the solutions implied by their models would be achieved. How these markets actually organize them, on the other hand, has been generally neglected.

Walras's famous *tâtonnement* theory[11] provides a significant case in point, for while it clearly demonstrates that it is possible to devise a theoretical market organized so as to clear along the lines suggested by traditional microeconomic analysis, it says

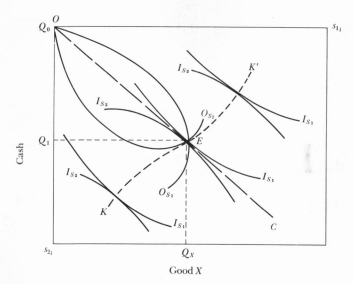

FIGURE 4   Exchange Under Competition.

sellers are tangent to each other, i.e., at a point where with a given exchange rate (price) between the two assets, the amount demanded by the members of S_2 is equal to the number of shares that holders, S_1, are willing to dispose. The specific exchange rate, line $0C$, yields the equilibrium price for good X in a perfectly competitive market, while Q_X constitutes the equilibrium amount transacted.

The locus of tangencies of the indifference curves of the two groups, KK', is the contract curve on which the rates of commodity substitution, defined as the ratio of marginal utility of cash to marginal utility of good X, are equal for the members of both sets.[9] From the point of view of economic efficiency, it is important to note that the equilibrium solution in a competitive market obtains on the contract curve, which traces all Pareto-optimal (economically efficient) solutions. Consequently, only exchange transactions conducted in competitive markets are economically efficient *per se*.

In an open market system, where sellers engage in production as well as exchange, the competitive model can be discussed with the help of demand and supply schedules. The basic behavioral assumptions of the model are quite similar to those mentioned in pure monopoly: Sellers are assumed to maximize their profits independently under a given production function, and buyers, constrained by the size of their budgets, are assumed to maximize their independent satisfactions. Moreover, both sellers and buyers are assumed to possess perfect information, thus insuring uniform prices throughout the market at any given time.

The short-run equilibrium of a perfectly competitive market is determined by the prevailing supply and demand schedules. Each seller takes the price as given and supplies that quantity which maximizes his profits. The well-known condition for profit maximization involves having each seller carry production to a point where marginal cost equals the market price. Algebraically, the necessary conditions for profit maximization are as follows:

$$\text{Maximize } \pi = p \cdot q - g(q) \qquad (2.6)$$

that is,

$$\frac{d\pi}{dq} = p - g'(q) = 0$$

or

$$p = g'(q)$$

To insure a local maximum,

$$\frac{d^2\pi}{dq^2} = -g''(q) < 0 \qquad (2.7)$$

that is, $g''(q)$ must be increasing. In fact, the condition in equation (2.7) must be fulfilled for a stable equilibrium to obtain. This, of course, implies that the competitive model is incompatible with economies of scale.

As represented in Figure 5, each seller faces a perfectly elastic demand for his services, AR_1, at the market price, P_1. In the short run, profits are maximized at q_1 units of output ($p = AR^1 = MC$), and the seller makes $(A - B)$ dollars of profit per unit. A distinguishing assumption of the competitive model, however, is the perfect mobility of factors of production. Thus, as long as price exceeds the average cost of production at the equilibrium level of output, additional sellers are attracted to the market. As the number of sellers increases, however, supply expands (represented by a shift from S_1S_1' to S_2S_2'). With the demand unchanged, this leads to a decrease in price to P_2, thereby eliminating any "windfall" profits in the market. The long-run equilibrium, consequently, is established at $p = MC = AC$, where the influx and exit of sellers ceases.

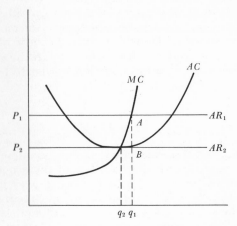

(A) Equilibrium of firm

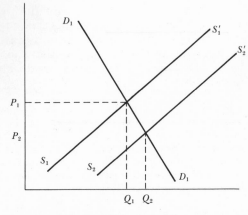

(B) Equilibrium of market

FIGURE 5   Equilibrium in Perfect Competition.

Since buyers maximize their satisfaction at the point where marginal utility of all goods and services is equal per dollar outlay, the competitive model guarantees a solution where rate of commodity substitution between any pair of goods services is equal to the ratio of their prices or the ratio of th marginal costs of production. This equality insures the e ciency of the market under a given distribution of origi

very little about the way real markets reach an equilibrium. The two fundamental elements of the *tâtonnement* process are (1) freedom for recontracting among buyers and sellers and (2) a market clearing decision rule administered by some central agency. The process begins, i.e., the market opens, at some price arbitrarily selected by the central agency. Sellers and buyers who desire to consummate transactions at that price submit their orders to the central agency, whose function is to calculate the total amounts supplied and demanded and to adjust price in accordance with the decision rule given by the pure exchange model, i.e., raise the price when there is excess demand and lower it when there is excess supply at the previously announced price. As long as there is excess supply or demand at a specific price, the orders submitted by buyers and sellers are not binding. In fact, both parties can submit revised orders and recontract as prices are adjusted by the central agency. All orders, however, become binding at the equilibrium price, i.e., the price where neither excess supply nor demand exists in the market.

Although it clearly represents a major contribution to the basic economic theory of markets, the *tâtonnement* process is of limited usefulness in helping us understand how real stock markets operate to bring buyers and sellers together. Even within its (intentionally) artificial context, the model leaves a considerable number of important procedural questions unanswered. For example, how does the central agency select the price at which the *tâtonnement* begins? Is it purely random, or are there decision rules by which the agency attempts to reduce the time required to reach an equilibrium price? Beyond this, who maintains the central agency and pays its operating costs?

In real securities markets, of course, the questions are even more complex. Unlike the participants in the *tâtonnement* model, real buyers and sellers of stocks do not necessarily come to the market simultaneously, nor do they all show a willingness to wait around while the equilibrium price is being arrived at by an iterative process. This being the case, the real-world counterparts to the *tâtonnement* model's central agency must develop fairly elaborate procedures for bringing buyers and sellers together and for smoothing out temporary imbalances in the incoming flow of buy and sell orders.

The need for these elaborate procedures, of course, suggests the existence of an important, yet often neglected, characteristic of stock markets, namely, the existence of transaction costs. Both the price theory models discussed in the preceding section and Walras's *tâtonnement* fail to provide an explicit treatment of these costs. Indeed, as mentioned above, one of the basic assumptions of these market models is that exchange transactions are free of any costs.[12]

Matters would be sufficiently complicated if the problem ended here. Unfortunately, it does not! In fact, it would appear that the economist's price theory models not only fail to provide a meaningful framework for understanding how real securities markets organize supply and demand and determine prices, but also frequently afford a highly distorted picture of what is actually taking place. In both the competitive and the monopolistic models, for example, a price change takes place as the result of a shift in either supply or demand or both.[13] Consider now the plight of the economics student who observes transaction-to-transaction variability in the price of a common stock. Understandably, he is prone to conclude that these price changes represent the results of adjustments in the underlying demand and supply conditions for the security, when in fact they may not.

A similar problem relates to interpretation of the behavior of stock prices. In perfectly competitive markets with no transaction costs, the random walk model of price changes would be expected to hold. That is, the expected price change of a stock in the future would be statistically independent of its previous price changes. As we shall demonstrate in a later chapter, however, transaction-to-transaction price changes can be expected to manifest considerable dependence when these costs are present.

We are not criticizing price theory models *in toto*, but merely arguing that the basis on which they are constructed and, particularly, their disregard for the transaction process *per se* limit their usefulness for rationalizing the existence of much ongoing activity of the stock market. As we shall argue below, on the other hand, these models can be extremely useful in organizing the analysis of these activities.

Simulation Models of Stock Markets

Recognizing that traditional price theory models are limited in their ability to provide an understanding of the processes by which real securities markets bring buyers and sellers together, economists have begun to turn to simulation models. In a recent study, George Stigler develops a simple, yet extremely interesting simulation approach to stock markets.[14] Within the framework of his model, Stigler is able to show how demand and supply are organized in a stock market where buy and sell orders lack continuity, i.e., where they arrive irregularly over time. In another study, West extends Stigler's approach to analyze the basic functions and objectives of the institutions prevalent in stock markets.[15] Moreover, he is able to demonstrate the influences of the market organization on the short-term behavior of stock prices.

Stigler's Model. Stigler starts with the demand schedule reproduced in Table 2–1, an outstanding supply of 710,000 shares, and thus an equilibrium price per unit between $29\frac{3}{4}$ and 30. He then assumes that the stream of incoming orders can be simulated by a series of two-digit random numbers. The first digit is used to determine the nature of the order—a bid if even, an ask if odd; the second digit determines the price specified by the order: $0 = 28\frac{3}{4}$, $1 = 29\frac{1}{4}$, and so forth.

The first two random numbers in his sequence are as follows:

(1) 28: a bid at $30\frac{1}{4}$
(2) 30: an ask at $28\frac{3}{4}$

At this point, Stigler comments, "A transaction occurs at $30\frac{3}{4}$ because the highest outstanding bid exceeds the seller's minimum ask."[16] In other words, the knowledge that there is a

TABLE 2–1
Demand Schedule for a Security

Price	Random Number	Aggregate Demand
$28\frac{3}{4}$	(0)	800,000
29	(1)	780,000
$29\frac{1}{4}$	(2)	760,000
$29\frac{1}{2}$	(3)	740,000
$29\frac{3}{4}$	(4)	720,000
30	(5)	700,000
$30\frac{1}{4}$	(6)	680,000
$30\frac{1}{2}$	(7)	660,000
$30\frac{3}{4}$	(8)	640,000
31	(9)	620,000

bidder at 30¾ effectively pre-empts the second tender from specifying a price of 28¾, as is implied by the last digit of the random number.

The next three random numbers are as follows:

(3) 95: an ask at 30
(4) 01: a bid at 29
(5) 10: an ask at 28¾

Once again the presence of an outstanding order, the bid of 29, causes the price determined by the fifth random number to be superseded by market circumstances. In this case, a transaction takes place between the fourth and fifth orders at a price of 29. Transactions data for the first hundred tenders (random numbers) in Stigler's simulation are reproduced in Figure 6.

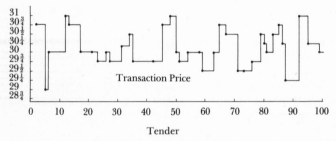

FIGURE 6   Hypothetical Sequence of Transaction Prices Generated by Sequence of Random Numbers.

What kinds of insights about the operations of securities markets can be obtained from the analysis of these data? Consider first the relationship between the stock's equilibrium price and the prices at which trading takes place. In this case, the equilibrium price is somewhere between 29¾ and 30, say 29⅞. Yet the particular flow of orders and the difficulty of matching them causes more than 60 per cent of all transactions to take place at prices outside of this range. Moreover, on several occasions the price moves from well below this range to well above it, or vice versa, from one transaction to the next.

In the previous section of this chapter, it was noted that an analysis of transaction-to-transaction price data based on a straightforward application of elementary price theory might easily lead to the (incorrect) conclusion that all variations result from adjustments in underlying supply and demand conditions.

One of the facts of life in real stock markets, however, is that some price fluctuations are not associated with basic shifts in supply or demand. The results of the simulation clearly demonstrate that a certain amount of price variation is perfectly compatible with the existence of an unchanging equilibrium price. More important, the model provides an insight into the causes of these price fluctuations.

In addition, the simulation results show that delays can occur in executing orders that specify a price limitation (limit order). The results provide concrete evidence concerning the reasons for these delays, and they also make it abundantly clear that the mere presence of potential buyers and sellers is not a sufficient condition for the consummation of a transaction. Consider, for example, the situation that obtains with the appearance of the fourth tender. At this point in the proceedings, both a buyer and a seller are present, yet no transaction takes place, nor should one, since the minimum asking price of the only existing seller is above the maximum bidding price of the only buyer.

In his 1964 article, Stigler makes no explicit reference to the brokerage function; yet his model provides an extremely good vehicle for gaining an understanding of the need for the broker's services and the functions he performs. Indeed, even without mentioning brokers, the model indicates the economic need that is fulfilled by the brokerage function. Someone, after all, must be on the receiving end of the simulated stream of buy and sell orders, someone must keep track of the unfulfilled bids and offers, and someone must, when appropriate, make transactions. In real securities markets this someone is, of course, a broker. It is the broker who acts as the focal point for incoming orders, keeps a record of unfulfilled bids and asks, and makes transactions. In fact, the brokerage function is typically described in terms of the performance of these services.

Brokers, in their capacity as agents for individual traders, both reduce the over-all cost of search in the market and provide the facilities needed to execute orders that require active solicitation or negotiation. The cost savings related to search can be illustrated by the situation that obtains in Stigler's model as the first two tenders arrive. If the two traders were obliged to make contact directly, the costs of executing a transaction could be prohibitively high. To illustrate further, let us suppose that there are m traders in the market, but the trader submitting the first tender is the only one interested in buying the issue in question at present. In this case, the potential seller who submits the second tender has only a probability of $1/m$ of making contact with the potential buyer in the absence of a broker. Assuming that each contact costs him t in terms of opportunity costs of the time used in searching for a buyer, his expected cost of consummating a transaction, $E(t)$, is given by the following expression:

$$E(t) = 1/m(t + 2t + 3t + \cdots + mt), \text{ or} \qquad (2.8)$$
$$= 1/m((m)(m+1)/2)t = (m+1)t/2 \qquad (2.9)$$

On the other hand, if there are n brokers (where $n < m$), the costs of search can be substantially reduced. If we let t^* represent the cost of having brokers make contact with each other, it can easily be shown that the expected searching costs for the potential seller, $E(t^*)$, is equal[17] to

$$t + \frac{(n-1)t^*}{2} \qquad (2.10)$$

as long as $n < m$ and $t \geq t^*$, $E(t^*) < E(t)$.

Indeed, even in the unlikely event that $t = t^*$[18], the presence of brokers can reduce the costs of search by $(m-n)t/2$. We say "unlikely event," of course, because of the expectation that t^* should be lower than t owing to the economies of specialization and scale associated with the search processes of brokers.

The situation that obtains with the appearance of the third and fourth tenders is appropriate for illustrating the function of brokers in facilitating negotiations between buyers and sellers. As originally submitted, these two tenders do not make it possible for a transaction to occur. The bid at 29 is less than the prevailing ask at 30. Under these circumstances, the traders can either simply wait for other tenders to appear or, alternatively, engage in negotiations designed to strike a happy medium. The presence of brokers encourages the development of negotiations by providing both sides with anonymity. When buyers and sellers do not know each other, it is less likely that either side will be able to take advantage of the situation and force the other party to accept an unfavorable price. This is especially important in the buying or selling of large blocks for institutional investors, where secrecy concerning the identity of a potential trader and the size of an order can improve bargaining power considerably.

In addition to facilitating negotiated transactions, brokers can also actively solicit orders to fulfill outstanding tenders that are entrusted to them. This is a very common function of brokers, especially in the so-called over-the-counter market for stocks. In the absence of brokers, the costs of soliciting offsetting orders would be prohibitive for small individual investors. Brokers, on the other hand, can perform this marketing function through their existing branch offices or correspondents at fairly reasonable costs. Moreover, in doing so, they can assist in the integration of all sectors of the stock market.

Extending Stigler's Simulation. The brokerage function provides the *modus operandi* for executing limit orders, reducing search costs, facilitating negotiations between buyers and sellers and soliciting orders. However, it does not guarantee continuity and liquidity in the absence of offsetting limit orders. Put differently, it does not insure that temporary imbalances in the flow of buy and sell orders will be dampened, thus increasing the possibility that traders on one side of the market will be able to do business even when offsetting orders fail to appear. In a real securities market, the task of smoothing out such imbalances is the function of individuals who are referred to as dealers. Unlike brokers, dealers act as principals, taking positions for their own accounts. Because Stigler's simulation model only provides for the submission of limit orders, it is not suitable for illustrating the need for the dealership function or the dealer's role. West, however, provides extensions to Stigler's model that make it possible to incorporate both.[19]

To demonstrate the need to extend Stigler's simulation market, West begins by asking what would happen if buyers and sellers were permitted to make a choice between setting a price limitation on their orders (a maximum price in the case of buyers, and a minimum in the case of sellers) and specifying that orders be transacted at the market. For illustrative purposes, he assumes that subsequent to the opening of the market, the following sequence of orders appears:

(1) an order to sell one share at a price of $30\frac{3}{4}$ or better
(2) an order to sell one share at the market price
(3) an order to buy one share at the market price

It should be fairly obvious to the reader that, in the absence of some extensions in the simulation, a basic quandary exists: Who is to trade with whom at what price? There can be no doubt that a trade should take place, since there are buyers and sellers offering somewhat compatible terms. The first and third orders, for example, could be 'crossed' at a price of 30¾. But where would this leave the second seller, who is willing, presumably, to part with his holdings for less than 30¾? Furthermore, if the second and third orders were to be crossed, at what price would trading take place? As West concludes, "clearly, the simulation does not provide straightforward answers to these questions."[20]

West then notes that one solution might be to have the third order specify a zero price, on the assumption that a waiting seller (order 2) is prepared to accept any offer. From a highly formalistic viewpoint, this approach would solve the problem. But it would do so only at the expense of common sense; for if the seller knew he risked a zero price, he would never have submitted a market order in the first place.

To cope with market orders, West expands the simulation's machinery for matching bids and offers and establishing prices. The reader will recall that the unmentioned broker who operates the market in Stigler's simulation simply notes down offers to buy and sell, provides information to potential buyers and sellers, and makes transactions. West now adds the services of an individual who stands ready to buy or sell stocks for his own account at stated prices when other traders are not in the market. In short, he augments the machinery for matching buy and sell orders by injecting a dealer, an individual who maintains limit orders on both sides of the market simultaneously.

Perhaps the first question that comes to mind is why anyone would be willing to maintain buy and sell orders simultaneously. To answer this, it is necessary to refer to the behavior of prices in Figure 6. The reader will remember that despite an unvarying equilibrium price in the neighborhood of 29⅞, transaction prices fluctuate quite substantially in the range from 29 to 31. It is these price fluctuations that provide a rationale for the presence of individuals who simultaneously maintain limit orders to buy and sell stocks. This point is perhaps best illustrated by recourse to an analogy. Suppose a truck driver observed that the prices of a particular commodity in New York and Chicago differed by more than the cost of shipping it from one to the other. Isn't it reasonable for him to begin purchasing the commodity in the cheaper city and shipping it to the dearer one for resale? Similarly, suppose now that someone were to observe the pattern of prices in Figure 6. Is it not reasonable for him to conclude that the average price of the security was about 30, and that a profit could be made by buying at slightly below that price and selling at slightly above it? For example, if he were to submit limit buy and sell orders at $29\frac{1}{2}$ and $30\frac{1}{2}$, respectively, he could make a profit of one point on each "round turn," i.e., each purchase and resale, or vice versa.

Having rationalized the presence of a dealer, we can now rather easily accommodate the submission of market orders. In the "quandary" situation mentioned above, for example, the arrival of the second order, that is, the order to sell one share at the market price, results in an immediate transaction at $29\frac{1}{2}$. In this case, the dealer acts as the buyer, offsetting the market sell order. When the third order is submitted, he is again involved in the transaction; this time, however, as the seller, providing the stock at a price of $30\frac{1}{2}$ to the person submitting an order to buy at the market.

By adding the service of an individual who maintains limit orders on both sides of the market, West makes it possible for the simulation to provide a straightforward understanding of what Demsetz calls "the neglected problem of 'immediacy' in supply and demand analysis."[21] As Demsetz puts this problem:

> Predictable immediacy is a rarity in human actions, and to approximate it requires that costs [of waiting] be borne by persons who specialize in standing ready and waiting to trade with the incoming orders of those who demand immediate servicing of their orders. The bid-ask spread is the markup that is paid for predictable immediacy of exchange in organized markets.[22]

The rationale for Demsetz's statement is apparent in the operations of the simulated market. Prior to the addition of an individual who stands "ready and waiting," the market does not provide for predictable immediacy.

Thus far, we have discussed the roles of brokers and dealers as though they always were performed by separate individuals. In real security markets, of course, the two roles are frequently performed by the same individual. The stock exchange "specialist" provides an important case in point. When brokers cannot cross buy and sell orders on the floor of the exchange by themselves, they normally transmit their unfulfilled orders to the specialist who, acting on an agency basis, executes the orders in the sequence in which they are received at the prevailing prices. In so doing, he provides a centralized brokerage service for the orders of other member brokers of the exchange. For providing this service, he receives a portion of the commission paid to the broker by the buyer or seller. It is the market-making function of the specialist, however, that needs special emphasis. By submitting standing limit orders, the specialist improves the market's continuity and resilience. Moreover, his activities tend to enhance the transaction-to-transaction stability of prices, since virtually all transactions outside the range of his bid and ask prices disappear.

The contribution of a dealer to the resilience of a market and to short-term price stability can be illustrated with the help of a more realistic simulation model, which accommodates not only limit and market orders but also tenders of different sizes. Let us simulate a flow of orders with a sequence of four-digit random numbers. The first digit determines the nature of the order (a bid if even, an ask if odd). The second digit determines the price specified for limit orders, $(0 = 28\frac{3}{4}; 1 = 29; 2 = 29\frac{1}{4};$ etc.). The third digit is used to determine whether the tender calls for the order to be executed at the price specified by the second digit, or instead calls for it to be executed at the market. We assume that there is an equal probability of market and limit orders, so that even numbers signify market orders and odd numbers, limit orders. Finally, the fourth digit determines the size of the tender. To insure that small orders dominate, we establish the following rules: 1 to 4 inclusive = one share; 5 to 7 inclusive = two shares; 8 and 9 = three shares; and 0 = four shares.[23] To illustrate, the random number 2382 produces a market order to buy one share. In this case, the price of $30\frac{3}{4}$ implied by the second digit is nullified by the fact that the third digit determines the tender is to buy at the market.

The results of operating the simulation for 50 rounds (tenders) are presented in Figure 7. These results are obtained under the assumption that a dealer is willing to place standing limit orders to buy or sell up to 4 shares at prices of $29\frac{1}{2}$ and $30\frac{1}{2}$, respectively. A comparison of Figures 6 and 7 reveals, as expected, that the presence of the dealer reduces the variability in transaction prices. The mean absolute deviation from the equilibrium price (taken as the closer of $29\frac{3}{4}$ or 30) is $.34 in Figure 6. In Figure 7 it is only $.25. In other words, price variability has been reduced more than 26 per cent by the dealer's presence.

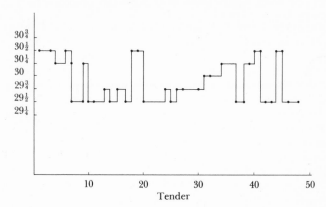

FIGURE 7   Hypothetical Sequence of Transaction Prices Generated by a
Sequence of Four-Digit Random Numbers.

We also see that the submission of orders of varying size
tends to generate transactions at more than one price. The
seventh order, for example, results in transactions at $30\frac{1}{4}$ and
$29\frac{1}{2}$. This order is an offer to sell up to four shares at the market.
When it is tendered, there is an unfulfilled limit order to buy
one share at the price of $30\frac{1}{4}$ or below. Thus, one transaction
for one share takes place at this price. The remaining three
units of the sell order are handled by the dealer at $29\frac{1}{2}$. The
dealer participates in slightly more than half of the transactions. In all, he handles forty-three shares of the stock, selling
twenty and buying twenty-three. His inventory, in other words,
increases by three units during the period covered by the
simulation.

Thus far, all of the price variability in the simulated models is
associated with movements around a stable and unvarying
equilibrium price. These price fluctuations are associated
with the difficulties in organizing an irregular inflow of tenders,
some of which specify prices and some of which do not. In real
stock markets, of course, prices change not only for these
reasons but also because of adjustments in the equilibrium
price level of the security. To complete our understanding
of stock markets we must now consider how such adjustments in
equilibrium price levels influence our simulated market. Changes in the equilibrium level of prices can be simulated in a variety
of ways. One possibility is to add an additional digit (or digits)
to our random numbers, specifying some distribution of price

changes from the initial equilibrium price. For illustrative purposes, however, we simply assume that after a stream of fifty tenders similar to the kind used in developing the data in Figure 7, demand shifts to the left, causing the equilibrium price to drop from a level of approximately $29\frac{7}{8}$ to approximately $26\frac{7}{8}$. We further assume that, when this change occurs, the distribution of limit orders shifts downward accordingly, and all unfulfilled limit orders specifying prices around $29\frac{7}{8}$ are cancelled. In other words, if the second digit 0 called for a limit order price of $28\frac{3}{4}$ prior to the shift in the equilibrium price, it would call for a price of $25\frac{3}{4}$ afterward.

What would be the impact of the change in the equilibrium price on the distribution of market orders? The answer to this question would seem to be dependent upon the dealer's behavior following the adjustment. If, for example, the dealer were able to make a correct adjustment instantaneously, i.e., if he were to judge correctly the direction and size of the price adjustment and change his bid-ask spread accordingly, it would follow that the distribution of limit orders might remain essentially as it was before the change in the equilibrium price. However, if the dealer is unable to change his bid-ask spread instantaneously, it would then follow that the distribution of limit orders could be expected to change. It would be likely that a failure of the dealer to reduce his bid and ask prices immediately by approximately the same amount as the drop in the equilibrium price would increase the number of market sell orders, both in relation to market buy orders and in relation to the total number of orders reaching the market. On the assumption that this basic logic is correct, let us suppose that the following events take place after the change in the equilibrium price:

1. The dealer maintains his bid-ask spread at $29\frac{1}{2}-30\frac{1}{2}$ for ten tenders, at which time he drops it to $26\frac{1}{2}-27\frac{1}{2}$. Admittedly, this is a very arbitrary assumption; it may suffice for illustrative purposes, but it would be more reasonable to hypothesize a staggered adjustment pattern, based perhaps on changes in the dealer's inventory.

2. During the period from the fifty-first to the sixtieth tender inclusive, i.e., when the dealer maintains his bid-ask spread at $29\frac{1}{2}-30\frac{1}{2}$, the probability that a market order is an ask rather than a bid increases from 0.5 to 0.8. It would be

reasonable to go further and assume an increase in the probability that any particular order will be a market order. To simplify matters, however, the assumption of a 0.5 probability that any order is a market order will stand.

3. When the dealer lowers his bid-ask spread to $26\frac{1}{2}-27\frac{1}{2}$, the probability that a market order is an offer will return to 0.5.

The results of operating the model for one hundred tenders, i.e., fifty tenders with equilibrium at $29\frac{7}{8}$ and the other fifty at $26\frac{7}{8}$, are summarized in Figure 8. As might be expected, the results for the first fifty tenders generally resemble those presented in Figure 7. Similarly, the results following the sixtieth tender resemble Figure 7, except for the difference in the general level of prices. The data for the tenders 50 to 60, however, reflect the rather different conditions associated with the process of adjusting from one price level to another. In particular, these data show the result of the dealer's inability to recognize and adjust instantaneously to the shifts in the equilibrium level. Accordingly, his inventory increases markedly. This result is produced, of course, by holding the dealer's bid price at $29\frac{1}{2}$ while lowering the price distribution of limit ask orders and increasing the number of market orders. In essence, the dealer acts as an artificial price support from the fifty-first through the sixtieth tender. Although dealers would hardly be expected to support prices in this manner for an indefinite period, it is not unusual for them to provide a stabilizing influence in the market. Baumol, for example, shows that in the case of transitory price declines the stock exchange specialists can support prices at halfway between the original equilibrium level and the equilibrium level after the decline, thereby maximizing their expected profits.[24]

The decision to have the dealer lower his bid-ask spread to $26\frac{1}{2}-27\frac{1}{2}$ on the sixty-first tender is completely arbitrary.[25] Nevertheless, the simulation results suggest what factors cause dealers in real markets to respond to changes in equilibrium prices. Most important, there is the pressure of inventory changes that develops between the fiftieth and sixtieth tenders. In general, dealers would prefer to maintain an even inventory position, deriving their profit from trading on the spread between the bid and ask prices rather than from holding net long or short positions.[26] This being the case, they might be expected

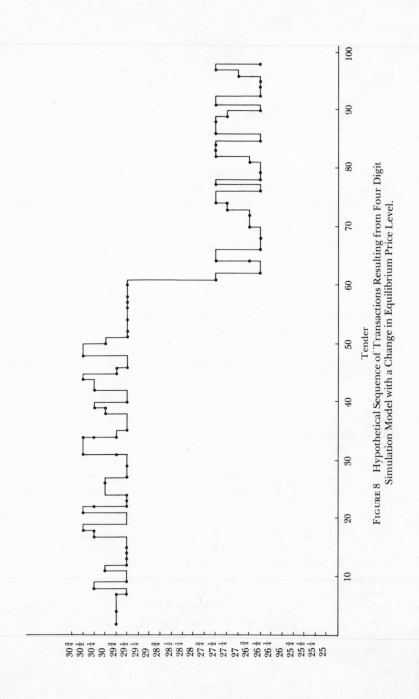

FIGURE 8 Hypothetical Sequence of Transactions Resulting from Four Digit Simulation Model with a Change in Equilibrium Price Level.

to respond to a marked increase in their long positions by lowering their bid and ask prices or reducing the sizes of their bids and offers.

In addition, it might be expected that changes in prices specified by increasing limit orders would cause the dealer to re-examine his spread policy. In the case under discussion, for example, the lower prices of incoming bids would almost certainly cause the dealer to ask whether the basic demand conditions for the stock had changed.

The reader will recall that the results presented in Figure 8 assume that any outstanding limit orders are cancelled when the equilibrium price changes following the fiftieth tender. At the time of the change in the equilibrium price, there are several outstanding limit orders specifying prices between $29\frac{1}{2}$ and 28. These orders cannot be executed so long as the dealer makes a market between $29\frac{1}{2}$ and $30\frac{1}{2}$. That is to say, no incoming sell orders can cross against these bids, because the dealer is prepared to buy at a price of $29\frac{1}{2}$. An interesting question to consider is how these orders might be handled if they are not cancelled. One obvious possibility would be to have the dealer sell to each of these bidders at the maximum price specified by the order. Under these circumstances, the price does not move in one step from $29\frac{1}{2}$ to $27\frac{1}{2}$, but rather "drifts" downward as the outstanding bids are executed.[27]

In all of the simulation models we have presented in this chapter, the distributions of limit and market orders, of prices, and of issue size are selected completely arbitrarily for the purposes of illustrating some of the concepts and problems to be taken up in detail in later chapters of this book. By now, however, it should be obvious to the reader that the possibilities for making alterations and additions to the simulation model are virtually limitless. Indeed, the technique itself is flexible enough to analyze a wide range of realistic problems related to the operation of the stock markets and marketing of particular security issues. One obvious possibility for adjusting the model would involve changing the shapes of distributions for various tenders. Demsetz makes a convincing case that distribution of limit bids and asks around the equilibrium price should be related to the time rate of transaction.[28] By incorporating this situation into the simulation model it would be possible to demonstrate that the dealer's ability to influence the width of the spread between his bid and ask prices is dependent on the shape of the distribution of limit orders, which is to say, the time rate of transactions. Similarly, another study might include experimenting with various rules concerning the reactions of dealers to changes in trading conditions.

Price Theory Models and Stock Market Analysis: A Concluding Comment

The simulation models just discussed are extremely valuable in illustrating a number of significant aspects of the processes by which supply and demand are organized and exchange transactions are consummated, but they do not provide a complete and self-sufficient basis for the study of the institutional framework and the costs associated with this process. For example, the simulations make no references to the determinants of the costs of providing broker and dealer services or the pricing of these services. On the other hand, the price theory models, which lack an explicit concern for the processes by which buyers and sellers are brought together, provide an excellent framework for analyzing the economics of these processes. By analyzing the markets for brokerage and exchange services within this framework, for example, we can develop hypotheses about the determinants of brokerage commissions and the spread between the bid and ask prices quoted by stock exchange specialists. Moreover, as we shall demonstrate in Chapters 4, 5 and 6, the implications of these hypotheses provide a basis for the empirical analysis of the costs of transacting in the stock market.

Notes

1. Some sections of this chapter are adapted from Richard R. West, "Simulating Securities Markets Operations: Some Examples, Observations and Comments," *Journal of Financial and Quantitative Analysis* 5, No. 1 (March, 1970): pp. 115–137.
2. George J. Stigler, *Five Lectures on Economic Problems* (London: Longmans, Green & Co., Ltd., 1949), p. 23.
3. Kenneth E. Boulding, *Economic Analysis*, (New York: Harper & Bros., 1955), p. 13.
4. Within this framework, a vertical structure such as the one in Figure 2 can be studied by considering each of the levels as a separate horizontal market.
5. Pure monopoly may result from a number of causes. Two of the more potent sources of monopoly power are economies of scale and barriers to the entry of potential competitors, e.g., legal barriers such as patents or franchises, or economic barriers, including exorbitant capital requirements.

6. It can be shown that the price elasticity of demand is the sum of all cross-elasticities and the income elasticity of demand.

7. As will be observed in the next section, the perfect competition model is not compatible with economies of scale (decreasing marginal costs through the relevant range of output). Then economies of scale become an important reason for the monopolization of the industry, commonly known as "natural monopoly."

8. $MR = qf'(q) + f(q) = (-p/e + f(q))$ where the price elasticity, $e = -p/qf'(q)$. Equivalently, $MR = p(1 - 1/e)$. For two demand functions with varying elasticities, e_1 and e_2, there will be two marginal revenues, MR_1, MR_2.

9. I.e, $\dfrac{\partial U_{s1i}}{\partial Q_{cash}} \Big/ \dfrac{\partial U_{s1i}}{\partial Q_x} = \dfrac{\partial U_{s2i}}{\partial Q_{cash}} \Big/ \dfrac{\partial U_{s2i}}{\partial Q_x}.$

10. William J. Baumol, *The Stock Market and Economic Efficiency*, (New York: Fordham University Press, 1965), pp. 5–6.

11. For an excellent discussion of Walras's theory of *tâtonnement*, see Don Patinkin, *Money, Interest and Prices* (New York, Harper and Row, 1965), pp. 38–43 and 531–40, Note B.

12. Within a reasonable interpretation, one may include costs of transacting in the monopoly and perfect competition models. For example, the production costs of the monopolist may also be thought to include the costs of exchange transactions, such that Total Cost = $g(q) + h(q)$, where the second expression represents costs of exchanging in a general functional form.

Similarly, in the perfect competition model exchange costs can be considered separately or within the framework of production costs. In this case, there exists additional profit opportunities for more efficient sellers in the short run. Sellers with lower costs of exchange will make profits in excess of their returns from production. In the long run, however, equilibrium conditions will require all sellers to undertake the same kind of exchange services and incur the same average costs of transacting.

Clearly, in this framework, the equilibrium mechanism and the conditions of equilibrium in the market will not be any different from what they are with zero costs of exchange. However, when the exchange process involves a series of functionally differentiated intermediaries operating under diverse conditions of competition, the simple treatment will not suffice to understand the organization of supply and demand in the market; nor will it be useful in examining the equilibrating mechanism. For example, it is very difficult to study price behavior of stocks simultaneously with the monopolistic behavior of transaction costs in some organized stock exchanges.

Indeed, only under very special circumstances can the costs of transacting be implicitly incorporated into price theory models. In general, these models give no explicit and systematic treatment for the costs of transacting, but rather avoid them by assuming frictionless markets where buyers contact sellers directly and at no cost.

13. In the case of monopoly, there is no supply schedule in the conventional sense. Hence, monopoly price may change as a result of a shift in demand or a change in the monopolist's marginal cost or both.

14. George J. Stigler, "Public Regulation of the Securities Market," *Journal of Business* 37 (April, 1964): 117–34.

15. West, "Simulating Securities Markets Operations."

16. Stigler, "Public Regulation of Securities Market," p. 127.

17. $E(t^*) = t + \left[\dfrac{1}{n}0 + \dfrac{1}{n}t^* + \dfrac{1}{n}2t^* + \cdots + \dfrac{1}{n}(n-1)t^* \right]$ or

$$= t + \frac{1}{n}\frac{(n-1)(n)t^*}{2} = t + \frac{(n-1)t^*}{2}$$

18. The probability of contact with a buyer or a seller, $1/m$, may be approximated by the ratio

$$\frac{\text{average number of daily transactions in a stock}}{\text{average number of daily transactions in the market}}$$

In this case, active issues will have the same effect as a lower m, that is, for active stocks, the probability of contacting the opposite side increases, while the number of necessary contacts for an assured execution decreases. Issues with thin markets, on the other hand, have the opposite influence on the cost of exchanging.

Similarly, with a small number of brokers, the cost of transacting will tend to decrease. Beyond a lower limit k, however, (where $n \geq k$) brokers may not be able to provide prompt execution services to their customers, which in effect implies higher costs in relation to the quality of these services.

19. West, "Simulating Securities Markets Operations," pp. 121–30.

20. *Ibid.*, p. 121.

21. Harold Demsetz, "The Cost of Transacting," *Quarterly Journal of Economics* 88 (February, 1968): 33–53.

22. *Ibid.*, pp. 35–36.

23. In this context, a "share" is equivalent to a round lot.

24. Baumol, *Stock Market and Economic Efficiency*, pp. 28–30. Analytically, Baumol summarizes his argument in the following figure, where P_i is the original equilibrium price, P_e is the equilibrium price at which the market would clear without dealer's participation and S is the market's excess supply schedule. The price decline is assumed to be temporary, so that the specialist expects it to return to its original equilibrium level, P_i.

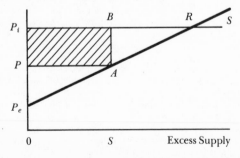

The largest rectangle, P_iBAP, inscribed within the triangle P_iP_eR reflects the maximum dealer profits assuming that he can later sell these OS shares at P_i. This rectangle has a corner at A where it can be shown that it corresponds to support price, $P = \frac{1}{2}(P_i + P_e)$.

25. The reader might expect that it would be more realistic for the dealer to move to the new level in several steps. The evidence concerning the behavior of stock price movements, however, suggests that rapid and, on the average, "correct" price adjustments are the general rule in highly organized stock markets.

26. This tendency is reported in *Report of the Special Study of the Securities Markets of the Securities and Exchange Commission*, U.S., 88th Cong., 1st Sess., House of Representatives Document 95 (Washington, D.C.: Government Printing Office, 1965), Part 2.

27. The problem of having to deal with outstanding limit orders in periods when the market is moving to a new level has received much attention and discussion over the years. In the SEC's *Special Study of the Securities Markets*, for example, it is a major subject for discussion in the sections devoted to the activities of stock exchange specialists. Among other things, the report discusses the so-called tick test and the "offsetting balance" tests. According to the tick test, the practice of cleaning up unfulfilled limit orders along the lines suggested in this paragraph would not be interpreted by the stock exchange as appropriate dealer behavior. See *Ibid.*, pp. 78–110. For a discussion of the problems associated with the tick test see Stigler, "Public Regulation of Securities Markets," pp. 124–33.

28. Demsetz, "The Cost of Transacting," p. 41.

3 The Organization of Trading Activities

In the last chapter, our simple simulation models introduced the reader to the basic operations of brokers and dealers in making markets for common stocks; this one will examine the ways in which these operations are organized in practice. We begin by providing a brief description of the two basic contemporary approaches to organizing trading in common stocks: the stock exchange and the over-the-counter market. Next, the factors that determine the allocation of securities between the stock exchanges and the over-the-counter market are considered. Against this background, we explore the question of whether the organization of trading activities has any systematic impact on stock price behavior, i.e., whether listing on one of the major exchanges influences a stock's value. Finally, we briefly discuss the use of computers as a vehicle for organizing trading in common stocks.

Organizing the Broker and Dealer Functions

At present, virtually all trading in common stocks in the United States takes place in one of two basic types of market structures: stock exchanges and over-the-counter markets. The fundamental purposes and functions of the two types of markets are similar, but their detailed practices and procedures differ considerably. To indicate both the similarities and the differences, let us briefly discuss the major characteristics of the exchange and the over-the-counter approaches to making markets in common stocks.

The Stock Exchange.[1] In the discussion of the simulated market models presented in the last chapter, almost nothing was said about how buyers and sellers of stocks communicated their orders to the individuals who performed the broker and dealer functions; presumably, they did so either by going to the location where trading took place or by transmitting their orders directly to the brokers and dealers who made the market in the stock they wished to trade. In the major stock exchanges, in contrast, investors are not permitted to be present during the trading process or to communicate directly with those involved in that process. Instead, they must gain access to the market-place by dealing through one of a limited number of persons who have the right to be present where trading takes place and to communicate with those making the market. This right is obtained by purchasing a "seat" on the exchange. At the close of 1969 there were 1,366 seats on the New York Stock Exchange and 650 seats on the American Exchange.

To facilitate the processing of orders submitted by investors, the exchanges have developed a high degree of specialization and division of labor among their members. On the NYSE and ASE, members are divided into five basic groups, four of which are primarily concerned with assisting in the execution of nonmember orders.[2] One of the four is composed of the so-called office partners. Although they rarely appear on the floor of the exchange during the hours of trading, the office partners play a critical role in the process of opening the exchange's trading facilities to the public. As mentioned above, only individuals who are members of the exchange have the right to communicate with the floor. If at least one of its partners or directors owns a seat, however, a brokerage house can be designated as a "member firm," thus permitting it to accept orders from the public. In the jargon of Wall Street, an exchange member who uses his seat for this purpose is an "office partner."

A second group of exchange members, the floor brokers, provides the next link in the chain that connects the public with the trading process. Indeed, it is the floor brokers who actually shepherd customer orders when they reach the floor of the exchange. The manner in which floor brokers receive orders depends on whether or not they are affiliated with a member firm conducting a public business. Floor brokers having such an affiliation obtain orders directly from the firm's offices. Those who do not work with a single member firm receive business from two sources: (1) brokerage houses that are not large enough to employ a floor broker on a full-time basis; and (2) member firms whose own floor brokers are too busy to handle all of the orders coming their way.

According to customs established many years ago, trading in listed stocks takes place in a standard-size quantity, generally referred to as a "round lot." Investors, however, are permitted to place orders in other than round lot sizes. When they do, the business is taken care of by a third group of exchange members: the odd lot brokers and dealers. The odd lot broker's task is quite similar to the floor broker's in that he acts on an agency basis. Unlike the floor broker, however, he acts as an agent not for a public customer but rather for one or two odd lot dealers. These dealers, in turn, buy and sell for their own accounts, hoping to make a profit on the inventory turnover.[3]

The fourth group of members is composed of the specialists. In terms of the over-all operation of the exchange, the specialists clearly play the dominant role: They have the primary responsibility for making the market and keeping it orderly. To perform this role, they act both as agents and as principals. In the former capacity, they match up public buy and sell orders forwarded to them by the floor brokers; in the latter, they trade for their own accounts.

The full significance of the specialist's role can best be appreciated against the background of the continuous auction process, which forms the backbone of the stock exchange method of market-making. The essence of the auction approach involves a physical congregating of buyers and sellers or, more typically, their agents, to match bids and offers and establish transaction prices. Auction markets take two basic forms: call and continuous. In a call auction market, goods are traded according to a pre-arranged order; when the trading in the first good is finished, trading in the second begins, and so on. Between calls for a particular good, brokers collect orders to be executed on the next round. Trading in a continuous auction market, on the other hand, takes place at any time during the hours the market is in operation. On the major stock exchanges, for example, individual securities are assigned to particular locations, or posts, on the trading floor and an exchange member, a specialist, is assigned the task of making a market for as long as the exchange is open to trading. Some years ago, several specialists often were assigned to a very active issue. More recently, however, the exchange has discouraged this practice, so that a single specialist is now assigned to make a continuous auction market in each stock on the list.

The processing of a typical public order begins with a call from a customer to an office of a member firm of the exchange. By wire or telephone, the firm transmits the customer's order to the floor of the Exchange, where a clerk carries it to a floor broker for appropriate action. Assuming that it is a round lot order, the broker moves to the post where the stock is traded and asks the specialist for the current quote; that is, for the best bid and ask prices available. If he is attempting to execute a limit order, the broker ascertains whether or not the current quote makes it possible for him to do business without delay. For example, if the broker holds a limit order to buy at 36 or better, and the current quote is 35 bid and 36 ask, he knows that conditions permit immediate action. Because of his obligation to obtain the best possible price for his client, the broker may begin the bargaining process by making a bid at $35\frac{1}{2}$ in the hope that another trader at the post will "take the bait." If this does not work, he generally, "hits the book," that is, offers to buy at the 36 ask price.

If, however, the limit order price specified by the public customer is outside of the existing quote, say $35\frac{1}{2}$ bid, the floor broker is not able to make an immediate transaction. Under these circumstances, he assigns the order to the specialist for processing if and when the stock's price moves into the appropriate range. In other words, the specialist takes over the brokerage function at this point, thus permitting the floor broker to move on to other business.

When a public customer places an order to buy or sell "at the market," the floor broker is normally expected to accept the prevailing quote on the opposite side of the market, in this case, the ask at 36. The rules of the Exchange actually permit him to attempt to get a somewhat better price for his customer; but they also imply that he may be liable for the difference between the price finally obtained, if higher than the price that prevailed when the order was placed. Understandably, this factor tends to discourage most floor brokers from attempting to do better than the current quote in any but the most unusual circumstances.

As we demonstrated in the preceding chapter, the ability of a a market to accommodate orders without a price limitation requires the existence of "reasonable" bid and ask prices at all times. In the absence of such prices, any prudent investor would be foolish not to specify a maximum buying or minimum selling price or to engage in some form of negotiation. On a stock exchange, it is the specialist's duty to maintain reasonable bid and ask prices throughout the hours of trading. When such prices are provided by the unfulfilled limit orders placed with him for execution, the specialist can simply act as a "traffic cop," giving out the current quotes to prospective traders and making transactions when conditions dictate. If limit orders fail to appear, however, or if they do not provide "reasonable" bid and ask quotations, the specialist is obligated to step into the breach, specifying prices at which he will buy or sell for his own account. Indeed, it is this obligation which guarantees that the stock exchange's auction market will be continuous in the sense that traders submitting market orders can be accommodated.[4]

Later in this chapter, and more particularly in Chapters 4 and 6, we shall explore the economics of the continuous auction market and the specialist's function in more detail. For now, however, let us turn to an examination of the basic mechanics of trading in the other major sector of the stock market, the over-the-counter market.

The Over-the-Counter Market. By comparison with the major exchanges, the outward appearance of the over-the-counter market for common stocks must make it seem disorganized, if not completely chaotic. Since it is not organized on an auction basis, the market has no trading floor, no building, no centralized location where buyers and sellers congregate to engage in trading. Nor does it have a well-defined division of labor or specialization among the myriad brokers and dealers who together make it function; on any given day, a firm in the over-the-counter market may simultaneously act as a broker in some issues, a dealer in others, and as a broker-dealer in still others.

Even the results of the market's deliberations are difficult to observe. Statistics on trading volume in the over-the-counter market are virtually nonexistent.[5] Beyond this, the prices of a large number of over-the-counter stocks found each day in the financial pages of leading newspapers are little more than nominal quotes; they do not necessarily represent the terms on which any trades took place.

Among the factors responsible for shaping the over-the-counter market's character and distinguishing it from that of the exchanges, the most important is freedom of access and behavior. The securities traded in the over-the-counter market do not have to meet any listing requirements. Nor is it necessary for those who perform the broker and dealer functions to buy a seat or in some analogous way obtain formal entry to the market place. Anyone with a telephone, some capital, a measure of intestinal fortitude and a registration with the Securities and Exchange Commission is free to become a participant in the over-the-counter market. Moreover, he is relatively free to dictate the terms and conditions of his participation. Competition, of course, may force him to pursue certain policies, but he is not, in general, bound by the kinds of rules and regulations that apply to stock exchange members.

Because of the comparative absence of formal constraints on the firms that participate in the over-the-counter market, the strength of the market in a particular stock is subject to considerable variation over time. If a large number of firms are actively making a two-way market in a stock, i.e., are providing firm bid and ask quotations for "reasonable" sized orders, buyers and sellers have little difficulty in taking or disposing of their positions. On the other hand, if firms are backing away from the market, either by widening their bid and ask spreads or reducing their willingness to take positions, or both, investors find it difficult to do business on reasonable terms. Indeed, when firms back completely away, as is sometimes the case if the market is characterized by extreme uncertainty, investors are faced with a situation in which orders either are refused outright or are accepted only on the basis that they will be transacted if and when offsetting orders appear. When this happens, of course, over-the-counter trading takes place strictly between investors, with the market-makers limiting their participation to providing brokerage services.

The over-the-counter market for a particular security has both a wholesale and a retail component. The wholesale portion of the market is composed of firms that have announced a willingness to take positions for their own accounts. The number of such firms varies considerably from issue to issue, depending primarily on the level of trading activity. Some idea of this relationship can be obtained from Table 3–1, which shows the average number of market-making firms and the trading volume for a sample of 200 stocks traded in the over-the-counter market early in 1962.

TABLE 3–1
Over-the-Counter Stocks Classified by Dealers Quoting a Two-Way Market and Activity (200 selected stocks on Jan. 18, 1962)*
(number of stocks)

Number of Dealers Quoting a Two-Way Market†	None	Less than 500	500 to 999	1,000 to 1,999	2,000 to 4,999	5,000 to 9,999	10,000 and over	All Stocks
None	32	5	—	—	—	—	—	37
1 to 2	20	14	1	2	3	2	—	42
3 to 4	8	14	5	5	2	1	—	35
5 to 6	2	7	6	6	3	—	1	25
7 to 8	2	10	5	3	9	1	1	31
9 to 10	1	2	—	2	3	2	—	10
11 to 14	—	—	—	1	3	7	4	15
15 and over	—	—	—	—	1	1	3	5
Total no. of stocks	65	52	17	19	24	14	9	200‡
Avg. no. of dealers per stock	1.3	3.8	5.0	5.6	7.8	9.9	13.2	4.6

*Adapted from *Special Study*, Chapter 7, p. 729.
†Based on quotations in National Quotation Bureau, Inc., the National Quotation Service, Jan. 18, 1962.
‡Includes three stocks listed on the New York Stock Exchange.

The fact that more than one firm often makes a wholesale market in a given stock has a number of important implications for the conduct of business in the over-the-counter market. First, it means there must be a considerable amount of communication between firms in the wholesale market. To avoid losing touch with its competitors' trading conditions, each firm must have up-to-the-minute knowledge of what other wholesalers are doing, that is, what prices they are quoting and what kinds of commitments they are willing to take. Since such information can be relied upon only when it represents the terms on which trades can actually be consummated, wholesale dealers sometimes make transactions with each other simply to keep abreast of market developments. Such transactions usually take place directly between dealers, but in some cases—for example, when a dealer wishes to avoid "tipping his hand"—they may be handled by an inter-dealer broker.

A second implication of the presence of multiple market-makers relates to the conduct of operations in the retail market, which forms the link between the wholesale market-makers and public customers. When a firm making a retail market in over-the-counter stocks is contacted by a customer, it can act on either a principal or an agent basis. If it happens to be one of the firms making a wholesale market in the stock for which an order is obtained, it will normally act in the former capacity. On the other hand, when it does not do a dealer business in the stock, the firm must work through the wholesale market to accomodate the customer's order. Since several firms make a market in most over-the-counter stocks, the retail broker can obtain a number of bid and ask prices. This characteristic of the over-the-counter market stands out in sharp contrast to the exchange markets, where the practice of assigning a single specialist to each issue means that only one quote is available.

Because the presence of reasonable bid and ask quotes cannot be quaranteed at all times in the over-the-counter market, most transactions are made on a negotiated basis. The public customer initiates the transaction by requesting information from a brokerage firm about the current state of the market. If the firm deals in the issue itself, it will supply the customer with a quotation directly. In all other cases, the firm will first communicate with a wholesale dealer to obtain a quotation that can be forwarded to the customer. On receiving the information forwarded by the retail firm, the customer must decide whether he is willing to trade on the basis of the prices quoted or prefers to try to obtain a better price. Of course, even if he decides to trade on the basis of the current quote, he may receive a better price if his brokerage firm is able to strike a bargain somewhere between a wholesale dealer's bid and ask prices. To this extent, the customer's decision to trade "at the market," so to speak, still represents the submission of a limit order at the qouted price.

Allocating Securities Between the Exchange and the Over-the-Counter Market

Why is it that some stocks trade in the over-the-counter market, while others are listed on an exchange? Beyond this, why do exchange-listed securities sometimes trade in the over-the-counter market?

While recognizing that a wide variety of factors probably have some influence on the determination of where a particular stock will trade, it is our contention that the primary determinant in the allocation process is whether or not trading can be effectively organized on a continuous auction basis. When conditions seem amenable to the establishment of a continuous auction market, a stock *usually* trades on an exchange; when these conditions are lacking, it trades in the over-the-counter market. Put somewhat differently, *most* stocks trading in the over-the-counter market do so simply because they are not well suited to trading on an exchange. To this extent, the allocation of securities to the over-the-counter market *typically* represents a "residual" type of determination.

In making these general statements we have been careful to use such words as "usually," "most" and "typically." Our reason for being so cautious is quite simple: Listing on an exchange is not something that comes as a natural consequence of a stock's having characteristics that permit the establishment of a viable continuous auction market. To the contrary, listing requires the submission of a formal application by a stock's issuer. This being the case, some issues that could easily be traded on a continuous auction basis continue to trade in the over-the-counter market purely because of a firm's reluctance to list.[6]

Most firms, however, are eager to apply for admission to exchange trading, hence the vast majority of stocks trading in the over-the-counter market do so for one of two reasons:

(1) They cannot meet exchange listing requirements, which are intended to exclude certain types of stocks that would be difficult to trade on continuous auction basis; or (2) they can meet the requirements, but still are ill-suited to trading on this basis. The full import of the second reason should not be missed by the reader. It implies that even in cases where the listing requirements are unable to weed out stocks on the basis of their suitability for trading on an exchange, "natural" economic forces take their place.

To understand how and why these forces work, we must explore in somewhat more detail the functioning of the continuous auction method of market-making. From the discussion in the preceding section, the reader will recall that the stock exchange specialist plays the pivotal role in operating a continuous auction market. To perform this role effectively, he must iron out temporary disparities between the inflows of buy and sell orders by buying and selling for his own account. Moreover, as organized in the New York and American Stock Exchanges, he must do so without attempting to solicit orders when trading volume is inadequate. In other words, in contrast to the over-the-counter dealer, who actively seeks out orders to adjust his inventory position, the specialist must rely on price adjustments or other changes in market conditions to induce a flow of orders that will offset his positions. When there is a relatively steady, well-balanced inflow of buy and sell orders, the specialist can meet his obligation with relative ease. Indeed, under these conditions the risks and costs associated with taking positions not only are manageable but also provide him with an opportunity to earn an excellent, if not unreasonable, return on his capital.[7]

When the inflow of orders becomes unsteady or unbalanced, however, the specialist's task becomes considerably more demanding and risky. The *Special Study* reported, for example, that specialists find it both difficult and unprofitable to make markets in inactive or "thin" stocks. According to the *Special Study*,

> Several specialists testified that they are reluctant to take positions in inactive stocks. The reason is fairly obvious; a position in an inactive stock with a thin book would tend to "lock in" the specialist. In such issues, he has no assured flow of orders through which he can quickly realize the "jobber's turn." Although he may buy at his own bid, the lack of a counter party within a reasonable time compels him to hold

the stock in inventory at the risk of market movements. By the time a counter party arrives in the market, extrinsic events may have changed the price to a point where the specialist can no longer realize a profit by selling at his own offer . . . . Thus, it seems that in inactive issues where the specialist participation may be most needed, the risks are the greatest while the chances of trading profit are lower, so that the specialist's incentive for making a close [spread between his bid and ask prices] and a continuous market are reduced.[8]

Similar problems result when the total quantity of shares bought and sold is relatively sizable, but the distribution of orders varies greatly over time, as, for example, in the case of stocks that are traded in large blocks. The *Special Study* comments on their problems as follows:

> [A] specialist purchasing a block faces the same economic problem as that present in dealing in an inactive stock, i.e., it may be some time before sufficient matching orders arrive, and until that time the specialist is left with an inventory at the risk of the market and with his capital "tied up."[9]

For this reason, it concluded that "blocks of shares are often too large to be readily and promptly absorbed through the routine procedures of the continuous auction market.[10] If anything, this may be an understatement; recent developments would seem to suggest that some blocks may be too large to be absorbed through the continuous auction market under any reasonable conditions. Additional comments on this general subject will be made in Chapters 6 and 9, which concern the determinants of specialists price policies and the impact of institutional investors on the structure of the stock market. For now, let us consider the factors that might be expected to influence the volume and size distribution of buy and sell orders for a particular common stock.

On purely *a priori* grounds, a strong case can be made that the primary determinants of order volume and distribution ought to be the amount of the issue outstanding and the characteristics of its ownership pattern. In particular, it seems reasonable that an issue with a large number of outstanding shares held by a substantial number of small investors ought to have a flow of orders that is relatively steady and well balanced between bids and asks, that is, a flow of many small orders. However, as the number of shares outstanding declines and/or the ownership becomes somewhat more concentrated, it might be expected that the time rate of transactions would decline and the average size

over-the-counter basis. Indeed, the so-called third and fourth markets, in which listed stocks trade on an over-the-counter basis, derive much of their *raison d'être* from the problems posed for the continuous auction process by the inflow of block orders.[13]

Thus far the discussion has focused on pointing out why certain types of stocks are *not* well suited for trading in one of the exchanges. We might equally well ask why these same stocks are better suited for trading in the over-the-counter markets. By looking momentarily at the organization of trading activities in another part of the capital markets, the market for United States government securities, we can obtain some interesting insights into this question. Over its lengthy history, the market for United States government securities has sometimes been organized on an exchange basis and sometimes on an over-the-counter basis. For almost fifty years, however, the bulk of the trading has taken place in the over-the-counter market; treasury bills, first issued in 1929, have not been listed on an exchange.

In 1958, a speculative buildup and decline in the government securities market led to a joint Federal Reserve–Treasury study of whether or not the market should be restructured along the lines of the stock exchanges or remain in its dealer (over-the-counter) form. The study reported that the respondents to a questionnaire on this subject, representing a wide range of interests and backgrounds in the financial community, "were virtually unanimous in the view that the present over-the-counter market is preferable to an exchange market."[14] While differing somewhat in details, the respondents' conclusions generally stressed the argument that the variability in the inflow of orders and the presence of considerable block trading are better accommodated in the over-the-counter market. They pointed out, for example, that "dealers maintain a close working relationship with prospective buyers and sellers and are in a position to seek them out when attempting to lodge a large sale to satisfy a large purchase or to execute a swap transaction."[15] More important, they questioned whether the same type of accommodations could be provided by an exchange market:

> In order to serve customers effectively, the dealers must maintain constant contact with potential sources of demand and supply throughout the country. . . . This intimate knowledge of nationwide customer needs is of considerable importance in making markets for long-term Treasury issues, particularly at times when market

conditions make the maintenance of large dealer positions exces-
sively risky. At such times, dealer transactions are largely confined
to matching up customers' bids and offers but their awareness of
individual investor needs throughout the country often enables
them to ferret out offsets to match incoming orders.... The dealer
mechanism, consequently, appears to contribute to the relative
ease with which transactions can be executed and hence to market
continuity. *A specialist on the New York Stock Exchange, on the other
hand, lacking these contacts with customers and other dealers, would have to
depend on a balanced inflow of purchase and sale orders from investors and
traders themselves. If this inflow became one-sided the exchange specialist
would be limited in his ability to execute orders until the needed price adjustments, or other conditions, induced a flow of offsetting orders.*[16]

Stating matters somewhat more succinctly, the respondents
argued, in effect, that the over-the-counter market's real virtue
is its emphasis on negotiation. In contrast to the specialist, the
over-the-counter dealer is not required to act passively, waiting
for incoming orders to provide him with opportunities to make
inventory adjustments. Nor is he faced with having to take a
position if he cannot match up a buyer and a seller. Instead,
the over-the-counter dealer is free to communicate with potential
buyers and sellers and, in general, to "shop" a deal aggressively.
For this very reason, the over-the-counter dealer can do a better
job than an exchange specialist in making a market for stocks
having order flows that are thin or unbalanced.

Trading Organization and Stock Price Behavior

One of the more interesting questions related to the organization of trading activities is whether listing on one of the major
stock exchanges has a positive influence on the market price
of common shares. On *a priori* grounds, there are several
reasons to expect that it might. To begin with, the fact that the
exchanges have listing criteria related to the profitability of a
company and the distribution of its shares means that listing,
in the words of one observer, "gives an investor reasonable
grounds to believe that the issue of securities was legal, that the
concern was legally organized, and that at the time of entering
it was a solvent growing concern with a relatively large issue of
securities well distributed."[17] Besides this, listing guarantees
that there will be daily information about the outcome of
trading activities. Each of these factors, of course, might be

expected to broaden investor interest in a stock listed on an exchange. The availability of daily price and volume information, for example, brings the name of the stock to the attention of many people who do not have access to over-the-counter quotations. More important, these data give investors some notion of the activity on a stock, thereby informing them of its probable marketability.[18]

Until quite recently there was little empirical evidence against which to weigh that *a priori* reasoning. The evidence that was available, however, tended to support the idea that listing has a positive influence on price behavior. On the basis of a study of the post-listing behavior of some stocks, Anna Merjos, for example, reaches the conclusion that, "generally speaking, listing on the American or on the New York Stock Exchange pays off in the form of higher prices."[19] A similar conclusion is drawn by John D. O'Connel.[20] O'Connel bases this judgment on an analysis of two types of data: (1) the behavior of the prices of stocks delisted from trading on the exchanges and (2) the differences in the behavior of the prices of stocks that were simultaneously traded on an exchange and in the over-the-counter market. Unfortunately, neither Merjos nor O'Connel attempts to control for the influence of variables other than listing that affect the behavior of share prices. Instead, both assume that any difference in the level of prices is solely the result of the impact of listing. This, however, is not a particularly reasonable assumption. The very fact that a company chooses to have its stock listed, or to move its listing from one exchange to another, suggests that it is experiencing marked changes in its business situation.

Furst's Study. A recent paper by Richard W. Furst presents the results of an analysis of listing that attempts to control for a number of financial and operating variables known to influence the behavior of stock prices.[21] The population Furst studies consists of 198 companies whose common shares moved from the over-the-counter market to the New York Stock Exchange between 1960 and 1965.[22] To isolate the influence of listing, Furst makes use of a multiple regression model developed some years ago by Myron J. Gordon.[23] In general terms, the model specifies that a stock's price is a function of its future income stream and the rate at which that stream is capitalized. In logarithmic form, the model appears as follows:

$$\log P = \log \alpha_0 + \alpha_1 \log D + \alpha_2 \log (1 + br)$$
$$+ \alpha_3 \log (1 + \sigma/A)$$
$$+ \alpha_4 \log (1 + h - ih/k)$$
$$+ \alpha_5 \log S \tag{3.2}$$

where P equals the price of a common share; D is the dividend per share; br is the average rate of growth of the firm's dividend per share; σ/A is a measure of the firm's earnings stability; $(1 + h - ih/k)$ is a leverage variable; and S equals corporate size.[24] To this basic valuation model Furst adds a dummy variable to take account of the effect (if any) of listing on the price of shares.

For each company in the sample, measurements of the dependent and independent variables are made for a date approximately six months prior to having its shares listed on the New York Stock Exchange, and for a date six months after the shares are listed. In the prelisting data, the dummy variable takes on a value of zero for each company. After listing, it is coded with a one. Furst then combines the data for the two dates and regresses price on the variables for dividend growth, earnings stability, and so forth. He reasons that if listing is an important factor, the coefficient of the dummy variable should be positive and statistically different from zero.

The results Furst obtains are summarized in Table 3-3. As these results indicate, the coefficient of the dummy variable is not significantly different from zero; nor is it even positive, as originally hypothesized.

On the basis of the results of his regression analysis, Furst concludes that "the widely held belief that a company will benefit from listing on the NYSE through obtaining a higher market price (for its stock) was not confirmed."[25] While we generally concur with this conclusion, we would point out that several aspects of Furst's study are subject to question. To begin with, the basic regression model does not perform as well for Furst as it does for Gordon. The multiple coefficient of determination in Furst's regression equation (R^2) is only 0.27. By comparison, Gordon's results show R^2 consistently above 0.85. To be sure, Gordon's tests are based on data from separate industry groups, while Furst combines data from a range of industries. However, even when his data are broken down into eight industry groups, Furst's R^2 lags considerably behind Gordon's. In no industry is the R^2 greater than 0.62;

TABLE 3–3

Regression Coefficients, Standard Errors, and *t*-ratios for the Independent Variables*

Variable	Coefficient	t-Ratio
Dividend	0.218	6.23
	(0.035)	
Growth rate	3.836	8.51
	(0.451)	
Earnings instability	−1.125	−2.14
	(0.526)	
Leverage	−0.653	−6.99
	(0.093)	
Size	0.215	8.23
	(0.026)	
Listing	−0.017	−0.99
	(0.018)	

NOTE: Multiple coefficient of determination = 0.27; degrees of freedom = 389; regression constant = 1.081; SE of market price variable = 0.172.

*Adapted from Richard W. Furst, "Does Listing Increase the Market Price of Common Shares?" *Journal of Business* 43, No. 2 (April, 1970): 174–80.

in five it is less than 0.60. Moreover, when the data for the two sample periods are analyzed separately, the coefficient for earnings instability has the wrong sign in the prelisting equation.[26]

Another potential source of concern in Furst's work relates to the stability of the regression coefficients of the dividend, growth, earnings instability, leverage, and size variables. Recognizing that his dummy variable test is valid only if it can be demonstrated that these coefficients do not change significantly over the year studied, Furst calculates prelisting and postlisting equations. He then tests the null hypothesis that the two equations come from the same population, using a well-known F test. The calculated value of F, 0.866, is much too low to reject the hypothesis with any degree of confidence.[27] Thus, Furst concludes that the equations are not significantly different.

As a separate test of the stability of the regression equation underlying Furst's model, we employed a test that examines each coefficient separately, rather than the equation as a whole.[28]

TABLE 3–4

Test of the Stability of the Regression Coefficients in Furst's
Two Cross Sections

Variable	y	Probability of Obtaining as Large a χ^2	Accept Hypothesis That All Samples Have the Same Coefficient?
Dividend	0.0008	> 0.90	Yes
Growth rate	2.243	< 0.15	Yes
Earnings instability	1.931	< 0.20	Yes
Leverage	0.492	> 0.40	Yes
Corporation size	2.426	< 0.15	Yes

Our results, reported in Table 3–4, require us to accept the hypothesis that each coefficient is the same in both equations; yet we feel it important to note that the probabilities associated with the χ^2 for earnings instability, growth, and size are much lower than the probability of obtaining an F of 0.866 in Furst's test. In other words, although we accept the null hypothesis in each case, we are somewhat less confident about our results. By itself, this latter point might not seem worthy of concern. However, its importance is magnified because the over-all "fit" of the model leaves so much to be desired. In short, the combination of the low multiple coefficient of determination and the *relative* instability of the regression coefficients causes us not to reject Furst's conclusions, but simply to view them with something less than complete confidence.

Van Horne's Study. As a prelude to describing his results, Furst mentions that both he and Anna Merjos conclude that stock prices tend to behave rather paradoxically around the time of listing. According to Furst, "there is a tendency for the market price to rise from about sixty days prior to listing; then the price falls back to about its prior level approximately sixty days after listing."[29] James Van Horne, in a recently completed study, subjects to empirical testing the null hypothesis that stocks do not experience superior or inferior price performance around the time of listing.[30] Van Horne's procedure involves attempting to isolate any abnormal price behavior by computing the difference between the return on newly listed stocks and the returns on closely related industry stock price indices over various time periods surrounding the date of listing. A test is applied to determine the statistical significance of the average differences.

Van Horne's sample is composed of 140 stocks that were newly listed on either the New York or American Stock Exchanges during the years 1960–67. To take account of both prelisting and postlisting price behavior, and to study price behavior during the "listing cycle," i.e., the period between application for listing (referred to as the registration date) and listing itself, Van Horne calculates price ratios for the following time periods: four months before registration to two months before registration; two months before registration to registration; registration to listing; listing to two months after listing; and two months before registration to two months before listing.

In his initial analysis, Van Horne finds that the average differences between the returns on newly listed stocks and the returns on closely related stock price indices are uniformly positive during the periods prior to listing. After listing, on the other hand, they are negative. More important, during the prelisting periods, the differences are statistically significant at rather high levels. The negative difference after listing, however, are not significantly different from zero.

Rather than drawing conclusions on the basis of his initial results, Van Horne wisely notes that several important factors detract from their validity. The most important factor is the failure to take account of transactions costs associated with buying and selling stocks. After making an approximate correction for the existence of these costs, he concludes that the results "seem to be considerably different":

Not only are the average differences between the stock price indices for listing stocks and those for industry averages lower than before, but the ratios are also lower. For the NYSE [portion of the sample], only the average difference between two months prior to registration and registration is significant at the 5 per cent level. One must remember that the price used [to calculate returns] for the registration date was the ask price. If a market participant were to buy a stock two months prior to registration and sell it at the registration date, the relevant price would be the bid price, in which case the average difference would not be significant.

For the ASE [portion of the sample], none of the changes in the average price of listing stocks, holding constant the effect of industry stock price movements, is significant.[31]

Beyond taking transactions costs into consideration, Van Horne notes that other factors, including higher risk character- istics and lower payout ratios of newly listed stocks, tend to bias the results in favor of superior price performance by newly listed stocks. After taking account of these factors, Van Horne concludes that his results do not support "the idea that stocks rise significantly in price after the announcement to list and continue to rise through the time of actual listing, after which they sell off."[32]

On the basis of the studies recently completed by Furst and Van Horne, it seems reasonable to argue that the existing evidence fails to establish that listing *per se*, or the process of listing, has any significant impact on either the short- or long- run behavior of stock prices. This is not to say that listing has no real value to either investors or issuers, but rather that this value has no systematic, measurable impact on the pricing of shares.

Automation and Market-Making

In recent years, the growth in block trading by institutional investors has led to a growing interest in the use of computers as a means of organizing trading in common stocks. Thus far, most of this interest has focused on the development of auto- mated trading information systems that use time shared comput- ers to transmit indications of buying or selling interest in various stocks. However, at least one operating system, called Instinet, already has the capability both to transmit information and to facilitate communication among potential buyers and sellers, leading to the submission of formal offers, negotiations, and the execution of transactions. Beyond this, there exist proposals to develop a fully automated "stock exchange" that would give the computer all of the obligations of today's specialists.

This section will briefly discuss the logic and mechanics of various automated methods of facilitating trading in common stocks. The simplest of these methods, the automated trading information system, is examined first, followed by the Instinet approach to market-making, and, finally, by the idea of a fully automated stock exchange.

At present, three automated information systems are in operation. The simplest (in terms of its operation), yet most revolutionary (in terms of its potential impact on the structure of the equities market), is the National Association of Securities Dealers' Automated Quotation system, or NASDAQ. The other two are the NYSE's Block Automation system and the AutEx system operated by the AutEx Service Corporation. All three systems are evolutionary, rather than revolutionary, in that they seek to tie the computer to existing institutions rather than to supplant these institutions. The developer of AutEx has stated, for example, that a basic premise underlying his system design has been that "the industry should not be forced into a new mold, since it is difficult enough to gain acceptance for automation without coupling this to basic reorganization or indeed revolution in the securities industry."[33]

The NASDAQ System. The NASDAQ system provides up-to-the-minute bid and ask quotations on some 2,400 over-the-counter stocks. In addition it relays daily closing prices to newspapers and wire services. In other words, NASDAQ permits over-the-counter dealers to transmit quotes via the computer, thus eliminating the need to phone back and forth constantly to keep up with changes in market conditions.

Here's how the system works. Over-the-counter market-makers with "Level III" service enter quotes into a central NASDAQ computer facility and update them as they see fit during the trading day. To obtain a quote a subscriber pushes the appropriate button on a receiving unit. Subscribers to "Level II" service, i.e., over-the-counter retailers, receive all bid and ask prices that are on file with the central computer. In addition, subscribers to "Level I" service, usually registered representatives and individual investors, obtain median bid and ask prices through such operating systems as Quotron.

The NASDAQ system does not eliminate the need for telephone contact between retail and wholesale dealers. That is, the system does not yet provide for the execution of trades. Nor does the system guarantee that quotes for a particular stock will be available at all times. It does, however, hold out the promise of improving the over-the-counter market's performance by providing more and better information about the state of the market at a particular time. For this reason, the system also presents a threat to the organized stock exchanges. Earlier in this chapter we noted that listed securities sometimes trade in the over-the-counter market for reasons related to the mechanics and cost of the auction market. Prior to the advent of NASDAQ, some firms tended to avoid trading listed stocks in the over-the-counter market because of a lack of firm quotes. With NASDAQ this problem is largely overcome. The NYSE and ASE are aware of the threat posed by the system and they have been able to keep listed stocks off it for the time being. Whether they will be able to do so in the long run depends on the outcome of antitrust suits filed on behalf of over-the-counter dealers who regard the prohibition as a restraint of trade.

The NYSE Block Automation System. Perhaps the simplest of the automated systems is that operated by the NYSE. Each of the system's subscribers, who may be either exchange members or nonmembers, including institutional investors, has a computer terminal for entering and receiving messages from the system. The typical "entry message" calls for the subscriber to give his identification, the name of the NYSE listed security he wishes to trade, and the amount he wishes to trade. If he is a non-member organization, he must also name the member broker who is handling the trade for him.

If the computer finds that it has interest on both sides of a given stock, i.e., buy and sell interest, it notifies the appropriate exchange member brokers, who then go about negotiating the terms of a trade. If an institutional investor has submitted one of the orders, the computer also notifies it of the match and of the name of the broker on the other side of the negotiation. When the two brokers in question agree on the terms of a trade, the final execution is made at the appropriate post on the floor of the exchange.

To permit subscribers to keep abreast of potential interest in various stocks, the NYSE system also has the capability of printing out a list of the securities named in all of the active buy and sell messages. However, information concerning the types of messages and the size of buy and sell interest is not provided.

The AutEx System. Like the NYSE system, the AutEx system incorporates the concept of broadening and accelerating the process of informing institutional investors of block interest in various stocks. The system, however, relies on two types of computer terminals. One type, available only to brokers, is used to send "interest messages" that specify the broker's name, the size, side (buy or sell) and name of the security, being "shopped."

According to AutEx, the issuance of an interest message "means that the broker is ready, willing, and able to trade as he designates at or near the current market price." Interest messages are received by institutional subscribers on the second type of computer terminal. However, the mere possession of a receiving terminal does not mean that a subscriber to AutEx will be notified of all interest messages. Brokers are free to specify the names of subscribers to whom a particular interest message should be sent. All over-the-counter brokers who are members of the National Association of Securities Dealers and all members of a registered stock exchange can subscribe to AutEx and receive a broker's terminal. Receiving terminals are available to "any organization which manages security portfolios on a professional basis and meets other minimal requirements."

To understand how the AutEx system operates, let us assume that a large institutional investor desires to sell, say, 50,000 shares of XYZ common stock. As the first step in the transaction process, he telephones his brokerage house informing it of the order size he has in mind and the price limitations he wants to specify. The brokerage house, being a subscriber to AutEx, enters an interest message in its terminal, giving its name, the name of the stock, the fact that it has a sell order and the information that it is trying to sell a large amount of stock. The institutional subscribers specified by the broker receive the interest message on their receiving units. If one of them decides that it might be interested in purchasing some XYZ, it makes arrangements to get in touch with the broker who entered the message. It can do this in several ways. One way is to send a message to the broker to call it. Another is to call the broker directly, and a third is to contact the broker via a second broker. This last alternative makes it possible for the institution to remain anonymous.

From this point onward, the negotiations take place very much as they would if the whole operation had taken place via telephone conversations. If the stock being traded is listed in an exchange, for example, the final transaction is usually made at the appropriate post on the floor. The computer's role, in other words, is strictly limited to bringing buyers and sellers to the point where trading can take place; no attempt is made to automate the process of negotiations, or to bypass the traditional institutional arrangements for making trades.

The Instinet System. As described in newspaper and magazine accounts, the Instinet system provides for trading in over 1,000 common stocks, many of which are listed on the New York and American Stock Exchanges.[34] Access to the system is limited to institutions and individuals who, by paying a monthly subscription fee, are able to correspond via teletype equipment with the system's computer headquarters. Subscribers are able to submit limit buy and sell orders for any stock included in the system. In addition, they can place "wild card" orders that merely specify the desire to buy or sell an unspecified amount of stock at a particular price or a specific amount at an unspecified price. Orders in the computer's "book" are, of course, available to all subscribers to aid them in forming orders. Finally, the system provides for subscribers to contact each other anonymously to engage in haggling over price or quantity.

To illustrate how the system works, let us suppose that a subscriber desires to sell up to 70,000 shares of the common stock of XYZ Corp. To begin with, the subscriber might ask the computer to give him a print out of all the existing orders to buy or sell XYZ, say, one order to sell up to 10,000 units at $66.20 and a second order to buy up to 15,000 units at $64.10. If our subscriber is particularly anxious to sell a part of his holding, he can do so simply by submitting a sell order for 15,000 at the current bid price of $64.10. Following this action several options remain. He can, for example, submit a sell order for the remaining 55,000 units at some particular price; alternatively, he can submit a sell order but withhold volume information. In the latter case, of course, he is indicating a willingness to haggle over trading terms.

With the exception of the important options relating to haggling, the Instinet system closely parallels the first simulation model discussed in Chapter 2. Like the model, the Instinet system provides a means for submitting limit orders, keeping a book of unfulfilled orders, and making trades when appropriate. Since it does not guarantee the existence of limit orders on both sides of the market at all times, the system, like the simple model, is unable to accommodate market orders. Indeed, it is this limitation that partially creates the need to provide for placing orders without price or volume information and for the use of bargaining.

In cases where demand exists on both sides of the market, the Instinet system, in effect, eliminates the need for a broker: The computer acts as the broker. Unless subscribers to the system accept the role of dealer in particular securities, however, it is still necessary for subscribers to deal at times with dealers who are willing to take positions for their own accounts. In other words, the Instinet system does not eliminate the need for someone to step into the breach when a subscriber wants to unload and no buyers are around. Some observers view this characteristic as a flaw, particularly as it relates to institutional business. No institution, they argue, can afford to divulge its desire to liquidate a position over the system if it is unsure that a transaction will take place; to do so might "tip off" the market that the stock is for sale, thus making it difficult to get any marketmaker, such as a third market dealer, to take on the block at any reasonable price.[35]

A Fully Automated Stock Exchange? Recently, one brokerage house executive, Mr. Charles E. Youngblood, argued that it should be relatively easy to devise a well-capitalized, publicly owned, fully automated stock market that would be capable of meeting simultaneously the trading needs of institutions and rank and file investors.[36] According to Youngblood, computerized markets should be able to service institutional demands simply by having "the Exchange [computer] itself assume the specialist's responsibility."[37] Presumably, this process would involve having the computer decide to take positions with the Exchange's capital, when crosses could not be made.

On the surface, this argument has much to recommend it. Its appeal is strengthened by the fact that the Exchange computer also could do most bookkeeping chores, thereby solving some of the stock market's "back office" problems. It is our judgment, however, that the stock market of the future will be even more difficult to automate fully than today's. Existing stock exchange practices, with their emphasis on relatively rigid rules for specialist behavior, continuity of price movements (i.e., small price changes from transaction to transaction), and continuous trading during the hours of exchange operation, might well lend themselves to computer programming. The market of the future, however, shows signs of being considerably more complex and probably will require that many existing rules of thumb be scrapped in favor of greater recourse to judgment. We shall have more to say on this subject in Chapter 9. For now, however, it should suffice to say that in coming years dealers will probably have to be free to decide when to trade and when not to trade; when to trade on both sides of the market and when to deal on only one side; and what price to quote. Furthermore, their quotations will typically be nominal, with transaction prices resulting from bargaining.[38] In short, the market of the future probably will need to embody many of the characteristics of today's over-the-counter markets, the most important of which is the negotiated basis for transactions.

While acknowledging the growing capabilities of electronic computers, we feel that it is quite unlikely that a system could be devised in the near future to perform these complex tasks satisfactorily.[39] How, for example, could the computer be programmed to decide whether or not to trade at a particular time and for a specific quantity, particularly given the important "tone and feel" characteristics of making a negotiated market? Then again, what price should the computer quote and how should it bargain with an institution that may have more stock to sell than it originally makes known? It is interesting to note that Mr. Youngblood did not attempt to deal explicitly with such questions as these! He did note that his proposed Exchange might be able to provide the computer with a marketing capability by incorporating the sales facilities of existing brokerage houses. This, however, would not solve the basic problem of giving the computer the data necessary to bargain effectively and make sensible positioning decisions. In a negotiated market it is not sufficient merely to have a marketing capability. Rather, that capability must be tightly linked (in terms of profits and losses) to the positioning function, since the latter's decisions are made largely on the basis of the intelligence it receives from the former.

The problem of devising a workable computerized stock market seems even more complex when regulatory considerations are added to the picture. Historically, the SEC has favored continuity of trading during exchange hours. On today's exchanges, for example, a specialist must continue to operate unless he receives permission to stop trading; then he must stop all trading. Would the SEC be prepared to sanction an exchange that operated according to the relatively informal rules of an over-the-counter market, where some trades are made, others are refused, and so forth? Frankly, we doubt it.

Notes

1. The discussion in this section is based in large measure on portions of the *Report of the Special Study of the Securities Markets of the Securities and Exchange Commission*, U.S., 88th Cong., 1st sess., House of Representatives Document 95 (Washington, D.C.: Government Printing Office, 1965) (hereafter referred to as *Special Study*), Part 2, especially Chapters 5 and 6.
2. The fifth group of members is composed of the floor traders. Floor traders are exchange members who buy and sell for their own accounts in the hope of achieving profits on their transactions. Except for the limited amount of liquidity they provide, the floor traders have little impact on the exchange's role in meeting the trading needs of rank-and-file investors. Moreover, in today's market, there are relatively few floor traders. At the close of 1969, for example, only thirteen floor traders were active on the NYSE. For a discussion of floor brokers' activities, see *Special Study*, Chapter 6, pp. 202–42.
3. The mechanics of odd-lot trading are conceptually simple but operationally complex. The *Special Study* reports that one student of the odd-lot process concluded that it takes nineteen steps to consummate an odd-lot transaction. For a detailed discussion of odd lot activities, see *Special Study*, Chapter 6, pp. 173–202.
4. Unfortunately, the word "continuous" often is also used to imply certain behavior of prices as well. In particular, it is used to imply "that a series of consecutive separate transactions . . . will involve minimum price variations or deviations." *Special Study*, Chapter 5, p. 16.
5. This deficiency should soon be remedied when the National Association of Securities Dealers begins to publish daily trading volume for a larger number of over-the-counter issues.
6. An example is the common stock of Anheuser-Busch.
7. A New York Stock Exchange specialist recently told one of the authors that his firm had not suffered a loss in any of its first fifty years in business. Few major nonfinancial corporations are in a position to make such a statement.
8. *Special Study*, Chapter 6, p. 87.
9. *Ibid.*, p. 129.
10. *Ibid.*, p. 128.
11. Harold Demsetz, "The Cost of Transacting," *Quarterly Journal of Economics* 82 (February, 1968): at 47.
12. Seha M. Tiniç, "The Value of Time Preference, and the Behavior of Liquidity Costs in the New York Stock Exchange" (unpublished doctoral dissertation, Cornell University, 1970).
13. On this point, see Chapter 9. See also C. Welles, "Can the New York Stock Exchange Survive?" *The Institutional Investor*, June, 1970, pp. 25 ff.
14. *Treasury–Federal Reserve Study of the Government Securities Market* (Washington: n.p., 1959), p. 75.
15. *Ibid.*, p. 26.
16. *Ibid.*, pp. 79–80. *Italics* added.
17. W. Eiteman, C. Dice, and D. Eiteman, *The Stock Market*, 4th ed. (New York: McGraw-Hill, 1966), p. 224.

18. As we shall demonstrate later, however, the amount of marketability also depends on factors other than the total amount of trading activity.
19. Anna Merjos, "Going on the Big Board," *Barrons*, May 1, 1967, pp. 9–10.
20. John D. O'Connel, "Case Evidence on the Value of a New York Stock Exchange Listing," *MSU Business Topics* 17 (Summer, 1969): 15–21.
21. Richard W. Furst, "Does Listing Increase the Market Price of Common Shares?" *Journal of Business* 43, No. 2 (April, 1970): 174–80.
22. During this period, some 239 companies made the move to the NYSE, but data problems made it necessary for Furst to drop 41 from his study.
23. Myron J. Gordon, *The Investment, Financing and Valuation of the Corporation* (Homewood, Ill.: R. D. Irwin, 1962).
24. The specific methods of calculating each of these variables are somewhat complex, and space considerations make it impossible for us to reproduce them here. The interested reader should see Furst, "Does Listing Increase Market Price?" pp. 176–77.
25. *Ibid.*, p. 180.
26. However, it is not significant.
27. The probability of obtaining an $F = 0.866$ or greater with Furst's sample size exceeds 60 per cent. The 5 per cent F level for this sample size is 2.10.
28. This test involves calculating the following statistic:

$$y = \sum_{t=1}^{T} \frac{(\beta_{it} - \beta_i^*)^2}{S_{it}^2}$$

where β_{it} = the partial regression coefficient of the ith variable in period t, and S = the standard error of β_{it}.

$$\beta_i^* = \frac{\sum_{t=1}^{T} \beta_{it}/S_{it}^2}{\sum_{t=1}^{T} 1/S_{it}^2}$$

According to Lawrence Fisher, who developed this test, the statistic y "has approximately the χ^2 distribution with $T-1$ degrees of freedom. Hence an improbably high value of y is cause for rejecting the hypothesis that the partial regression coefficients are estimates from the same population." See Lawrence Fisher, "Determinants of Risk Premiums on Corporate Bonds," *Journal of Political Economy*, June, 1959, p. 29.
29. Furst, "Does Listing Increase Market Price?" p. 126.
30. James Van Horne, "New Listings and Their Price Behavior," *Journal of Finance*, September, 1970, pp. 783–794.
31. *Ibid.*, p. 790.
32. *Ibid.*, p. 792.
33. A. F. Kay, "An Appraisal of Three Block Information Systems" (mimeographed paper), pt. 6.
34. Descriptions of the Instinet system have recently appeared in several magazines, e.g., *Fortune*, April, 1969, p. 168.
35. This point has been made to one of the authors by a number of institutional investors and block traders.
36. Charles E. Youngblood, "The Argument for a Publicly Owned Stock

Exchange," *Financial Analysts Journal*, November–December, 1969, pp. 104A–104D.

37. *Ibid.*, p. 104B.

38. An excellent discussion of the factors surrounding the position policies of dealers in negotiated trading markets can be found in Ira Scott, *The Government Securities Market* (New York: McGraw-Hill, 1965), pp. 118–37.

39. On the other hand, it seems quite likely to us that it will be possible in the future to automate fully the trading in odd lots and, indeed, small round lots.

4 The Theory of
Transaction Costs

In the preceding two chapters, we demonstrated the need for brokers and dealers in organizing supply and demand in stock markets, specified the types of functions they perform, and discussed the factors that influence their organizational characteristics. In this chapter and the next two, we are concerned with the analysis of the costs associated with brokerage and dealership activities, i.e., the costs of transacting. This chapter will present a theoretical discussion of transactions costs, focusing on the demand and supply for broker and dealer services. On the basis of this discussion, we analyze the costs of transacting on the NYSE in Chapters 5 and 6.

Pure Exchange

The theory of pure exchange provides a convenient vehicle for introducing the idea of transaction costs into the competitive market model. Let us assume that there are a large number of small traders, each of whom is endowed with a portfolio of assets consisting of various stocks and cash. At any given time these traders may rearrange their portfolios of stock or sell all or part of their holdings for cash. They can change the composition of their portfolios, however, only by trading in the stock market. In other words, trading takes place in a closed system where investible funds are neither increased nor decreased[1] and where the prices of securities are determined by the net over-all effect of independent actions of numerous buyers and sellers, with no individual buyer or seller able to exert any control over prices. We further assume all buyers and sellers possess complete information about the number of shares offered in the market and the price of shares.

Let Q_{ij} represent the actual number of shares of the jth security in ith investor's portfolio, where $i = 1, \ldots, n$, and $j = 1, \ldots, m-1$. If we treat cash as a security with a price per share of unity, then $j = 1, \ldots, m$. Now, let us define q_{ij} as the desired number of shares of the jth stock (or cash) the ith investor would like to possess, where q_{ij} is determined on the basis of expectations concerning the returns and the riskiness of the jth security.[2] Once q_{ij} is determined, the difference between the number of shares he desires to hold, q_{ij}, and the number of shares he already owns, Q_{ij}, represents his excess demand, D_{ij}, for a particular stock or cash. Algebraically,

$$D_{ij} = q_{ij} - Q_{ij}, (j = 1, \ldots, m) \tag{4.1}$$

if $q_{ij} > Q_{jj}$, then $D_{ij} > 0$, representing a desire to purchase an additional D_{ij} shares of jth stock. Similarly, $q_{ij} < Q_{ij}$ implies $D_{ij} < 0$, reflecting the desire to sell D_{ij} shares of the jth stock. Note that for every distinct asset in the portfolio, there will be an equality such as (4.1).

At any given time the market value of the ith portfolio, V_i, will be the sum of the values of all securities and cash. Algebraically,

$$V_i = \sum_{j=1}^{m} P_j Q_{ij}, \quad j = (1, \ldots, m) \tag{4.2}$$

where P_j is the price of the jth security. In a market with no transaction costs, e.g., in the competitive market model, complete liquidation of the portfolio will return V_i dollars to the investor. Therefore, the sale of a part or the whole of the portfolio and its immediate repurchase, or the purchase of other securities, will not alter the total monetary value of the portfolio unless the relative prices of stocks are altered in the market.

We have observed, however, that exchange transactions are not costless. In real stock markets, buyers and sellers do not usually make contact directly, but rather use the services of brokers and dealers in adjusting their portfolios. Since both of these services are purchased at a positive price, we can no longer expect that the sale of the portfolio i will return V_i dollars to its owner. In fact it will yield C_i dollars, when $C_i < V_i$. The difference between the market value of the portfolio and the return to the owner, E_i, represents the cost of transacting, that is, the value of the specialized marketing services the owner purchases in association with selling his assets. In algebraic terms,

$$E_i = V_i - C_i \tag{4.3}$$

or, alternatively,

$$E_i = \sum_{j=m+1}^{3m} P_j q_{ij} \tag{4.4}$$

where $j = (m+1, \ldots, 2m)$ represent the brokerage services associated with the m stocks; and $j = (2m+1, \ldots, 3m)$ represent the dealer services associated with these stocks; and P_j and q_{ij} represent the prices and quantities of these services. In nearly *every* transaction, the trader purchases the services of a broker. For this reason, we shall henceforth refer to the service provided by brokers as exchange services. When a trader wants to avoid delays in making a transaction, he also purchases the services of a dealer. Since the dealer's primary role is to provide traders with marketability, we shall henceforth refer to his services as marketability services. In any event, because there are two services that the trader may purchase during each transaction in a particular security, there must be $2m$ $(j = m+1, \ldots, 3m)$ possible services that he may consume in total. If a particular investor does not transact in all of the securities, the corresponding quantities, $q_{.j}, \ldots, q_{.k}$ are equal to zero.

Our model implies, of course, that the traders being considered do not themselves specialize in selling brokerage (exchange) or dealership (marketability) services, but rather are interested in buying and selling securities in the market. This being the case, they do not usually possess the necessary facilities or membership privileges (in the case of organized markets), with which to provide these services to other traders. In other words, the marketability services they may occasionally sell (in the form of limit orders) are incidental to their transactions in securities. Therefore, the excess demand, D_{ij}, $(j = m+1, \ldots, 3m)$ of the traders for these services cannot be negative. Algebraically,

$$D_{ij} = q_{ij} \quad (j = m+1, \ldots, 3m) \tag{4.5}$$

implies consumption of services.

Since there are no exogenous influences on the trading endowment, the sum of the value of the shares the trader would like to possess and the value of the exchange and marketability services he wants to buy is limited by the value of his original portfolio. In algebraic terms, this implies

$$\sum_{j=1}^{3m} P_j q_{ij} = \sum_{j=1}^{m} P_j Q_{ij} \tag{4.6}$$

If we rearrange (4.6) and express the consumption of transactions services as a separate term, we obtain

$$\sum_{j=1}^{m} P_j(q_{ij} - Q_{ij}) + \sum_{j=m+1}^{3m} P_j q_{ij} = 0 \tag{4.7}$$

Substituting from (4.1) and (4.5), we can write this equation in terms of the excess demands for all assets and services as follows:

$$\sum_{j=1}^{m} P_j D_{ij} + \sum_{j=m+1}^{3m} P_j D_{ij} = \sum_{j=1}^{3m} P_j D_{ij} = 0 \tag{4.8}$$

In short, equation (4.8) states that the total value of the excess demands for each trader must equal zero, which is just another way of saying that the value of total purchases has to equal the value of total sales for each investor. In effect, then, (4.8) constitutes the budget constraint of the ith trader; each of the n traders faces a similar budget constraint, the size of which varies with the initial distribution of endowments among traders.

Now, the utility function of the ith trader can be represented in terms of his excess demand for various securities, cash and transactions services:

$$U_i = f(q_{i1}, q_{i2}, \ldots, q_{im}, q_{im+1}, \ldots, q_{i3m})$$
$$= f(D_{i1} - Q_{i1}, \ldots, D_{im+1}, \ldots, D_{i3m}) \tag{4.9}$$

Maximization of this utility function subject to the endowment constraint in (4.8) is equivalent to maximizing U_i^*, when

$$U_i^* = f(D_{i1} - Q_{i1}, \ldots, D_{im} - Q_{im}, \ldots, D_{im+1}, \ldots, D_{i3m})$$
$$+ \lambda \left(\sum_{j=1}^{3m} P_j D_{ij} \right) \tag{4.10}$$

The first order conditions for a maximum are:

$$\frac{\partial U_i^*}{\partial D_{ij}} = \frac{\partial U}{\partial D_{ij}} + \lambda P_j = 0$$

$$\frac{\partial U_i^*}{\partial \lambda} = \sum_{j=1}^{3m} P_j D_{ij} = 0$$

(4.11)

If the second order conditions for maximum are also satisfied, the equilibrium for each individual investor is reached when[3]

$$\frac{\partial U_i}{\partial q_{ij}} \bigg/ \frac{\partial U_i}{\partial q_{ik}} = \frac{P_j}{P_k} \quad \text{(for } k \neq j\text{)}$$

(4.12)

In other words, given the market prices for securities, the initial portfolio endowments and the prices of the transactions services for each stock, an individual engages in exchange transactions until the rate of marginal substitution for every pair of securities and transactions services equals the ratio of their prices.

At this equilibrium, the excess demand functions of each trader for every stock and transactions services can be derived from $(3m + 1)$ equations in (4.11). For example,

$$D_{ij} = f(P_1, P_2, \ldots, P_m, P_{m+1}, \ldots, P_{3m})$$

(4.13)

where the excess demand for each stock and transaction service is a function of prices of all securities and the prices of transactions services for all stocks. The excess demand function in (4.13) provides some insight concerning the trader's demand for exchange and marketability services, and the relationship between transactions costs and the demand for individual securities. The excess demand function suggests, for example, that exchange and marketability services for a particular stock are, in essence, goods complementary to that stock. Thus, if an increase in the price of either service (with all other prices unchanged) reduces the amount demanded by traders, it also reduces the demand for the stock itself. In short,

$$\frac{\partial D_{ij}}{\partial P_{m+j}} < 0 \quad \text{and} \quad \frac{\partial D_{ij}}{\partial P_{2m+j}} < 0 \quad \text{(for } j \leqslant m\text{)}$$

(4.14)

where $j = 1, \ldots, m$ represents various stocks, $j = m + 1, \ldots, 2m$ stands for the exchange services corresponding to these stocks respectively, and $j = 2m + 1, \ldots, 3m$ is the marketability services for each stock.[4]

Along these same lines, we can see that there can be sets of exchange and marketability services that are substitutable for others. Of course, when exchange and marketability services for one stock are substituted for another's, the stock will also be substituted. The major significance of transaction costs in this respect is that they introduce additional demand interrelationships (cross elasticities), which cannot be analyzed in terms of a theory that assumes exchange transactions to be costless. It can be seen, for example, that even if the price relationships among securities are unaltered, substitutions in the portfolios of investors may still take place because of variations in the relative prices of exchange and/or marketability services.

Having introduced the idea of transaction costs and the demand for transactions services into the framework of pure exchange, we now turn to an analysis of the demand and supply of exchange and marketability services. Although theoretical in nature, this analysis is presented with an extremely practical objective in mind, that is, developing a framework that can be used to study the NYSE's pricing of these services in the next two chapters.

Exchange Services

Brokers provide investors with a variety of services. In Chapter 2 we demonstrated that they can reduce the cost of search for traders, facilitate negotiations, and solicit orders. Beyond this, they often provide investors with investment counsel, research reports, and so forth. In principle, it might be possible for us to analyze the demand and supply for these various services separately. However, because the price brokers normally charge for their services, referred to as the brokerage commission, varies only with the amount of a stock being bought or sold, it seems more appropriate to consider them collectively.

The Demand for Exchange Services. In the previous section, we demonstrated that the demand for exchange services for a given stock is a function of their price, the prices of exchange services for other stocks and the prices of the various stocks themselves.

However, if we hold the latter two sets of prices constant, the demand for exchange services becomes solely a function of their own price. That is,

$$D_j = f(P_j) \text{ for } j = m+1, \ldots, 2m \qquad (4.15)$$

where D_j is determined by summing the excess demands for these services by all investors at each price level. Following the so-called law of demand, we assume that the demand curve for exchange services is downward-sloping to the right. Thus, a decrease in the price of these services causes the amount demanded to increase, and vice versa.

How much the quantity demanded changes in response to a price change depends on the price elasticity of demand for exchange services. Generally speaking, a good's price elasticity tends to increase (become more elastic) as the number of close substitutes increases. Since stocks with similar risk characteristics and expected returns would seem to constitute close substitutes in many investors' portfolios, it might be expected that the exchange services associated with buying and selling such stocks also would be highly substitutable. If this is so, it seems logical to hypothesize that the demand for exchange services for most securities is relatively elastic. Put somewhat differently, it seems reasonable to argue that if the price of exchange services for a given security were increased, many traders would switch their trading activity to securities with similar risk and expected return characteristics and lower transaction costs.

The NYSE recently presented the SEC with an analysis concluding that the *aggregate* transaction demand for securities is relatively inelastic.[5] Since the framework of our analysis is constructed in terms of the individual security, it is not well suited to studying the matter of aggregate demand or aggregate elasticity. Nevertheless, on purely practical grounds, we find it somewhat difficult to accept the NYSE's conclusion. If the price of exchange services for all securities were to be raised, for example, the higher costs of trading would almost certainly cause some speculators to turn from pursuing the profit opportunities presented by short-term price fluctuations. Even if the increased costs were not sufficient to eliminate completely the potential trading profits from short-run speculative activity, many speculators might find the *reduced* profit potential incompatible with the risk involved. Similarly, many small investors who engage in trading primarily on the basis of their liquidity status might find that changing the composition of their portfolios had become costly enough to consider shifting their investable funds to other types of assets.

In the final analysis, of course, the elasticity of demand for aggregate transactions services is a matter for empirical investigation. To the best of our knowledge, however, no one has yet attempted to make such an investigation.

The Supply of Exchange Services. Generally speaking, the supply of any good or service primarily depends on two factors: (1) the costs associated with producing that good or service and (2) the competitive structure of the industry in question. Within a short-run context, the costs of providing exchange services can be thought of as having two components, one fixed, the other variable. The fixed component comprises all costs that do not change with the amount of exchange services being provided; it includes the costs of licenses, dues, fees, office maintenance, and some communications, as well as some clerical and administrative costs. The variable component is made up of all costs that change with the amount of services provided; it includes clearance charges, commission fees, variable communication charges, and certain clerical costs. Algebraically, the total short-run costs of providing exchange services can be summarized as follows:

$$TC = F + f(q) \tag{4.16}$$

where TC is total cost, F is fixed costs and $f(q)$ is the variable cost, or the cost that changes with the amount of services, q. The average fixed cost, average variable cost, and marginal cost of exchange services are respectively:

$$AFC = F/q; \quad AVC = f(q)/q; \quad MC = f'(q) \tag{4.17}$$

Average total cost is equal to the sum of average fixed and average variable costs.

If the structure of the brokerage industry approximated the competitive market model, a firm's short-run supply of exchange services would be given by the marginal cost curve above its point of intersection with average variable cost. The summation of the marginal cost curves of all firms would represent the short-run industry supply of these services.

In the long run, of course, all of the broker's costs are variable. In response to changes in the amount of business transacted, he can alter the size of his facilities, the number of his clerical employees, and the administrative staff. Thus, the relevant supply schedule for a given firm, again assuming a competitive market structure, would be the long-run marginal cost curve. Similarly, the long-run industry supply curve would equal the sum of the marginal cost curves of the individual firms.

The slope of the long-run cost curve depends upon the nature of returns to scale for the individual firms. If constant returns are present, it is parallel to the quantity axis. If increasing returns prevail, it has a negative slope in relation to the quantity axis. Decreasing returns, on the other hand, produce a positive slope.

The Pricing of Exchange Services. In a market with a large number of brokers, each operating on a scale that was small relative to the aggregate, the price of exchange services might be expected to obtain at such a level that neither excess supply nor excess demand occur. In particular, if constant or increasing long-run costs were present, the problem of price determination might be expected to approximate the simple competitive market solution discussed in Chapter 2.

The presence of economies of scale, on the other hand, would introduce significant complications to the problem of price determination. Consider, for example, the hypothetical situation depicted in Figure 9. Since the long-run marginal cost

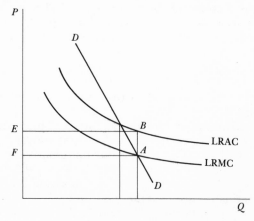

FIGURE 9   Economies of Scale and Exchange Services.

is assumed to decline throughout the relevant range of output, equating marginal costs with demand would produce a price level that would not be high enough to permit producers to cover all their fixed costs. In fact, it would result in a loss of *BA* per unit of output, or a total loss of *ABEF*.[6] In the long run, of course, the existence of economies of scale implies a tendency toward monopoly. Thus, unless they are accompanied by some form of regulation, these economies should lead to a determination of prices along the lines of the monopoly market solution described in Chapter 2. Since the NYSE maintains that the brokerage industry is, in fact, subject to increasing returns to scale, we shall return to the analysis of pricing exchange services under these conditions in the next chapter.

For now, however, let us conclude this section by noting one implication of the discussion to this point. We have been assuming that the prices of exchange services can be effectively analyzed in terms of supply and demand conditions. As long as supply conditions are dependent on the cost of providing exchange services, we might expect to find that the price of these services would vary from security to security. We noted in Chapter 2, for example, that brokers probably can execute orders in active stocks more cheaply than in inactive stocks, implying that the price of exchange services ought, perhaps, to be a decreasing function of trading activity. Of course, we recognize that other factors also have an impact on the cost of supplying exchange services and will defer further discussion of this particular subject to a later chapter.

Marketability Services

In a monetary society, the noun "marketability" is used to connote the ease with which an asset can be exchanged for cash. In this context, the ease or convenience of exchangeability is usually measured in terms of (1) the "waiting time" involved in disposing of an asset and (2) the difference between the price actually received and the underlying equilibrium price, i.e., the price that would prevail if all buy and sell orders arrived at the market simultaneously, as is implied by conventional price theory models.[7] Other things being equal, the shorter the waiting time, the greater an asset's marketability. Similarly, the smaller the difference between the price received and the equilibrium price, the more marketable the asset.

Many factors influence marketability, including the organizational structure of the market in which an asset is traded and the nature of the asset itself. Standardized assets, for example, do not require personal examination prior to making transactions, and thus can usually be traded with shorter delays (waiting time). Similarly, a highly organized, active market with a large number of transactions per unit of time tends to reduce delays in executing orders. Market organization, of course, often tends to be a function of such factors as an asset's standardization. Other things being equal, it is easier to establish a highly organized, active market in assets that are homogeneous, have low carrying costs, and so forth.

In comparison with many assets, most common stocks are highly marketable. They have extremely low carrying costs and are relatively standardized. A prudent investor may want to obtain information about a company before he decides to buy or sell its stock, but he does not ordinarily want to examine the goods physically before making a transaction. Nor does he care which hundred shares he buys or sells, as all are homogeneous for a given firm. Of course, the marketability of stock differs considerably from firm to firm and market to market. The stocks of firms with a large number of shares outstanding and little concentration in shareholder ownership, for example, tend to be more marketable than those of closely held, small enterprises.

In the remainder of this section, we shall be primarily concerned with exploring the demand and supply for the marketability services for a given common stock. As we mentioned earlier, these services are provided by dealers to traders who desire to reduce the waiting time associated with making transactions.

The Demand for Marketability Services. For reasons that are rather obvious, there are often considerable advantages to being able to consummate a transaction quickly. Yet, as we have noted several times, a fundamental fact of life in real securities markets is that offsetting public orders need not appear simultaneously. If we assume for the time being that there are no institutions that specialize in offsetting temporary imbalances in the inflow of orders, it becomes apparent that those who desire immediate exchange can usually obtain it only by providing incentives to the other side of the market in the form of price concessions. In the case of investors who desire to exchange stock for money without delay, this incentive takes the form of a lower selling price. For investors who desire to obtain a position immediately, it takes the form of a higher bid price. Immediacy of exchange, in other words, normally bears a positive cost in the absence of offsetting orders in the market. Furthermore, this cost tends to be a function of the probable waiting time involved in making an exchange: The longer the probable waiting time, the larger is the cost of obtaining an immediate exchange.

The relationship between probable waiting time and the cost of immediate exchange to investors who desire marketability can be stated somewhat more formally with the aid of "time differentiated" demand and supply schedules.[8] In Figure 10, the supply schedule, S_{t_0}, represents the number of shares offered at various prices by investors who desire immediate

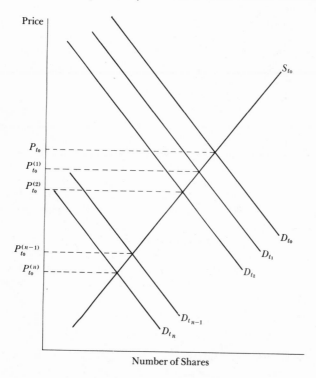

FIGURE 10 The Determination of Marketability Discounts.

exchange at time period t_0. The schedules, D_{t_0}, D_{t_1}, etc., represent a number of possible time differentiated demand curves. In essence, these curves represent the demand at time t_0 of buyers who are willing to wait various periods of time in order to improve their chances of obtaining better trading terms. The amount that sellers who desire immediate exchange must pay to avoid delays depends on which of these demand curves is "applicable." In the case where D_{t_0} obtains, for example, there are no costs associated with making an immediate sale, since there are also buyers in the market who want to make immediate purchases. This situation comes very close to representing the conditions that are assumed to exist in the economist's basic supply and demand model.

However, if there are no "immediate" buyers at t_0, the relevant demand curve becomes one of the time differentiated curves, D_{t_1}, D_{t_2}, etc. In this case, the seller who seeks an immediate transaction must be willing to take a lower price to avoid a delay. To illustrate, let us assume that the relevant demand curve facing our immediate sellers is D_{t_1}. Following the logic above, this curve represents the demand at t_0 of buyers who hope to obtain a somewhat lower purchase price by waiting one period.[9] Faced with this demand situation, sellers who enter the market have two alternatives: (1) They can wait for the appearance of buyers who desire immediate exchange, thus obtaining a price of P_{t_0}, or (2) they can make transactions now with buyers represented by D_{t_1}. Since the latter alternative results in a transaction price of $P_{t_0}^{(1)}$, the difference between P_{t_0} and $P_{t_0}^{(1)}$ represents, in effect, the discount needed to attract buyers who are willing to wait in order to improve trading terms. Along these same lines, if sellers who desire immediate execution must cater to buyers who are willing to wait even longer, say two periods, they must offer a larger discount of $(P_{t_0} - P_{t_0}^{(2)})$. As might be expected, the size of the discount varies directly with the length of the waiting time that may be avoided by catering to buyers who are willing to wait in order to obtain more favorable trading terms. Algebraically,

$$(P_{t_0} - P_{t_0}^{(1)}) < (P_{t_0} - P_{t_0}^{(2)}) < \cdots < (P_{t_0} - P_{t_0}^{(n-1)}) < (P_{t_0} - P_{t_0}^{(n)})$$
$$(4.18)$$

By analogous reasoning, we can easily analyze the situation facing investors who desire to buy stock without any trading delays. In Figure 11, this case is presented graphically. The

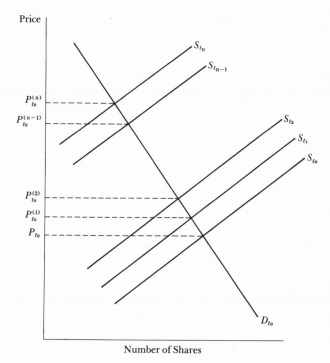

FIGURE 11 The Determination of Marketability Premiums.

demand curve D_{t_0} represents the number of shares bid for at various prices by investors who desire immediate executions. If there are no "immediate" sellers in the market at t_0, these investors must pay a premium price to induce holders of stock to dispose of their shares immediately. As expected, this marketability premium increases as the buyer deals with sellers who are willing to wait longer to obtain favorable trading terms. That is,

$$(P_{t_0}^{(1)} - P_{t_0}) < (P_{t_0}^{(2)} - P_{t_0}) < \cdots < (P_{t_0}^{(n-1)} - P_{t_0}) < (P_{t_0}^{(n)} - P_{t_0})$$
(4.19)

The reader should note that the size of the premium, or discount, in the case presented above, is partially determined by the relative positions of the time differentiated demand and supply schedules, which are determined, in turn, by the preferences

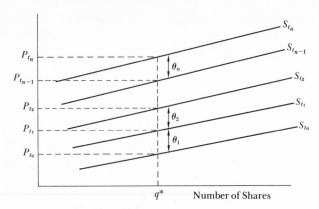

(a) Marginal Value of Time Preferences
on the Supply Side

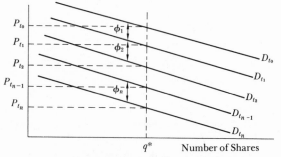

(b) Marginal Value of Time Preferences
on the Demand Side

FIGURE 12   The Marginal Value of Time Preferences.

of traders on both sides of the market and the values they assign
to the incremental value of avoiding delays in making trades.

The value of time preferences for the demand and supply
sides of a market is presented in Figure 12. The supply schedule
S_{t_0} again represents the desire for immediate exchange of
stocks for money, while S_{t_1}, S_{t_2} and S_{t_n} indicate the supply of
traders who are willing to wait various time periods in order to
obtain more favorable terms. For a given number of shares,
q^*, the ordinates of the time differentiated supply functions
can be expressed in terms of the prices implied by S_{t_0}, the "im-

mediate" supply function. That is,

$$P_{t_1} = P_{t_0} + \theta_1,$$

$$P_{t_2} = P_{t_0} + \theta_1 + \theta_2, \tag{4.20}$$

$$\vdots$$

$$P_{t_n} = P_{t_0} + \sum_{i=1}^{n} \theta_i$$

When looked at in this way, θ_i represents the value sacrificed by waiting one less time unit or, alternatively, the value obtained by waiting one more time unit, that is, the *marginal* value of time preference for sellers. Since consumption and investment opportunities, as well as risk exposure, may change over time, the various θ_i need not have the same value: The marginal value of time preferences may be an increasing, decreasing, or constant function of the waiting time involved in executing tenders. In the case of a trader who has an increasing marginal value of time preference, there is a willingness to provide larger discounts to avoid each incremental of waiting time. Thus,

$$\theta_n > \theta_{n-1} > \cdots > \theta_2 > \theta_1 \tag{4.21}$$

Analogously, decreasing and constant marginal value of time preferences imply

$$\theta_n < \theta_{n-1} < \cdots < \theta_2 < \theta_1 \text{ and } \theta_n = \theta_{n-1} = \cdots = \theta_2 = \theta_1 \tag{4.22}$$

respectively.

On the other side of the market, traders who have potential demand for the stock exhibit time preferences for purchases with marginal values of ϕ; once again, the marginal values of time preferences, ϕ_i, may be an increasing, decreasing, or constant function of waiting time.

In the previous section of this chapter, we analyzed the demand for exchange services for a given security as a function of their price, the price of exchange services for other stocks, and the prices of the stocks themselves. Thus far in this section, our analysis of the demand for marketability services has emphasized the role of time preferences. While superficially different, these two approaches are actually based on the same logic. After all, the values traders assign to time preference or immediacy of exchange in a given stock are determined in large measure by the attractiveness of alternative investment opportunities. In effect, then, the prices of all other stocks and the prices of exchange and marketability services for other stocks play a major role in determining the values investors place on immediacy of exchange in a given security. Thus, whether we assume that all of the prices are held constant or that the marginal values of time preference on both sides of the market are constant, we can argue that the demand for marketability services in a given stock is a function of the price of those services. Algebraically then,

$$D_j = f(P_j) \text{ for } j = 2m+1, \ldots, 3m \qquad (4.23)$$

where, D_j, the market demand for marketability services, is obtained by summing the individual excess demands of individual traders at varying prices.[10]

A careful examination of Figures 10 and 11 reveals that the amount of marketability services demanded in the market is a decreasing function of their price. The rate of change in quantity demanded with respect to price depends, of course, on the elasticity of demand for these services, which is determined by the functional relation between the marginal values of time preferences and the waiting time. From Figures 10 and 11 and the inequalities in (4.18) and (4.19), it also is apparent that the prices and quantities of marketability services to buyers can be represented as the negative values of the corresponding services to sellers. (See Figure 13.) Thus, it is possible to carry on the analysis for only one of these services, since any conclusion derived also holds for the other.

A somewhat more intuitive feeling for the analysis of the time differentiated supply and demand schedules can be obtained by referring back to the simulation models developed in Chapter 2. The reader will recall that the models or, more precisely, one of the models, provided for the submission of two types of tenders: (1) limit buy or sell orders and (2) market buy or sell orders. When a limit order arrived at the market, it could only be executed if there was an offsetting limit or market order. This being the case, traders who submitted limit orders were, in effect, giving notice that they were willing to wait some time before consummating a trade. Moreover, the farther their limit order price was from the underlying "market" price, the greater was their willingness to wait in the anticipation of obtaining more favorable trading terms. Market orders, on the other hand, were submitted by traders who desired immediate exchange and were willing to obtain it by trading at a price that was sufficiently away from the "market" price to interest one of

Price of Marketability to Sellers

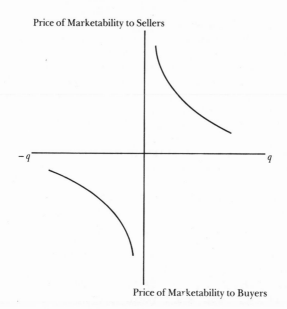

$-q$ q

Price of Marketability to Buyers

FIGURE 13   Demand for Marketability by Sellers and Buyers.

the traders who was willing to wait. The relationship between the operations of the simulated market and our time differentiated demand and supply analysis should now be apparent; the time differentiated schedules are the analytical counterparts to the simulation's limit and market orders. D_{t_0} and S_{t_0}, for example, represent the demand and supply schedules for market orders in the market at a given time. Similarly, $D_{t_1}, D_{t_2}, \ldots, D_{t_n}$ and $S_{t_1}, S_{t_2}, \ldots, S_{t_n}$ represent limit buy and sell orders. It follows, of course, that changes in the demand for marketability services should manifest themselves as variations in the relative importance of market orders.

The Supply of Marketability Services. Thus far in the analysis we have been assuming that the marketability demands of traders are met solely by the incoming supply of limit orders. Needless to say, this assumption implies that the supply of marketability ceases to exist when limit orders fail to appear. Indeed, it is this implication that led us to argue in Chapter 2 that the accommodation of market orders depends upon the presence of an individual who places standing limit orders on both sides of the market, that is, who provides a constant supply of marketability services. As we have already seen, there are individuals in all sectors of the stock markets who specialize in providing marketability services to traders. On the stock exchanges, the primary and continuous suppliers of these services are the specialists; in the over-the-counter markets, the wholesale dealers constitute the source of marketability. Although the operating procedure differs considerably, the economic functions performed by both of these groups are similar. In particular, both facilitate the execution of market buy and sell orders by their willingness to trade on either side of the market at quoted prices. Traders who desire immediate disposal of their shares, for example, sell them to the dealer at his bid price. Similarly, traders interested in the prompt acquisition of shares can purchase them from the dealer at his ask price.

Since the demand for marketability services arises from the disparities of time preferences among traders, the function of the dealer is, in effect, to balance the supply and demand of stocks over time. In doing so, the dealer incurs inventory carrying costs. It is the behavior of these costs and the economic organization of the market for marketability services that serve as the primary determinants of the supply of marketability service. In Chapter 6 we shall discuss the behavior of these costs and the organization of dealer activities within the context of the New York Stock Exchange specialist system. Let us, therefore, leave this subject temporarily to focus on the manner in which the price of marketability services is established in the market.

Price of Marketability Services. In the presence of dealers, the market situation can be represented by two pairs of demand and supply schedules, such as those shown in Figure 14. Schedules D_{t_0} and S_{t_0} reflect the market buy and sell orders of traders and D_{t_k} and S_{t_k} represent limit buy and sell orders specified by dealers.[11] Both sets of schedules are assumed to be linear in order to illustrate the determination of the price of marketability more conveniently. This assumption does not, however, restrict the generality of the argument.

The demand and supply situation can now be summarized as follows:

$$\left.\begin{array}{l} D_{t_0} = q_{t_0}^d = \alpha_0 - \beta p \\ D_{t_k} = q_{t_k}^d = \alpha_k - \beta p \end{array}\right\} \quad \begin{array}{l} \text{Time differentiated} \\ \text{demand functions} \end{array} \quad (4.24)$$

$$\left.\begin{array}{l} S_{t_0} = q_{t_0}^s = \sigma_0 + wp \\ S_{t_k} = q_{t_k}^s = \sigma_k + wp \end{array}\right\} \quad \text{Time differentiated supply functions} \quad (4.25)$$

From basic economic theory, we know that the price of the stock is determined by the intersection of the supply and demand curves that obtain in the market. In the case where demand and supply conditions are represented by D_{t_0} and S_{t_0}, the market clearing relationship implies

$$q_{t_0}^d = q_{t_0}^s \qquad (4.26)$$

Substituting from equations (4.24) and (4.25) enables us to write

$$\alpha_0 - \beta p = \sigma_0 + wp \qquad (4.27)$$

Solving for p yields

$$p = \frac{\alpha_0 - \sigma_0}{\beta + w} = P_{t_0} \qquad (4.28)$$

In Figure 14, this situation is represented by the intersection of the demand and supply schedules D_{t_0} and S_{t_0}. In Demsetz's words, this intersection "shows the conventional view of equilibrium price."[12] By this Demsetz means, of course, that it represents the intersection of the market order demand and supply curves under the assumption that buyers and sellers arrive at the market simultaneously. He quickly adds, however, that in reality schedules such as D_{t_0} and S_{t_0} "do not illustrate *always present* market orders; rather, they measure time rates of demand and supply for which, at any given time, no market orders need be present."[13]

If the market is characterized by the presence of market demand orders but no market supply orders, buyers must look to dealers for accommodation. In this case the market is defined in terms of schedules D_{t_0} and S_{t_k}. The market clearing condition therefore implies

$$q_{t_0}^d = q_{t_k}^s \qquad (4.29)$$

Again substituting from equations (4.24) and (4.25) and solving for p yields

$$p = \frac{\alpha_0 - \sigma_k}{\beta + w} = P_A \qquad (4.30)$$

In terms of Figure 14, P_A is the price associated with the intersection of the market demand curve D_{t_0} and the dealer supply curve S_{t_k}.

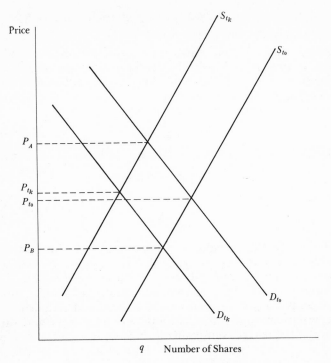

FIGURE 14 The Pricing of Marketability Services.

Analogously, when there are market sell orders but no market buy orders, sellers must look to dealers for servicing, in which case the market is characterized by D_{t_k} and S_{t_0}. Here the market clearing condition implies

$$q^d_{t_k} = q^s_{t_0} \qquad (4.31)$$

Substituting and solving for p we obtain

$$p = \frac{\alpha_k - \sigma_0}{\beta + w} = P_B \qquad (4.32)$$

Referring once again to Figure 14, we see that P_B is the price associated with the intersection of the market supply curve S_{t_0} and the dealer demand curve D_{t_k}.

By comparing the price that obtains when market buy and sell orders are present simultaneously with the prices that result when a dealer's services are needed, we can define the price of marketability services to sellers and buyers. For example, the price of these services to stock sellers, P_{LS}, is given by the difference between P_{t_0} and P_B. That is,

$$P_{LS} = P_{t_0} - P_B \tag{4.33}$$

Substituting from equations (4.28) and (4.32) gives us the following expression:

$$P_{LS} = \frac{\alpha_0 - \alpha_k}{\beta + w} \tag{4.34}$$

By similar logic, of course, we can define the price of marketability to buyers, P_{LB}, as the difference between P_A and P_{t_0}. That is,

$$P_{LB} = P_A - P_{t_0} \tag{4.35}$$

Again, by substitution,

$$P_{LB} = \frac{\sigma_0 - \sigma_k}{\beta + w} \tag{4.36}$$

From equations (4.34) and (4.36), it can be seen that the price of marketability services depends on both the slopes of the demand and supply curves and the horizontal distance between the time differentiated schedules. The comparative levels of P_{LS} and P_{LB} are a function of the relative sizes of $(\alpha_0 - \alpha_k)$ and $(\sigma_0 - \sigma_k)$. When they are equal, for example, the price of marketability services to sellers and buyers is the same.

If the market equilibrium price is defined not as P_{t_0}, but rather as the average of P_{t_0} and P_{t_k}, it can easily be shown that $P_{LS} = P_{LB}$ regardless of the relative sizes of $(\alpha_0 - \alpha_k)$ and $(\sigma_0 - \sigma_k)$.[14] In effect, P_{t_k}, which is associated with the intersection of D_{t_k} and S_{t_k} represents the price at which buyers and sellers submitting limit orders would do business "on the average." By averaging P_{t_0} and P_{t_k}, then, we obtain a price that again represents a kind of market equilibrium. That is,

$$\frac{P_{t_0} + P_{t_k}}{2} = \frac{\alpha_0 + \alpha_k - \sigma_0 - \sigma_k}{2(\beta + w)} = P_M \tag{4.37}$$

Once again, solving for the price of marketability to sellers in terms of the difference between the market equilibrium price,

P_M, and P_B, we have

$$P_{LS} = P_M - P_B \qquad (4.38)$$

Substituting from equations (4.37) and (4.32) and simplifying yields

$$P_{LS} = \frac{\alpha_0 - \alpha_k + \sigma_0 - \sigma_k}{2(\beta + w)} \qquad (4.39)$$

Similarly, we can solve for the price of marketability to buyers in terms of the difference between P_A and P_M. Substituting and simplifying, we can write the following equation:

$$P_{LB} = \frac{\alpha_0 - \alpha_k + \sigma_0 - \sigma_k}{2(\beta + w)} \qquad (4.40)$$

From equations (4.39) and (4.40) it is obvious that $P_{LS} = P_{LB}$ for all values of $(\alpha_0 - \alpha_k)$ and $(\sigma_0 - \sigma_k)$.

In a market with large numbers of relatively small dealers supplying marketability services, an individual dealer cannot exert any influence on the market price of these services. Therefore, the demand for the services of each dealer is perfectly elastic at the equilibrium price of these services. Put somewhat differently, when the dealership sector of the market approaches the conditions of a perfectly competitive market, a dealer's own supply and demand for a particular security are perfectly elastic at the corresponding ask and bid prices, which are determined by the interaction of aggregate demand and supply of marketability services. Moreover, the difference between the ask and bid prices, the bid-ask spread, is equal to the marginal cost of carrying inventories.[15] The relationship of the price of marketability services, and the dealer's supply and demand curves under perfect competition are presented in Figure 15. Since marketability services are a perfectly homogeneous good, the only conditions necessary for achieving the competitive solution are (1) a relatively large number of dealers supplying these services for each issue and (2) ready dissemination of information about their bid and ask quotations.

But what if there is only one dealer making a two-way market? How would he set his bid and ask prices and how much depth of marketability would he provide? In view of the fact that stock exchange specialists enjoy monopolistic privileges in individual issues, this question is extremely relevant to the analysis of the pricing of marketability services.[16]

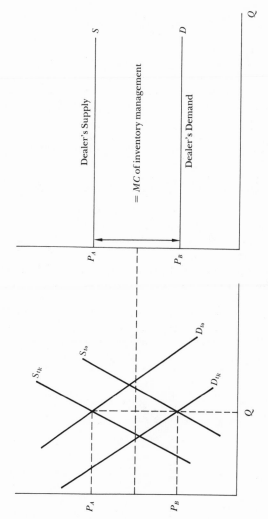

FIGURE 15   Dealer's Bid and Ask Quotations Under Competition.

When a single firm undertakes the market-making function and all other traders submit market buy and sell orders, the dealer is likely to behave as a monopsonist in buying stock and as a monopolist in selling it. The dealer knows that his own actions influence the price he pays for stock and the price he receives. He is aware, for example, that he must pay a higher price per share to increase his acquisitions and ask a lower price per share to increase his sales. Consequently, he regards $ME_{S_{t_0}}$ in Figure 16 as the marginal cost of purchasing from traders who desire immediate disposal of their shares. To this cost he adds the marginal cost, MC, of carrying these shares as his inventory, which we assume, for simplicity, is constant over the relevant range of trading volume. Hence the dealer's total marginal cost is equal to $MC + ME_{S_{t_0}}$. To maximize his profits from two-way trading, the dealer buys and sells that number of shares which equates his marginal cost to his marginal revenue function, $MR_{D_{t_0}}$. In Figure 16, this profit-maximizing quantity is q^* shares. The price the dealer pays for these shares is indicated by the point P'_B. Analogously, when he sells these q^* shares to traders who have outstanding market buy orders, he receives P'_A. The dealer's bid-ask spread, $P'_A - P'_B$, equals the sum of the prices of marketability services to sellers and buyers. As might be expected, the bid-ask spread of a monopolist-monopsonist dealer is greater than the spreads established in a competitive market.

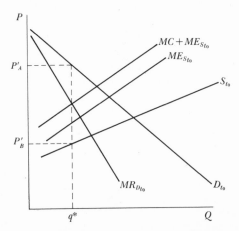

FIGURE 16   Bid and Ask Quotations of a Monopolistic Dealer.

A comparison of bid-ask spreads in competitive and monopolistic markets provides insight into the variability of transaction-to-transaction price variability of stocks. In discussing the simulation models in Chapter 2, we indicated that with a dealer in the market, the variability of transaction prices is substantially reduced, since the prices vary only within the limit set by the bid and ask quotations of the dealer. Hence, price variability tends to be lower when the bid-ask spread is narrow. In a competitively organized market, therefore, the prices of marketability services tend to be lower, the quantity of services supplied higher, and the transaction-to-transaction price variability less than they would be in the case of monopolistic organization.

Time Differentiated Schedules vs. Shifting Schedules. To avoid any confusion, we should perhaps point out that the time differentiated demand and supply schedules we have been discussing should not be interpreted as shifting schedules. Shifts in demand and supply schedules reflect the changes in the expectations of investors as to the "intrinsic" value of stocks. The time differentiated schedules, on the other hand, reflect variations in the demand for immediacy on the part of traders who possess a given set of expectations.

Changes in the equilibrium price of an issue result from shifts in its supply or demand schedules. A decrease in supply, *ceteris paribus*, results in a simultaneous downward shift in S_{t_k} and in S_{t_0}, as indicated in Figure 17. Depending on the relative changes in S_{t_k} and S_{t_0}, $(P_A - P_B) \lessgtr (P'_A - P'_B)$. For example, as long as the changes in supply fail to alter the time preferences of traders, the decline in the market price does not affect the bid-ask spread of the issue.

Shifts in D_{t_k} and D_{t_0} also alter the market price, P_M. Once again, however, whether or not these changes alter the magnitudes of bid-ask spreads depends on the relative changes in D_{t_k} and D_{t_0}. In short, the marketability status of stocks is affected by changes in their market prices only if these changes alter the relative composition of limit and market orders submitted by traders. The same conclusion can be reached by examining the algebraic formulation of P_{t_0}, P_{t_A}, and P_{t_B} in equations (4.28), (4.30), and (4.32).

By now it should be clear that the distinction between (1) changes in marketability prices and (2) changes in the price of the stock, due to the altered demand and supply condition, is

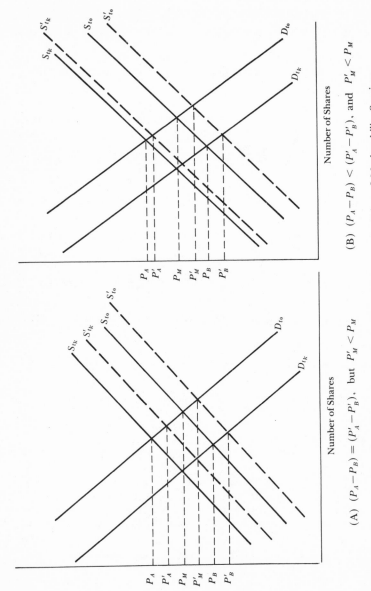

(A) $(P_A - P_B) = (P'_A - P'_B)$, but $P'_M < P_M$

(B) $(P_A - P_B) < (P'_A - P'_B)$, and $P'_M < P_M$

FIGURE 17 Changes in Market Price vs. Changes in Price of Marketability Services.

crucially important in evaluating the efficiency of stock markets.[17] The behavior of the prices of marketability service and the depth of marketability supply are closely related to the efficiency of the market, but the volatility of stock prices due to changing investor evaluations does not necessarily reflect any unfavorable implications about market performance *per se*.

Transaction Efficiency: A Concluding Comment

Economic efficiency is defined as the condition of Pareto optimality. Under this condition, the allocation of goods and services is efficient, since any reallocation among consumers lowers at least one individual's satisfaction.[18] Pareto optimality is achieved when the marginal rates of substitution between all pairs of goods and services are (1) equated for all consumers and (2) equal to the ratio of their respective prices. Furthermore, the prices must be equal to the corresponding marginal costs of production. This equality is obtained only in perfectly competitive markets, and therefore perfect competition is the only form of market organization which is absolutely efficient.

However, we often speak of markets as being more or less efficient in relative terms. We do this by focusing on the extent to which a market's price corresponds to marginal production costs. The closer price approaches production cost, the more efficient the market. The efficiency of a stock market in supplying the exchange and marketability services, then, can be assessed by the potential discrepancies between the prices charged for these services and the marginal costs of providing them. The closer the prices of these services are to their corresponding marginal costs, the more efficient is the market. For example, we can represent the total transaction costs incurred by traders as the sum of the values of exchange and marketability services. Algebraically, the total transaction cost may be represented as follows:

$$E_{ij} = [P_j^{(1)}q_{ij}^{(1)} + P_j^{(2)}q_{ij}^{(2)}] \qquad (4.41)$$

where $P_j^{(1)}$ is the price of the exchange service and $P_j^{(2)}$ is the price of marketability service for the jth stock. Similarly, $q_{ij}^{(1)}$ and $q_{ij}^{(2)}$ are the quantities of these services purchased (in number of shares) by the ith trader in the jth security. Note that in all exchange transactions $q_{ij}^{(1)} > 0$, but $q_{ij}^{(2)}$ may equal zero. In other words, traders do not necessarily purchase marketability services in every transaction.

Now if we let $MC_j^{(1)}$ and $MC_j^{(2)}$ equal the marginal costs of providing exchange and marketability services, the efficiency of brokers and dealers can be assessed by comparing the percentage deviation of prices from their corresponding marginal costs in each market. In other words, given

$$P_j^{(1)} - MC_j^{(1)} = W_j^{(1)} \quad \text{and} \quad P_j^{(2)} - MC_j^{(2)} = W_j^{(2)}$$

the ratios

$$\frac{W_j^{(1)}}{P_j^{(1)}} \quad \text{and} \quad \frac{W_j^{(2)}}{P_j^{(2)}}$$

can be used to assess the relative efficiencies with which exchange and marketability services are provided.[19] If the marginal costs of supplying these services are the same for brokers and dealers in different markets, a simpler measure of relative efficiency is the reciprocal of the prices of exchange and marketability services in various markets.[20] That is,

$$E_L = \frac{1}{P_L} \quad \text{and} \quad E_E = \frac{1}{P_E} \tag{4.42}$$

where, E_L and E_E represent the efficiencies with which marketability and exchange services are marketed. Then the over-all transaction efficiency of a stock market will be E_M, where

$$E_M = \frac{1}{P_L + P_E} = \frac{1}{\text{total transaction cost/share}} \tag{4.43}$$

In short, stock markets that enable traders to complete their exchange transactions with minimum delay and lowest possible costs are regarded as relatively efficient.

Notes

1. Only the single market exchange equilibrium is considered here. In fact, this constitutes a partial equilibrium analysis, since the prices of commodities in other markets and the incomes of the traders remain unaltered. In the general, multimarket equilibrium, this assumption is relaxed so that the over-all endowment of each individual, including his factor endowments (work vs. leisure) and consumption, can be included in the model. Analysis of multimarket exchange would not only yield solutions for the composition of the portfolio but also determine its over-all size. Since all markets are

interrelated, the size and composition of each endowment would be a function of the prices of all consumption and investment opportunities. Not all multimarket exchange systems necessarily have stable equilibrium solutions. Discussions of systems with stable solutions are found in J. R. Hicks, *Value and Capital*, 2d ed. (Oxford, England: Clarendon Press, 1946), pp. 314–17, and in Kenneth Arrow and Gerard Debreu, "The Existence of an Equilibrium for a Competitive Economy," *Econometrica* 22 (July, 1964): 265–90. A detailed analysis of pure exchange can be found in Peter Newman, *The Theory of Exchange* (Englewood Cliffs, N.J.: Prentice-Hall, 1965).

2. For a risk-averting investor, a solution for q_{ij} is obtained by examining the effects of the jth stock on the expected return and the variance of the ith portfolio. Comprehensive analysis of the "expected return-variance" model of portfolio selection is presented in Harry M. Markowitz, *Portfolio Selection* (New York: John Wiley, 1959), and in William F. Sharpe, "Capital Asset Prices: A Theory of Market Equilibrium Under Conditions of Risk," *Journal of Finance* 19 (September, 1964): 425–42.

3. From (4.1) above,

$$\frac{dD_{ij}}{dq_{ij}} = 1. \quad \text{Therefore,} \quad \frac{\partial U_i}{\partial q_{ij}} = \frac{\partial U_i}{\partial D_{ij}}$$

4. For an investor whose demand for various stocks is determined by the expected value-variance rules of portfolio selection, there may also be some stocks that are mutually complementary. However, our major concern here is with the effects of transaction costs on demand for securities, rather than the demand interrelationships of various securities.

5. New York Stock Exchange, "Economic Effects of Negotiated Commission Rates on the Brokerage Industry's Practices and the Market for Corporate Securities" (unpublished report), August, 1968, p. 100.

6. Under marginal cost pricing, smaller, less efficient firms are hit hardest. They often are unable to sustain operation and cease operations, thus leaving the industry dominated by one or very few large firms whose losses are smaller because of their size. If, on the other hand, the price is set at a point where it is high enough to cover average cost, buyers consume a socially undesirable amount of service. It is possible, however, to increase the welfare of the consumers if producers price their product at their marginal cost and the difference between *LRAC* and *LAMC* is subsidized by an external agency. When the price is equal to *LRAC*, the consumer can be regarded as subsidizing the industry's firms that, because of their higher costs, should not remain in business.

7. Smidt notes that if there is no waiting time involved in the exchange transaction, the marketability of an asset can be expressed in terms of the following ratio:

$$\frac{\text{Actual sales price } (P)}{\text{Market price } (P_M)}$$

See Seymour Smidt, "A New Look at the Random Walk Hypothesis," *Journal of Financial and Quantitative Analysis* 3 (September, 1968): 240.

8. The idea of incorporating a time dimension into the demand and supply analysis was introduced by Harold Demsetz, "The Cost of Transacting," *Quarterly Journal of Economics* 82 (February, 1968): at 36.

9. In actuality, of course, the buyers along D_{t_1} *expect* to wait one period on the

average. In other words, they deal in probabilistic, rather than deterministic, terms. A deterministic presentation, however, simplifies matters considerably without any loss of generality.

10. The quantity of marketability services is measured in terms of the number of shares for which immediacy is desired.

11. Within this context, traders who submit limit orders may be viewed as temporarily taking on the dealer activity.

12. Demsetz, "Cost of Transacting," p. 36.

13. *Ibid.*

14. The question of whether P_M is a "better" measure of the market equilibrium price than P_{t_0} is moot. As noted above, Demsetz argues that P_{t_0} is the price associated with the "conventional" view of equilibrium. Tiniç, however, argues in favor of the use of P_M on the grounds that it is "determined where there is no excess demand or supply, whether immediate or waiting." Seha M. Tiniç, "The Value of Time Preference, and the Behavior of Liquidity Costs in the New York Stock Exchange" (unpublished doctoral dissertation, Cornell University, 1970), p. 32.

15. The bid-ask spread, S, can be calculated either as the difference between P_A and P_B or as the sum of P_{L_S} and P_{L_B}.

16. Even with a single dealer in the market, pure monopoly or monopsony prices will not necessarily obtain. First, the dealer may purposely keep his bid–ask spread lower than the optimum monopoly-monopsony margin to discourage potential dealers from entering the market. Second, individual traders may submit limit orders on both sides of the market, inside the dealer's quotes, thereby reducing his volume of business. Finally, substitutability of stocks may curtail monopoly spreads. Nevertheless, the analysis of monopolistic bid and ask quotations increases our knowledge about the operation of markets where there are substantial deviations from the conditions of perfect competition.

17. There seems to be some confusion about this point. See, for example, John F. Lyons, "What Happens When Liquidity Disappears," *The Institutional Investor* 3 (November, 1969): 29 ff. The author uses the following ratio as a measure of the marketability of various common stocks:

$$\text{marketability} \atop \text{ratio} = \frac{\displaystyle\sum_{i=1}^{n} V_i P_i}{\displaystyle\sum_{i=1}^{n} \frac{\Delta P_i}{P_{i-1}}} = \frac{\text{value of transactions}}{\text{percentage change in} \atop \text{daily closing price}}$$

Here, V_i is the trading volume on the ith day, P_i is the closing price, and n is the number of days included in the sample under investigation. Higher marketability ratios are claimed to reflect more marketable stocks. This misleading conclusion is due to the failure of the author to differentiate between the price variability of stocks and the price of marketability services. A large number of small transactions all in the same direction may change the price of a security substantially, resulting in very low marketability ratios, without actually affecting the price of marketability services. In other words, good marketability does not imply a market where equilibrium prices of securities are invariant. A large number of small orders in the same direction, for example, is a likely indication of investors' altered appraisal of the issue and would result in a changed equilibrium price of the stock without necessarily affecting its marketability at all.

18. Paul A. Samuelson, *Foundations of Economic Analysis* (New York: Athaneum, 1967), p. 212.

19. Small values for $W_j^{(1)}$ and $W_j^{(2)}$ indicate relative weakness of monopoly power and better approximation of the competitive equilibrium. See Abba P. Lerner, "The Concept of Monopoly and the Measurement of Monopoly Power," *Review of Economic Studies*, June, 1943, pp. 157–75.

20. George J. Stigler, "Public Regulation of the Securities Market," *Journal of Business* 37 (April, 1964): 117–34, at 129.

5 Brokerage Commissions in the New York Stock Exchange

In the last chapter we presented a largely theoretical analysis of the costs of transacting. In this chapter[1] and the next, in contrast, our objective is to consider the behavior of transactions costs and the efficiency of the institutional arrangements for providing transactions services in more operational terms.

While we shall present a few intermarket comparisons, our primary focus is on the costs of transacting in the New York Stock Exchange (NYSE). The NYSE is singled out for several reasons. First, it is by far the most important of the nation's stock exchanges, accounting for nearly $\frac{3}{4}$ of the trading that takes place in an exchange context. Moreover, because the other exchanges are largely patterned after the NYSE, their operations are strongly influenced by what it does. Finally, a wealth of information about trading conditions in the NYSE makes it an ideal subject for empirical analysis.

In this chapter we are primarily concerned with the cost to investors of exchange services in the NYSE. Since this cost is equal to the commissions charged for brokerage services, the study of commissions constitutes the focal point of our analysis. We begin with a brief review of the history of commission rates in the NYSE. Because these rates have consistently reflected the Exchange's policy of charging a fixed minimum commission to nonmembers, we next present and analyze the NYSE's theoretical arguments in favor of fixed commission rates. Since the Exchange's defense of minimum commissions is based largely on a statistical analysis of brokerage house costs and economies of scale in the provision of brokerage services, we follow the theoretical discussion with a review of three empirical studies of the cost structure of brokerage houses, including the Exchange's own study. Finally, we consider how brokerage commissions might be determined in the NYSE in the absence of a fixed minimum commission policy and comment on the recently announced SEC proposals for the elimination of fixed commissions on transactions involving stocks having a value of $100,000 or more.

Fixed Minimum Commissions: The Background

On May 17, 1792, twenty-four brokers of the securities issued by the fledgling federal government of the United States signed what was to become known as the Buttonwood Tree Agreement, thereby establishing the forebear of today's New York Stock Exchange (NYSE). According to the terms of that agreement:

> We, the subscribers, brokers for the purchase and sale of public stock, do hereby solemnly promise and pledge ourselves to each other, that we will not buy or sell from this day for any person whatsoever, any kind of public stock at a less rate than one-quarter percent commission on the specie value, and that we will give a preference to each other in our negotiations. In testimony whereof we have set our hands this 17th day of May, at New York, 1792.[2]

In the years that followed the signing of the Buttonwood Tree Agreement, the Exchange's members developed a complex body of rules and procedures to govern their trading activities; but they never wavered in their support of the basic anticompetitive characteristics embodied in the original agreement. Moreover, until quite recently these characteristics remained virtually unquestioned by the courts and the nation's regulatory agencies. Indeed, despite being obviously inconsistent with the spirit if not the letter of U.S. antitrust legislation, these characteristics drew strength from such laws as the Securities Exchange Act of 1934, which specifically exempted the NYSE and other national stock exchanges from certain provisions of the statutes designed to inhibit anticompetitive practices.

Between 1792 and 1919, the fixed minimum commission charged to nonmembers was calculated on the basis of a flat rate of the par value of the stock traded. This method was discarded in 1919 in favor of a sliding scale per share based on its dollar value. The sliding scale approach was continued for the next twenty-eight years, with across-the-board increases in the schedule of rates taking effect in 1938 and 1942. In each case the reason for the increase given by the Exchange was the rising costs of providing brokerage services and the declining volume of trading activity.

In 1947 the Exchange made a second drastic overhaul in the method of calculating minimum commissions. This time the sliding scale per share on the value of the share was replaced with a sliding schedule based on the value of a round lot. In effecting the changeover, the Exchange also took the opportunity to make still another general increase in the level of rates. Two more increases were made in the next eleven years, the first in 1953 and the second in 1958.

A third major change in the Exchange's approach to calculating commissions was instituted in December, 1968. Breaking with a tradition that dated from its origin in 1792, the Exchange instituted a system of volume discounts on transactions of more than 1,000 shares.

At present, then, the commission per round lot charged nonmembers depends on both the price of the shares and the number of round lots being traded. The exact commission is calculated on the basis of the schedule presented in Table 5–1. From this table, the reader can see that the marginal commission rate per round lot on orders of 1,000 shares or less declines over four steps with the dollar value of the transaction.[3] On that

TABLE 5–1
Minimum Brokerage Commissions (nonmember rates)*

On First 1,000 Shares (per Round Lot)		On Excess over 1,000 Shares (per Round Lot)	
Money Involved	*Commissions*	*Money Involved*	*Commissions*
First $400	2% + $3	$100 to $2800	$\frac{1}{2}$% + $4
Next $2000	1%	$2800 to $3000	same as $2800
Next $2600	$\frac{1}{2}$%	Above $3000 to $9000	$\frac{1}{2}$% + $3
Above $5000	$\frac{1}{10}$%	Above $9000	$\frac{1}{10}$% + $39

*Commerce Clearing House, *New York Stock Exchange Guide*, Article XV, pp. 1,091–94.

portion of an order exceeding 1,000 a second declining marginal
rate based on the dollar value per round lot applies. Beginning
from a lower base, this second rate declines somewhat slower
than the first.

Today the NYSE still operates as a voluntary association
with stringent barriers to entry, and a minimum commission
rate that differentiates between members and nonmembers.
How long it will continue to do so is an open question. Very
recently, the SEC rejected several features of an Exchange
proposal concerning the fixing of commission levels. More
important, it proposed that commission rates on orders involving securities valued in excess of $100,000 be open to negotiation
between a broker and his client. Still more recently, it told the
Exchange that negotiated rates on orders in excess of $500,000
must be instituted no later than April 1, 1971.[4] When put into
effect, the SEC's mandate will clearly signal a major turning
point in the methods by which commissions are determined.
The history of the minimum commission issue, however,
suggests that it will be sometime before a resolution is obtained
concerning the methods of calculating charges for orders of
less than $500,000. In the meantime, the various arguments
presented by the Exchange and its critics will continue to be
a source of discussion and debate.

The Exchange's Case: Background and a Brief Summary

It is one thing for an industry to charge a minimum price for
its product or service and another to attempt to justify charging
it. Thus, it is not altogether surprising that the Exchange made
no real attempt to provide a formal economic rationale for its
minimum commission policy until pressured to do so by the
Department of Justice (DOJ) in 1968. In the spring of that year,
the Securities and Exchange Commission (SEC) invited "all
interested parties" to comment on various proposals of the
NYSE to revise its commission structure. In a sharply worded
brief, the DOJ responded that there was a "basic question
about whether rate fixing by the NYSE is required or justified
by the objectives of the Securities Exchange Act."[5] Moreover,
it went on to conclude that "upon the information now available,
the Commission could proceed to eliminate the fixing of
commission rates upon transactions by institutional investors

and upon other transactions above a specified dollar value."[6]
In addition, the brief argued that although there is "significant
uncertainty as to the effect and feasibility of eliminating all
rate fixing on smaller transactions . . . this does not appear to
justify the present system of minimum rates but it is possible
that maximum rates may be warranted for the protection of
investors."[7]

In response to the DOJ brief, the NYSE submitted a lengthy
economic analysis of the brokerage industry, concluding that
the policy of minimum commissions was justified.[8] Since the
submission of that brief, the SEC has held several rounds of
hearings, taken testimony from scores of witnesses, and accepted
replies and responses from the various parties.[9] Its recent
rejection of the NYSE's proposal concerning revisions in the
level and structure of minimum commissions indicates that the
original DOJ memorandum has already had an important
impact on the SEC's approach to commission rate-setting. As
mentioned above, however, the NYSE's history is one of un-
dying support for the minimum commission. Thus, while it is
possible for the Exchange to reverse its thinking at this late date,
it seems more likely that it will attempt to revise or, at the very
least, amend the SEC's position. In any event, it seems clear
that the NYSE's case in support of the minimum commission
will continue to be heard in the months and, probably, years to
come.

In the remainder of this section, we shall briefly summarize
the major arguments of that case. This is not an altogether easy
task. To begin with, the brief in which they are contained is
more than 100 pages long. More important, it is rambling,
redundant and generally lacking in brevity. We will endeavor,
however, to present the Exchange's case fairly and completely,
leaving it to the interested reader to judge for himself after
studying the brief in its entirety.

The Exchange's basic strategy for justifying minimum
commissions involves arguing that undesirable, indeed catas-
trophic, consequences could result from a system of competitively determined rates. Many such consequences are spelled
out in the brief. Virtually all of them fit into two categories:
(1) those related to the structure of the continuous auction
method of market-making employed by the Exchange and (2)
those related to the structure of the brokerage industry.

Following a brief introduction and summary, the NYSE
takes up the first set of consequences. According to the Ex-

change, the elimination of minimum commissions, i.e., the substitution of competitive rate-setting for the existing policy, would lead to a decline in the incentives for brokerage firms ①
to be members of the NYSE and eventually to a significant
reduction in both the number of firms holding membership and
the volume of trading channeled to the floor of the Exchange ②
for execution. These developments would, in turn, lead to a splintering of the auction market for NYSE listed stocks and make it difficult if not impossible for the Exchange to maintain ③
its policies related to self-regulation and surveillance. To quote
the Exchange's brief:

> The New York Stock Exchange auction market would be weakened
> as the Big Board shrinks to an association of floor brokers and
> specialists, and as an increasing proportion of trading is down in
> brokers' offices. . . . Increased trading in over-the-counter markets,
> which we believe would result from the abolition of minimum
> commissions, would not only lead to poorer executions, but would
> deprive the public of many of the NYSE regulatory safeguards,
> including the close surveillance of trading.[10]

The other group of consequences that the NYSE alleges would result from the abolition of minimum commissions concerns the brokerage industry. According to the Exchange, the economic characteristics of the industry are such that competitive rate setting would lead to destructive competition, particularly during periods of reduced trading activities. This competition, it is alleged, would result in a significant increase in the degree of concentration in the industry in the long run, with no guarantee that the more efficient firms would survive. Other probable long-run consequences are said to include (1) a reduction in both the quantity and quality of research and ④ ancillary services provided by brokers and (2) the development ⑤ of price discrimination favoring large institutional investors. In summary, it is the Exchange's position that the elimination of fixed rates would lead to the domination of the brokerage industry by one or a few "discount execution houses" having the power to engage in price discrimination and offering few if any ancillary services such as research or investment counseling.

Analyzing the Exchange's Case

So much for generalities; let us now turn to the more difficult tasks of describing and analyzing the Exchange's reasons for predicting that competitive rate setting would have such dire consequences. We shall begin with the arguments concerning the structure of the equities market and then take up the Exchange's logic concerning the brokerage industry.

The Structure of the Equities Market. As mentioned in the preceding section, the Exchange contends that the elimination of fixed rates would lead to deterioration in the central auction market for listed stocks. The reasoning behind this conclusion can be gleaned from the following statement from its brief:

> At the present time, the existence of minimum commissions represents a primary incentive for retaining NYSE membership. A member may trade on the floor of the Exchange by paying the prescribed charges to floor brokers, while the nonmember must pay the higher commission rate applicable to the public. Without some effective rate differential between members and nonmembers, the incentive to join the NYSE—thus bringing trades to the NYSE floor, and thereby contributing to the liquidity of the market—would quickly disappear. The entire complexion of the marketplace would change.[11]

In pondering this statement, the reader must be careful not to misread the first sentence. It does not state that the minimum commission system represents a primary incentive for paying a high price for obtaining or retaining a seat on the Exchange. If it did, no reasonable man could disagree; clearly, the existing system has had much to do with making the seats on the NYSE valuable capital assets. The sentence, however, makes a very different point—namely, that the minimum commission system provides an incentive for retaining memberships *per se*, that is, retaining them at any price. Indeed, it is this point that leads to the conclusion that members would leave the Exchange if the system were eliminated. In this form, the sentence is generally lacking in credibility, both in regard to its implications for the number of firms holding seats on the Exchange and for the volume of trading being brought to the Exchange.

On the matter of the number of memberships, Harold Demsetz has argued convincingly as follows:

> Should minimum commissions be abolished, the price of a seat would fall to the level necessary to equate the quantity of seats demanded to the quantity supplied. If the number of memberships allowed by the NYSE should remain unchanged, the price of a seat would fall to

that price required to keep the allowed number of seats filled. . . . If memberships were open to all who desired to pay the cost of providing such membership . . . the number of seats would increase or decrease to the extent required to produce (brokerage) services at the lowest possible cost. Whether this number of seats will (*sic*) be smaller or larger than presently is the case, depends on how stingy the NYSE has been in deciding how many seats it now allows.[12]

Demsetz then adds his own judgment that, since the NYSE has arbitrarily limited the number of seats, the number of memberships would probably increase under an open membership policy and competitive rate-making.[13]

To a large degree Professor Demsetz's conclusions concerning the membership question stem from his analysis of the impact of the elimination of fixed rates on the volume of trading that would flow to the Exchange. Like virtually all other academic economists who have studied the subject, Demsetz concludes that competitive rate-setting would, if anything, increase rather than decrease the volume of trading brought to the floor of the Exchange for execution. The logic behind this conclusion is really very simple: To the extent that the current level of commissions is above the cost that member firms incur in performing brokerage services for nonmembers, the relative attractiveness of other markets, e.g., the regional exchanges or the so-called third market, is improved; if commissions were permitted to seek a competitive level more in line with this cost, the attractiveness of the NYSE would be enhanced rather than impaired. This point is even attested to in a recent report prepared by a consulting firm retained by the Exchange. In discussing the level of commissions on large orders, the report makes the following observation:

> One apparent consequence of the high profitability on large orders has been the growth in over-the-counter trading of New York Stock Exchange–listed stocks on the "third" market, where brokers and dealers, not bound by the Stock Exchange commission minimum, are willing to reduce their effective commissions on large-volume transactions; the competitive advantage they gain thereby tends to divert stock trading away from the New York Stock Exchange.[14]

In terms put forth by the NYSE, the logic of those who feel that the elimination of fixed rates would enhance the attractiveness of the NYSE implies that an "effective rate differential between members and nonmembers" would be equal to the cost of having the former provide brokerage services to the latter. That many traders would be willing to pay this differential seems rather obvious—they now pay an even higher rate. Indeed, assuming that the demand for the Exchange's services is not completely inelastic, it seems clear that some traders would be willing to buy even more brokerage services (engage in even more trading) at a competitively determined rate.

Some economists who have commented on the NYSE's arguments concerning the impact of the elimination of fixed rates on the structure of the equities market go beyond merely arguing that competitively determined rates would make the Exchange seem more attractive in relation to the regional exchanges or the third market. Baxter, for example, concludes that competitive rates would almost certainly make the NYSE the only viable marketplace for the stocks listed on it.[15] His reasoning is that the dealer function, i.e., the specialist function, is a natural monopoly. This being the case, the NYSE specialist would become the only dealer in a listed stock if brokerage commissions on the Exchange were equal to the cost of providing brokerage services to non-members. According to Baxter, this is not now the case simply because the excessive level of fixed commissions makes it advantageous for some investors to trade away from the Big Board.[16] We question this appraisal and will have more to say about it in Chapter 9.[17]

For now, it should suffice to make the following observations. First, as long as the costs of bringing orders to the Exchange and of executing them on the floor compare favorably with the costs of crossing them elsewhere, memberships will be valuable. Second, so long as the price of brokerage services is above their cost, the Exchange's attractiveness, relative to other markets, will be diminished. Third, when the costs of executing orders on the Exchange do not compare favorably with other markets, no system of commissions, short of subsidized commissions, will be able to stop the erosion of the Exchange. In sum, then, regardless of the relative merits of the Exchange method of market-making, fixing minimum commissions above the rate that would prevail under competition cannot be supported on the grounds that it contributes to the health and maintenance of the continuous auction market; if anything, it does just the opposite.

Prior to considering the Exchange's arguments concerning the impact of competitive rate-setting on the structure of the brokerage industry, we wish to comment briefly on the NYSE's other major point related to minimum commissions and the conduct of exchange operations. That point concerns the costs of the NYSE's activities related to self-regulation and market surveillance. The Exchange's brief, if we interpret it correctly, asserts that in the absence of minimum commissions some members would leave the Exchange in order to avoid these costs.[18] For reasons similar to those expressed above, we find this argument completely unpersuasive. At present, commission rates are more than sufficient to cover these costs, yet many investors continue to patronize the Exchange. Presumably, then, they might even patronize it more at lower rates, still sufficient to cover the costs of self-regulation and surveillance. If this were the case, it seems difficult to believe that members would want to leave the Exchange because of the level of these costs.

Of course, it does not follow from this that the Exchange's current level of expenditures on self-regulation and surveillance are "optimal." The fact that it is not possible to observe any systematic improvement in the price of securities that move from the over-the-counter market to the NYSE[19] would seem to imply that investors do not feel the greater self-regulation and surveillance of the Exchange reduces risk or improves price stability, as is alleged. It might be interesting to find out how much the Exchange would spend on these aspects of its operations in the absence of regulatory pressures. If the evidence from the over-the-counter market is any guide, we suspect that fewer resources would be devoted to regulation and surveillance. It might be suggested, however, that this would not be a valid test of the economic worth of these services because of welfare problems related to "free riding," the desire for option demand, and the so-called tyranny of small decisions.[20] Of course, if this is true, it might also be argued that the amount of resources currently being spent on these activities in the over-the-counter market is less than optimal, in which case we would do well to consider increasing the amount of surveillance now being done by the over-the-counter market. If this were done, the Exchange could no longer argue that its expenses in this regard put it and its members at a comparative disadvantage vis-à-vis the over-the-counter market.[21]

The Structure and Behavior of the Brokerage Industry. The Exchange's arguments concerning the impact of competitively established commissions on the structure and behavior of the brokerage industry are to a considerable degree intertwined. We shall endeavor, however, to disentangle them somewhat and to give each its due. Our first subject will be the allegation that competitively established commissions would lead to a deterioration in the quantity and quality of ancillary brokerage services provided to investors, followed by the argument that, in the industry shakeout accompanying the elimination of fixed commissions, the most efficient firms would not necessarily survive. Finally, we shall consider the assertion that the demand and cost conditions of the industry are such that negotiated rates would lead to (1) destructive competition, (2) the loss of capacity to meet peak load demand, and eventually (3) the possibility of excessive concentration in the industry.

The quantity and quality of ancillary brokerage services. In the section of its brief entitled "Summary of Major Conclusions," the Exchange makes the following statement:

> Minimum commission rates have enabled member firms to provide individual investors valuable services in the form of financial information on specific companies, as well as important research, advisory and communications facilities. The elimination of minimum commission rates would probably deprive investors of these services.[22]

In the body of its brief, the NYSE takes considerable pains to suggest that the loss of research and related ancillary brokerage services would have dire consequences for both individual investors and the public at large. But it provides very little logic to support its conclusion that these services would be eliminated. Indeed, the Exchange's case rests almost entirely on two arguments: first, that the tyranny of small decisions would operate in the market for these services and, second, that the cost structure of providing these services is such that the prices charged for them would not be sufficient to break even. Let us consider the second argument first.

According to the Exchange, the cost characteristics of providing investment research involve high fixed costs and low variable costs. In particular, the cost of disseminating completed research is said to be "close to zero." But "since a competitive market will not charge a positive price for information beyond the cost of dissemination,"[23] it would not be possible to support research without minimum commissions. The fallacy involved in this argument hardly requires elaborate discussion. If it were true, neither *Consumer Reports* nor any of the myriad of market letters advertised in the *Wall Street Journal* and other financial publications could possibly turn a profit. The fact that many of the latter have survived and prospered over the years would seem, therefore, to belie the Exchange's case. The fact that such services, as well as investment advisory services and nonbrokerage investment research firms, can survive in the face of competition from NYSE members who provide "free" services suggests that there is little reason to fear that investors are (or would become) unwilling to pay for ancillary brokerage services on a direct basis. If this is true, then the Exchange's other major argument, that is, the argument related to the tyranny of small decisions, also lacks substance.

This is not to say, of course, that investors would continue to buy as much service on a direct payment basis as they now receive as a part of a tie-in sale. Under the prevailing fixed minimum commission schedule, traders do not necessarily pay for what they desire. Some traders pay for the costs of services for which they may have no demand, e.g., investment counsel and research; others, who need elaborate and specialized research services, are not satisfied with the standard information they now receive and must either make additional payments to specialized research organizations or engage in research on their own. With competitive pricing, each member firm could attempt to provide those brokerage functions in which it enjoyed a comparative advantage. As a result, some would offer only execution and clearance, charging commission rates reflecting the costs of providing these services. Analogously, others might specialize in research and investment counseling or might offer any combination of brokerage services for which they felt they could develop sufficient patronage.

Competitive rate-setting and survival. A second major theme of the NYSE's case is that negotiated commissions would produce a shakeout in the brokerage industry that would not necessarily eliminate the least efficient firms. According to the Exchange:

> A large portion of the securities commission business is handled by firms with substantial interests in other activities. The normal economic incentive of earning a reasonable return on commission business is considerably diluted for these firms. The test of survival would be the degree of dependence on commission business and size; not efficiency. The abolition of minimum commissions would eliminate the smaller firms, regardless of their efficiency.[24]

There seems to be little doubt that competitive rate-setting would be accompanied by the failure of some firms engaged in the brokerage business. This, however, is not the issue. Rather, the issue is whether or not the failing firms would be those that now perform brokerage functions inefficiently.

As an approach to evaluating this argument, we might begin by asking why conglomerate investment banking firms would pursue pricing policies that would drive smaller, yet efficient, firms out of business. One possibility is that they might do so in the belief that the losses or lower profits associated with aggressive pricing of brokerage services would be more than made up by increases in profits in other lines of commerce resulting from the attraction of added brokerage business. We have no idea whether or not this is a real possibility, but if this is the basis for a larger firm's power to eliminate smaller rivals, it suggests that the former is in fact more efficient in an over-all sense. Put somewhat differently, it suggests that the larger firm's lower charges for brokerage services are justified on the grounds that they either increase revenues or decrease costs in related investment banking activities by an amount great enough to justify the lower returns (or "losses") that accrue to the brokerage operations *per se.* This implies, of course, that there are significant joint cost and return characteristics in the industry and that it is inappropriate to attempt to measure the efficiency of a firm in the brokerage area without taking other activities into account. The NYSE's brief appears to recognize that there may be joint cost and return characteristics in the industry. It states, for example, that in 1966 large, multiproduct investment houses "obviously maintained their brokerage facilities as an adjunct to other services rendered in the financial market."[25] Unfortunately, however, the brief then goes on to suggest that this implies such firms "were relieved of the normal economic incentive of earning a reasonable return on that business."[26]

In many industries it has been alleged that, even in the absence of joint costs and returns, large multiproduct firms can drive smaller rivals in individual lines of commerce out of business by predatory pricing. The logic is that the large firm "subsidizes its predatory operations with profits from other markets until the predation creates conditions [i.e., monopoly power] which will repay the original subsidy."[27] At times, the Exchange's brief seems to be arguing along these lines. To be profitable, however, predatory pricing tactics must be accompanied by barriers that prevent the entry of new rivals;[28] yet the only barrier that the NYSE's brief identifies is the presence of economies of scale in the brokerage industry. As we shall see below, its evidence in support of such economies is not very persuasive; certainly, it is not persuasive enough to give the predatory pricing argument any viability.

Destructive competition in the brokerage industry. The next section will present a rather detailed analysis of the Exchange's empirical analysis of economies of scale. Before doing so, however, let us consider its logic concerning the implications of the existence of such economies.

According to the Exchange, the presence of economies of scale in combination with wide fluctuations in the demand for brokers' services would be prone to produce destructive or "cutthroat" competition in the industry. In the short run, this would lead to wide fluctuations in the price of brokerage services and the elimination of many relatively efficient firms; in the longer run, it would increase concentration and make it difficult for the industry to attract the capital needed to meet the growth in demand, particularly at times of peak load.

By itself, the problem of having to deal with fluctuating demand is neither unique to the brokerage industry nor sufficient grounds to advocate some form of price-fixing or stabilization. When combined with economies of scale, however, it may provide the basis for such an argument. At least, it has provided the basis in other industries. Not long ago the British cement industry, for example, convinced the British Restrictive Practices Court that it required a price-fixing arrangement on the grounds that it would otherwise be difficult to attract capital because of wide fluctuations in price.[29] F. M. Scherer, however, recently demonstrated that the case in favor of price stabilization requires more than a combination of economies of scale and fluctuating demand. In particular, he pointed out it requires that short-run marginal cost be quite inelastic in the range over which demand can be expected to fluctuate and, usually, that demand become less elastic during troughs. In the brokerage industry we have virtually no evidence on which to base judgments concerning the behavior of demand elasticity in relation to shifts in the demand schedule. The NYSE asserts in its brief that the demand for brokerage services is highly inelastic, but it offers no evidence to support this judgment.[30] More important,

the Exchange never argues that demand becomes even more inelastic when demand contracts. The burden of its case, then,
would seem to rest on its arguments concerning economies of
scale and the cost structure of brokerage houses. If there are
significant economies of scale and if short-run marginal cost is
extremely inelastic in the range over which demand fluctuates,
the NYSE's case for some form of price stabilization cannot be
rejected out of hand. If there are not such economies, however,
the Exchange is left with nothing more than the argument that
firms in the industry would have difficult problems in reacting to
fluctuations in demand. And while this is obviously true, it is
neither unique to the brokerage business nor a sufficient basis
for fixing prices through collusive arrangements.[31]

The price discrimination argument. As a final prelude to considering the empirical evidence concerning the behavior of
brokerage house costs, let us briefly comment on one more argument put forward by the Exchange to support minimum commissions. The argument to which we refer concerns the possibility
that competitive rate-setting would lead to price discrimination
favoring large institutional investors.[32] In a recent critique of the
Exchange's case for minimum commissions, Baxter notes that
"this argument perverts the economic meaning of the term
'discrimination.'"[33] He then goes on to make the following
comments:

> It is true that under competitive conditions lower rates per share and
> per dollar of transaction will apply to large transactions than to small
> ones, but this is not discrimination. The only economically sensible
> meaning of discrimination is that the price-cost ratio for one trans-
> action is different from the ratio for another.... The NYSE argu-
> ment is essentially an argument in favor of discrimination: big, rich
> institutional investors should pay high price cost ratios and poor,
> little individual investors should pay low ones.[34]

In general, we subscribe to Baxter's views concerning the Exchange's case. We would point out, however, that if there are
economies of scale sufficient to create monopoly or oligopoly,
the circumstances necessary for true price discrimination might
obtain. To conclude that price discrimination would take place
under even these circumstances, however, is tantamount to
arguing that the DOJ would stand idly by while one or a few
brokerage houses abused market power.

The Nature of Brokerage Cost Structures

Recognizing that its case in support of minimum commissions depends in large measure on the nature of brokerage costs, the New York Stock Exchange devotes considerable space in its brief to a statistical analysis of these costs. In this section, we shall summarize the Exchange's analysis, consider the theoretical merits of its approaches and techniques, and present some alternative results developed by H. Michael Mann[35] and Harold Demsetz.[36]

The NYSE Study. The NYSE's cost study attempts to (1) determine the fixed and variable components of total costs of providing brokerage services, (2) define the shape of the long-run marginal cost function, and (3) establish the relationship between efficiency and firm sizes.

Fixed vs. variable costs. The Exchange's study utilizes two different methods in determining the relative importance of fixed costs in the brokerage industry. The first consists of an *a priori* allocation of various items of brokerage costs into two categories: those that do not vary within a year and those functionally related to the output of the firm. On the basis of this *a priori* allocation, the distribution of fixed and variable costs in 1966 is presented in Table 5–2.

To avoid the bias introduced by this arbitrary classification of various cost items, the study employs a second method of de-

TABLE 5–2
Distribution of Variable and Fixed Costs*

Costs	*(With all clerical and administrative costs as fixed)*		*(With 75% of clerical and administrative costs as fixed)*	
	Millions of Dollars	*Per Cent*	*Millions of Dollars*	*Per Cent*
Variable	708.6	49	818.6	56
Fixed	745.5	51	635.5	44
Total	1,454.1	100	1,454.1	100

*Adapted from *Economic Effects of Negotiated Rates on the Brokerage Industry, the Market for Corporate Securities and the Investing Public* (NYSE Study), August, 1968, p. 56.

termining the distribution of variable and fixed costs. This procedure involves estimating a multiple regression equation in which the dependent variable is total expenses (X_1), and the independent variables are (1) the number of transactions handled by each firm (X_2), and (2) six "dummy" variables $(D_1$ to $D_6)$ to account for variations in firm size.[37] Algebraically,

$$X_1 = \alpha_0 + \alpha_1 X_2 + \alpha_2 D_1 + \alpha_3 D_2 + \alpha_4 D_3 + \alpha_5 D_4 + \alpha_6 D_5 + \alpha_7 D_6 \quad (5.1)$$

The results of the regression analysis are presented in Table 5-3.

TABLE 5-3

Estimated Coefficients of the Regression Equation*

Regressors	Coefficient	Standard Deviation	t-Ratio†
α_0	493,564	180,785	2.73011
X_2	20.654	0.8508	24.2777
D_1	925,208	331,687	2.7894
D_2	2,329,820	422,010	5.52076
D_3	1,652,270	578,703	2.85512
D_4	9,656,700	1,050,620	9.19146
D_5	8,690,310	1,433,370	6.06285
D_6	26,530,600	3,676,550	7.21617

*Adapted from NYSE Study (August, 1968), p. 58.
†All coefficients are significant at 5 per cent level; the R^2 for the equation is 0.942.

The coefficient of X_2 (the number of transactions) represents the variable cost of a transaction. Thus, according to the regression results, a brokerage firm incurs a cost of $20.654 for each transaction it consummates on behalf of a customer. The reader should note that the equation does not distinguish between various sizes of transactions but rather assumes that the variable cost of completing a transaction is invariant with respect to order size. Neither does the variable cost of a transaction vary among firms of different sizes.

The fixed costs for firms in each of the seven classes are determined by adding the coefficient of the appropriate classification variable to the intercept term α_0. The resulting distribution of fixed and variable costs for each of the classes is presented

TABLE 5–4

Distribution of Fixed Costs in the Brokerage
Industry*

Class	Number of Firms	Fixed Cost	Average Total Cost	Per Cent Fixed Cost
I	195	493,564	884,439	55.8%
II	83	1,418,772	2,725,437	52.1%
III	47	2,823,384	5,778,125	48.9%
IV	26	2,145,834	8,449,294	25.4%
V	9	10,150,264	25,286,670	40.1%
VI	7	9,183,874	35,255,910	26.0%
VII	2	27,024,164	105,419,428	25.6%

*Adapted from NYSE Study, p. 59.

in Table 5–4. These data indicate that nearly 90 per cent of the firms in the Exchange's sample have a cost structure in which fixed costs constitute about 50 per cent of total costs. This, according to the Exchange, supports its *a priori* classification.

The long-run average and marginal cost functions. Beyond trying to determine the composition of total costs, the Exchange's study also attempts to explore the shapes of the long-run average and marginal cost functions. Two approaches are employed. The first involves studying how the average cost of brokerage firms varies in response to changes in volume. Using data from 1965 and 1966, the Exchange divides 347 brokerage firms into three groups:

(1) those showing a decline in transactions executed
(2) those showing increases in execution of less than 25 per cent
(3) those showing increases of more than 25 per cent.

The Exchange's results are summarized in Table 5–5. According to its brief, these results are consistent with the argument that economies of scale are present in the brokerage industry, i.e., that marginal cost is below average cost. In particular, after adjusting these data for inflation in costs it concludes that 202 of the 347 firms have average costs above marginal costs.[38]

The Exchange's second approach involves the statistical estimation of the total cost function for the brokerage industry.

TABLE 5–5
Changes in Number of Transactions and Average Total
Costs*

Class	Percentage Increase in Number of Transactions	Number of Firms With Average Total Cost:		
		Decreasing	Increasing	Total
I	Less than 0.0%	1	56	57
II	0.0% to 25%	37	159	196
III	Over 25%	62	32	94

*Adapted from NYSE Study, p. 56.

Once the total cost function is estimated, the shapes of long-run marginal and average cost schedules are calculated from the estimated equation. Again multiple regression models, with total expense (X_1) as the dependent variable and the number of transactions (X_2) as the explanatory variable, are utilized in estimating the shape of the total cost function. Two functional forms are estimated:

$$X_1 = \alpha_0 + \alpha_1 X_2 + \alpha_2 X_2{}^2 \tag{5.2}$$

$$X_1 = \alpha_0 + \alpha_1 X_2 + \alpha_2 X_2{}^2 + \alpha_3 X_2{}^3 \tag{5.3}$$

Since the cubic term in equation (5.3) is insignifica'nt, the Exchange relies on equation (5.2) for its analysis.

The estimated coefficients for these two equations are presented in Table 5–6. The long-run marginal cost implied in this equation, i.e., $dX_1/dX_2 = 31.34 - 2.16 \times 10^{-6}X_2$, is a decreasing

TABLE 5–6
Estimated Long-Run Total Cost Function*

Equation	Regressors				
	Intercept	X_2	$X_2{}^2$	$X_2{}^3$	R^2
(5.2)†	476,393	31.3445	-1.082×10^{-6}		0.934
	(159,397)	(0.77604)	(1.65×10^{-7})		
	2.98871	40.3903	-6.54007		
(5.3)	381,229	33.1050	-2.926×10^{-6}	2.6873×10^{-13}	0.934
	(182,405)	(1.81578)	(1.277×10^{-6})	(2.506×10^{-13})	
	2.09002	18.2318	-1.69392	1.07242	

*Adapted from NYSE Study, pp. 52–53.
†All coefficients are significant beyond 5 per cent level in the equation.

function of the number of transactions. In other words, the equation states that there are increasing returns to scale within the estimated range (see Figure 18). Once again, the size of the transaction is assumed to exert no influence on the costs of providing brokerage services.

Efficiency and firm size. The NYSE's study also tests for the relationship, if any, between the efficiency of brokerage firms, as measured by net profit on gross security commission income, and the relative importance of a firm's brokerage business, as measured by the percentage of net income derived from brokerage activities. The correlation coefficient is not statistically different from zero (-0.0640).[39] Similarly, the study finds no systematic relationship between inefficiency and the size of the firms, where the latter is measured by the total commission income (correlation coefficient $= 0.0339$).[40] On the basis of these findings, the study concludes that competitive brokerage commissions might enable large — but not necessarily efficient — firms to dominate the brokerage industry.

Mann's Study. When the statistical cost analysis developed by the NYSE appeared in the summer of 1968, it did not win unanimous acceptance among economists. To the contrary, criticisms concerning the economic and econometric merits of the study soon appeared. One of the more thorough and damaging attacks was presented by H. Michael Mann, who used the Exchange's own cost data to reach conclusions that contradicted its contention concerning economies of scale in the brokerage industry. Mann's critique takes issue with all three aspects of the NYSE's study. It concludes that the Exchange's analysis overestimates the importance of fixed costs, overstates the significance of economies of scale, and implies too great a probability that competitive rate-setting would result in the rise of a few very large brokerage houses.

Fixed vs. variable costs. According to Mann, the Exchange's statistical evaluation of fixed costs (Table 5–4) does not conform to its assumptions concerning the economies of scale set forth in equation (5.2). In analyzing the fixed and variable components of the total costs, the Exchange assumes that the variable costs of providing brokerage services are the same for firms of different sizes. Yet in the second regression equation, it

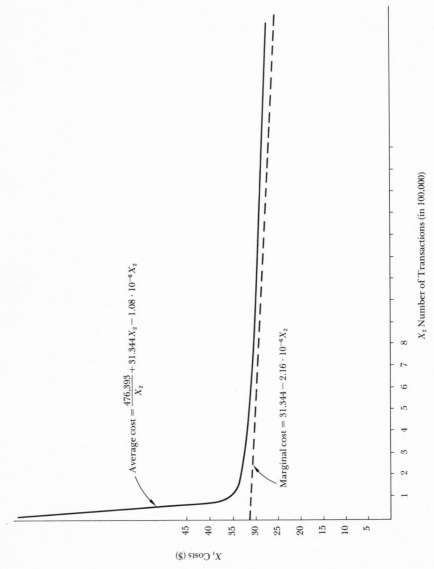

$\text{Average cost} = \dfrac{476.393}{X_2} + 31.344X_2 - 1.08 \cdot 10^{-6}X_2$

$\text{Marginal cost} = 31.344 - 2.16 \cdot 10^{-6}X_2$

X_2 Number of Transactions (in 100,000)

X_1 Costs ($)

FIGURE 18 Long-Run Average and Marginal Cost Functions (as estimated by the NYSE using data from 1966)

attempts to establish a cost structure in which variable costs decline with output. To eliminate this inconsistency, Mann adds a regressor to equation (5.1) that takes cognizance of the variability of out-of-pocket costs among firms of diverse outputs: the number of transactions squared. With the addition of this variable, the estimating equation becomes

$$X_1 = \alpha_0 + \alpha_1 X_2 + \alpha_2 X_2{}^2 + \alpha_3 D_1 + \alpha_4 D_2 + \alpha_5 D_3 + \alpha_6 D_4 + \alpha_7 D_5 + \alpha_8 D_6$$

$$(5.4)$$

The estimated coefficients of this equation are presented in Table 5-7. The reader will note that when the fixed component of the total costs is tabulated for firms in different classes

TABLE 5–7

Estimated Coefficients of Equation (5.4)*

Regressors	Coefficients	Standard Deviation	t-Ratio
Intercept	384,539	202,015	1.906†
X_2	26.76	3.34	8.12‖
$X_2{}^2$	0.000000877	0.000000465	1.886†
D_1	670,530	377,876	1.775†
D_2	1,604,478	587,438	2.73§
D_3	−202,214	1,086,306	−0.185
D_4	5,760,251	2,306,300	2.49‡
D_5	2,543,144	3,557,315	0.71
D_6	19,488,135	5,268,765	3.69‖

*Adapted from H. Michael Mann, "A Critique of the NYSE's Report on the Economic Effects of Negotiated Commission Rates on the Brokerage Industry, the Market for Corporate Stocks and the Investing Public" (hereafter: Mann's Study), presented to the SEC in autumn, 1970, p. 44.

NOTE: $R^2 = 0.94$ (sample size: 347 firms)

†Significant at 0.05 level.

‡Significant at 0.01 level.

§Significant at 0.005 level.

‖Significant at 0.0005 level.

(Table 5–8), there is a significant difference between the results obtained from the Exchange's model (Table 5–5) and those from Mann's revised version. In particular, Mann's results reflect a lower fixed-variable cost ratio in the brokerage industry.

Mann also points out that there are additional problems with the measurement of brokerage output and the allocation of costs.[41] First, the number of transactions is not a very accurate

TABLE 5–8
Distribution of Fixed Costs in Brokerage Industry
(Revised Model)*

Class	Number of Firms in Class	Fixed Costs	NYSE Estimate of Fixed Costs (From Table 5–4)
I	181	384,539	493,564
II	78	1,055,069	1,418,772
III	46	1,989,017	2,823,384
IV	24	182,325	2,145,834
V	9	6,144,790	10,150,264
VI	7	2,927,683	9,183,874
VII	2	19,872,674	27,024,164

*Adapted from Mann's Study, p. 45.

measure of the actual volume of business conducted by broker-age firms: It does not differentiate between transactions consummated by a single firm and transactions handled by more than one, as occurs, for example, when a firm doing a public business calls on a "two-dollar" broker for assistance. A second problem concerns the allocation of costs. According to Mann, the Exchange's data "include a substantial proportion of costs allocated between security commission business and other business."[42] But, as Mann comments, most allocations "may or may not bear any reasonable relation to actual costs."[43] A third problem is statistical in nature: when only one year's data are used in estimating costs, there is always a reasonably high probability that the results may not be representative of typical capacity utilization, i.e., that firms may not be in short run equilibrium.

Long-run marginal cost curve and economies of scale. Mann also criticizes the NYSE's approaches to the analysis of the long-run total and marginal cost schedules in the brokerage industry. He begins by pointing out that the results of the Exchange's first test, the one comparing volume and average costs, are consistent either with the presence or absence of economies of scale. To quote Mann: "A mere decrease in cost with an increase in output over a period of one year tells us nothing for certain about whether the firm is experiencing economies or diseconomies of scale at the end of the second year."[44] As an added point, Mann notes that the results presented by the Exchange are quite sensitive to the "arbitrary classification of firms into groups."[45] By dividing them into two groups (those that had volume increases and those that did not) a very different picture is obtained: On an inflation-adjusted basis, less than half of those with volume increases experience decreasing average costs.

The bulk of Mann's remarks are concerned with the Exchange's regression analysis. To begin with, he notes that the Exchange's model suffers from heteroscedasticity. Thus, he presents a weighted version of the Exchange's model in which the regression is deflated by the number of transactions.[46] In this form, the quadratic term (X_2^2) is found to be statistically insignificant, causing Mann to contend that there are no economies of scale implicit in the sample data. After deflation, the estimated regression equation is as follows:

$$X_1 = 342{,}986 + 25.57\,X_2 + 0.00000434\,X_2^2 \qquad (5.5)$$
$$ (10{,}653) \quad\ (3.62) \quad\ \ (0.00000864)$$
$$ 3.12 \qquad\ \ 7.06 \qquad\ \ 0.502$$

where X_1 is the total expenses and X_2 is the number of transactions.[47] Mann also criticizes the Exchange's use of the number of transactions as a measure of output. "Surely," he notes, "a transaction of 100 shares of a five-dollar security is not the same output as a transaction of 100 shares of a $600 security."[48] This comment, of course, suggests to Mann "that a more meaningful measure of output is the number of dollars [of commissions] transacted."[49]

When Mann uses the total commissions as the measure of brokerage output, he obtains the following results:

$$\frac{X_1}{X_3} = 18{,}319\,\frac{1}{X_3} + 0.8830 + 0.0000000001 X_3$$
$$\phantom{\frac{X_1}{X_3} = } (7{,}228) \quad\ (0.0131) \ (0.0000000009) \qquad \text{and } R^2 = 0.02 \qquad (5.6)$$
$$\phantom{\frac{X_1}{X_3} = } 2.54 \qquad\ \ 6.79 \qquad\ 0.11$$

where X_1 = total cost and X_3 = total commissions. In this form, the association between output and the average cost per dollar of commission business is very low. This result is to be expected, since the size of commissions is highly dependent on the price of an issue, while the costs of providing brokerage services need not change with the price of issues. On the basis of these results, Mann contends that "average costs are decreasing only to the extent necessary to spread 'fixed costs' over an increasing number of units of output."[50] More important, he concludes that "economies of scale are unimportant in the brokerage industry."[51]

Optimum firm size and the brokerage industry. Mann's critique also considers the profitability of 347 member firms during 1966 and analyzes the distribution of average cost per transaction for firms of differing sizes. On the basis of his results, he concludes that the optimum size of a brokerage firm is around 300,000 transactions per year,[52] implying that in a competitive market firms would strive to achieve this optimum size. Thus, according to Mann, competitive pricing would have resulted in 150 brokerage firms, supplying exchange services to traders making 45 million transactions in 1966. Mann, of course, recognizes that in actuality firms might not all be of the same size, but rather might differ somewhat, with some specializing in institutional orders, others doing a retail business, and so forth.[53] Nevertheless, his general conclusion is that there is little reason to expect that competitive rate setting would result in the dominance of the brokerage business by a few very large firms.

Demsetz's Analysis of Scale Economies. Mann's conclusions are supported by Demsetz, who also uses the Exchange's data to determine the average total cost per transaction for brokerage firms of different sizes. Interestingly, although Demsetz does not engage in a statistical analysis of brokerage costs, his "rough and ready" examination of the cost structure yields results very similar to those obtained by Mann.

Demsetz analyzes the average total cost of transactions for each of the seven classes of brokerage firms specified in the NYSE's study. He first determines the number of transactions for the average-sized firm in each class.[54] (See Table 5–9.) The average total cost per transaction is then determined by dividing the total cost figures for the average firm in each class, given in Table 5–4, by the transactions data in Table 5–9.

An examination of Demsetz's findings in Table 5–10 suggests that the average cost per transaction decreases with rising trading volume up to the level of 200,000 transactions per year; above this level the average cost per transaction appears to be quite constant. The reader will note the similarity of this average cost function with Mann's statistically estimated average cost schedule.

TABLE 5–9
Average Number of Trans-
actions in Each Group*

Class	Number of Transactions
I	19,000
II	63,000
III	143,000
IV	306,000
V	735,000
VI	1,250,000
VII	3,800,000

*Adapted from statement of
Harold Demsetz before the SEC,
August, 1969 (Demsetz statement),
p. 16.

TABLE 5–10
Average Total Cost per
Transaction*

Class	Average Cost per Transaction
I	$46
II	$43
III	$40
IV	$28
V	$34
VI	$28
VII	$28

*Adapted from Demsetz
statement, p. 17.

It must again be emphasized, however, that these analyses do not distinguish between transactions of differing sizes. Furthermore, these findings are only a first approximation of the actual average cost: There will be differences resulting not only from the size variation of transactions but also from the diverse costs characteristics in each class. As it is constructed, the intraclass variations in costs cannot be captured in the analysis.

Critique and Summary of Empirical Analysis. In concluding this section it seems appropriate to comment briefly on the quality of the econometric analyses and the question of whether this quality is high enough for us to put much faith in the "pro" and "anti" regression arguments. Perhaps the major potential problem in both the NYSE's and Mann's studies is that of multicollinearity. Equations (5.2) and (5.3) (calculated by the NYSE) and (5.4) and (5.5) (calculated by Mann), all have higher order terms of a common independent variable, which can lead to multicollinear relationships. The important question, of course, is not whether multicollinearity is present but rather how severe it is. Unfortunately, neither study provides data on the intercorrelation between independent variables. Given the sample sizes and the wide range of variation in X_2, however, the likelihood that collinearity is a severe problem should not be excessive.

Certainly, some of the differences in conclusions reached by the NYSE and Mann cannot be attributed to the results of intercorrelation. The difference in the sign of the coefficient of $X_2{}^2$ in equations (5.2) and (5.4), for example, cannot be explained on this basis. These two equations differ only in that (5.4) has six dummy variables not included in (5.2). These, however, are orthogonal and should not introduce any statistical problems.

Perhaps the major point to note is that, over all, the studies of the NYSE, Mann, and Demsetz tend to be reinforcing. For example, both Mann's study and Demsetz's tend to suggest that the brokerage industry does not experience substantial economies of scale. Moreover, even the NYSE's study fails to reflect significant dispersion between the average and marginal costs of providing brokerage services (see Figure 18). Thus, particularly when the differentiation of brokerage services is recognized, the minor increases in returns-to-scale need not give rise to a concern over destructive competition following the elimination of minimum commission rates.

The Competitive Pricing of Brokerage Services

In view of the SEC's recent proposal to abolish rate-fixing on orders having a value in excess of $100,000, it behooves us to consider how the rates charged by brokers might be determined under competitive conditions. Following the logic of basic price theory, we would argue that competitive rate-setting should be based largely on the demand for transactions services and the costs of supplying them. Among the factors that might be expected to influence the latter, the following three would appear to be among the most important: (1) the level of trading activity in an issue, (2) the average size of transactions and (3) the number of dealers making a market.

The Level of Trading Activity. It can easily be shown that, when there is a large number of traders interested in buying and selling an issue, the expected cost of finding a match and crossing orders decreases substantially.[55] Finding matching buy and sell orders in stocks with thinner markets, on the other hand, entails greater costs of search and longer time on the part of the brokers. On theoretical grounds, therefore, it would seem logical that the average cost of executing an order ought to be an inverse function of the level of trading activity in an issue. Hence, in a competitive market, where commissions reflected cost differences in providing brokerage services, rates might be expected to vary inversely with the level of trading activity.

The level of trading activity might also be expected to influence the unit cost of providing investment research and trading information. After all, issues with a large number of outstanding shares and active markets permit brokerage firms to spread these fixed costs of research over more customers. Thus, whether research services are sold separately or as a part of a "bundle" of brokerage services, the rates charged for their dissemination ought to vary inversely with trading volume.[56]

The Average Transaction Size. The existing fixed minimum commission schedule of the NYSE provides a modest discount to traders making large block transactions. These discounts, however, were determined rather arbitrarily and do not necessarily reflect the actual decreases in the marginal costs of servicing the incremental round lots of a large order. In a competitive market one of the major determinants of the commission rates applicable to diverse-sized orders would be the relationship between these costs and the size of transactions. To the best of our knowledge, the behavior of marginal cost of brokerage services for orders of different sizes has not yet been empirically established. We suspect, however, that this cost tends to decrease up to a point, remain stable over some range, and then start increasing. Of course, statistical analysis might not be expected to capture the positively sloped portion of the function, since traders can always avoid this range by submitting smaller orders.

The Number of Dealers Making Markets. One of the important contributions that dealers make to the market is greater continuity: by standing ready to position securities, dealers smooth out temporary imbalances in the inflow of buy and sell orders. Furthermore, they tend to give the flow of orders a focus, thereby reducing the time and effort that would otherwise be necessary in obtaining information about prevailing prices, outstanding tenders, and the over-all condition of the market in an issue. For both of these reasons, the number of dealers making a market for a stock might be expected to influence the ease with which brokers can facilitate transactions. Thus, it seems logical to expect that the commission rates charged to traders would vary inversely with the number of dealers making a market.

Some Evidence from the Over-the-Counter Market. In an attempt to develop some empirical evidence on the relationship between brokerage commissions and the variables just discussed, we analyzed some data from the over-the-counter market, where no minimum commission policy exists. These data were drawn from the SEC's *Special Study of the Securities Market* and reflect trading conditions that prevailed on January 18, 1962, for 200 issues traded in the over-the-counter market.[57] Unfortunately, the *Special Study* did not include information about the size distribution of transactions. Trading activity figures and the number of dealers making two-way markets, however, were presented in the *Special Study*.

To investigate the relationship between commissions and these two variables, we developed the following two multiple regression models:

$$B = \alpha_0 + \alpha_1 P + \alpha_2 V + \alpha_3 D; \tag{5.7}$$

$$B = \lambda_0 + \lambda_1 P + \lambda_2 \ln V + \lambda_3 D; \tag{5.8}$$

where B = average brokerage commissions incurred by traders in a stock ($\times 200$)

P = the average price of an issue

V = trading activity measured in number of shares

D = number of dealers quoting prices in the market

The estimated coefficients of these two regression equations are presented in Table 5–11. In general, the findings seem consistent with our earlier judgment that brokerage commissions in a competitive market would vary inversely with trading activity and number of dealers in the market.

TABLE 5–11
Brokerage Commissions, Trading Activity and Number of Dealers

		Regressors					
Equation	Intercept	P	V	ln V	D	R^2	F-test
(5.7)	119.66	0.959	−0.0020	—	−1.797	0.29	7.09§
	(17.79)	(0.312)	(0.0011)	—	(0.882)		
	6.728§	3.070§	−1.874*	—	−2.036†		
(5.8)	279.644	0.941	—	−21.05	−1.565	0.32	8.26§
	(73.05)	(0.303)	—	(8.468)	(0.874)		
	3.828§	3.101§	—	−2.486‡	−1.792*		

*Significant at 0.05 level.
†Significant at 0.025 level.
‡Significant at 0.01 level.
§Significant at 0.005 level.

In the case of the coefficients for the D variable, however, we are somewhat reluctant to conclude unequivocally that the results imply the relationship between commissions and dealer activity hypothesized above. Our caution in this regard stems from not knowing whether the *Special Study* data on over-the-counter commissions were completely purged of dealership margins. If they were not, that is, if the commission data included returns for dealer services as well as broker services, it may be that the relationship between B and D reflects competitive factors in the provision of dealership services. In other words, it may be that the inverse relationship between B and D in Table 5–11 is based on the impact of variations in dealer competition on the size of dealer returns. To the best of our knowledge, the data for commissions are *net* of any returns to dealers; yet the rather "casual" practices of the over-the-counter market, whereby commissions are sometimes hidden in the price of shares, may be reflected in these data. For this reason we would prefer to remain cautious in our interpretation of the results in Table 5–11.

Based strictly on the costs of providing brokerage services, there is little reason for a functional relationship between brokerage commissions and the price of an issue. How, then, can the relationship between B and P in Table 5–11 be explained? The answer, we believe, stems from factors related to the elimination of bias in trading activity among issues, where the transaction costs per dollar of stocks bought or sold was minimized. If, for example, traders were faced with a flat commission per round lot traded, they would tend, presumably, to seek out issues that met their desires concerning expected return and risk and also produced the lowest possible transactions costs. All else being equal, of course, such issues would tend to be relatively high-priced, thus producing a bias toward trading in these issues. The resulting trading imbalance, however, would tend to correct itself by two distinct mechanisms: first, by changes in equilibrium prices of issues and, second, by changes in commission rates charged for issues. In other words, the commission rates and the prices of the two issues would change in such a way that at the resulting equilibrium levels all stocks offered for exchange would be executed, and there would no longer be an incentive for investors to concentrate their trading activity in issues of any particular price level. This logic, of course, implies a positive relationship between the price of shares and the level of commissions. However, it does not necessarily imply *equal* percentage commissions for all stocks. The cost of transacting is only one of the very large number of factors that determine the price level of a stock, and certainly it is not the most important of all these variables. Inherent risk characteristics, expected return, and portfolio considerations may dominate price formation and changes. Thus, only in the very exceptional case where all of these characteristics were the same and the cost of providing brokerage services was the same would commissions, as a percentage of stocks prices, be identical.

A Concluding Comment

In sum, the analysis presented in this chapter leads us to conclude that the elimination of minimum commissions would lead to lower transactions costs for investors without the undesirable consequences spelled out by the NYSE. To be sure, it seems clear that the substitution of negotiated rates for the minimum commission system would lead to a "shake out" in the brokerage business. But this is probably as it should be anyway; the current system tends to protect a large number of inefficient, marginal firms. There is little evidence, however, to support the notion that negotiated rates would lead to "destructive competition" and the eventual domination of the industry by one or a few gigantic firms. The kinds of economies of scale necessary for this simply do not appear to exist. In short, the minimum commission policy of the NYSE does not seem capable of justification on economic grounds, but rather represents a monopolistic pricing scheme designed to inflate artificially the profits associated with the brokerage business.

Notes

1. After completing a first draft of this chapter, we became aware of William F. Baxter's paper "NYSE Commission Rates: A Private Cartel Goes Public," *Stanford Law Review*, April, 1970, pp. 675–712. Many of the points raised by Baxter paralleled our own thinking. On certain critical issues, however, we differed with his presentations and conclusions. At a later stage in this book, these differences will be made clear. Before proceeding, however, we would like to acknowledge our debt to Professor Baxter: His excellent article has been of invaluable assistance in revising this chapter and preparing a paper based on the revised version. See R. West and S. Tiniç, "Minimum Commission Rates on New York Stock Exchange Transactions," *Bell Journal of Economics and Management Science*, 1971.

2. *Report of the Special Study of the Securities Markets of the Securities and Exchange Commission*, U.S., 88th Cong., 1st sess., House of Representatives Document 95 (Washington, D.C.: Government Printing Office, 1965) (hereafter referred to as *Special Study*), Part 2, p. 295.

3. A minimum service charge of $15.00 or 50 per cent of accrued commissions was established for transactions involving 1,000 shares or less in April, 1970. With this additional service charge the effective discount for orders exceeding 1,000 shares is increased.

4. For a discussion of the SEC statement, see *The New York Times*, October 23, 1970. p. 1. See also *Wall Street Journal*, February 12, 1971, p. 2.

5. *Comments of the United States Department of Justice: Inquiry into Proposals to Modify the Commission Rate Structure of the NYSE*, SEC Release No. 8239, Washington, D.C., 1968, p. 2.

6. *Ibid.*, p. 7.

7. *Ibid.*, p. 3.

8. *Economic Effects of Negotiated Rates on the Brokerage Industry, the Market for Corporate Securities and the Investing Public*, report submitted by the New York Stock Exchange to the SEC in August, 1968 (hereafter referred to as NYSE study).

9. The NYSE submitted a second brief in May, 1969, in response to the testimony of DOJ witnesses and the DOJ's reactions to its original analysis.

The second brief made no new points and instead re-emphasized the ones made in the 1968 brief.

10. NYSE study, pp. 6-7.
11. *Ibid.*, pp. 22-23.
12. Statement of Harold Demsetz before the SEC, August, 1969 (hereafter referred to as Demsetz statement), pp. 4-5.
13. *Ibid.*, p. 6.
14. *Reasonable Public Rates for Brokerage Commissions: A Report Prepared by National Economic Research Associates, Inc., for the New York Stock Exchange*, February, 1970, Chapter 3, p. 8.
15. Baxter, "NYSE Commission Rates," pp. 704, 708-9.
16. *Ibid.*, p. 704.
17. See Chapter 9, below.
18. See NYSE study, pp. 26-30.
19. Cf. R. Furst, "Does Listing Increase the Market Price of Common Shares?" *Journal of Business* 43, No. 2 (April, 1970): 174-80; and J. Van Horne, "New Listings and Their Price Behavior," *Journal of Finance*, September, 1970.
20. On these questions, see Paul A. Samuelson, "The Pure Theory of Public Expenditures," *Review of Economics and Statistics* 36 (November, 1954): 388-89: Burton A. Weisbrod, "Collective Consumption Services of Individual Consumption Goods," *Quarterly Journal of Economics* 78 (August, 1964): 475-76; and Alfred E. Kahn, "The Tyranny of Small Decisions," *Kyklos* 19 (1966): 23-46.
21. Cf. Baxter, "NYSE Commission Rates," pp. 707-8.
22. NYSE study, p. 8.
23. *Ibid.*, p. 105.
24. *Ibid.*, p. 7.
25. *Ibid.*, p. 73.
26. *Ibid.*
27. F. M. Scherer, *Industrial Market Structure and Economic Performance* (Chicago: Rand McNally, 1970), pp. 273-74.
28. See *Ibid.*, pp. 274-76, and John S. McGee, "Predatory Price Cutting: The Standard Oil (N.J.) Case," *Journal of Law and Economics*, October, 1958, pp. 137-69.
29. *In re Cement Makers' Federation Agreement*, L.R., 2 R.P. 241 (1961). See also A. Beacham, "Some Thoughts on the Cement Judgment," *Economic Journal*, June, 1962, pp. 335-43.
30. NYSE study, pp. 88-95.
31. Cf. Baxter, "NYSE Commission Rates," esp. pp. 699-703.
32. NYSE study, pp. 83-88.
33. Baxter, "NYSE Commission Rates," p. 694.
34. *Ibid.*, 694-95.
35. H. Michael Mann, "A Critique of the NYSE's Report on the Economic Effects of Negotiated Commission Rates on the Brokerage Industry, the Market for Corporate Securities and the Investing Public," presented to the SEC in autumn, 1970 (hereafter referred to as Mann study).
36. Demsetz statement.
37. The 369 brokerage firms in the sample are grouped into seven classes on the basis of their annual transaction volume as follows:

		Values of Classification Variables
Class I	0 to 40,000 transactions	all D's are zero
Class II	40,000 to 100,000 transactions	$D_1 = 1$, others are zero
Class III	100,000 to 200,000 transactions	$D_2 = 1$, others are zero
Class IV	200,000 to 500,000 transactions	$D_3 = 1$, others are zero
Class V	500,000 to 1,000,000 transactions	$D_4 = 1$, others are zero
Class VI	1,000,000 to 1,800,000 transactions	$D_5 = 1$, others are zero
Class VII	over 1,800,000 transactions	$D_6 = 1$, others are zero

38. NYSE study, p. 58.
39. *Ibid.*, p. 67.
40. *Ibid.*, p. 68.
41. Mann study, pp. 24–30.
42. *Ibid.*, p. 26.
43. *Ibid.*
44. *Ibid.*, p. 32.
45. *Ibid.*
46. One of the assumptions of the classical regression model is the constant variance of the random disturbances. If the variance of the disturbances is not constant for all values of the independent variables (a case known as heteroscedasticity), the assumption is violated and the efficiency of estimation is reduced. Thus Mann increases the efficiency of the estimates by deflating X_1 by the number of transactions. See Mann study, p. 37.
47. The $R^2 = 0.75$. The terms in parentheses are the standard deviation of the estimated coefficients, and the figures on the following line are the t-ratios of the coefficients.
48. Mann study, p. 39.
49. *Ibid.* The reader, however, should note that use of total brokerage commissions as a surrogate measure for firms' output suffers from the same drawback as the Exchange's measure—that is, commissions as a measure of output fail to discriminate between the costs of transactions of varying sizes.

     Brokerage commissions are a function of the number of transactions executed by the member firms, the size of these transactions, and the prices of the securities involved. Thus, two brokerage houses that generate the same amount of revenue need not have similar cost structures, especially if one of them specializes in executing and clearing a small number of large tenders while the second receives most of its commissions from servicing a large number of small tenders. In fact, Mann's measure may confound the problem by incorporating the effects of price on the costs of offering exchange services.

     The relationship between the price of a security and the cost of servicing a tender is discussed in a later section of this chapter.
50. *Ibid.*, p. 41.
51. *Ibid.*
52. *Ibid.*, p. 51.

53. *Ibid.*, p. 56.
54. *Ibid.*, p. 16.
55. See Chapter 4, above.
56. For a discussion of the factors affecting the level of trading activities, see Chapter 3, above.
57. *Special Study*, pp. 725–28.

6 The Specialist and the Price of Marketability Services in the New York Stock Exchange

The theoretical discussion of transactions costs in Chapter 4 stressed that the supply of marketability services results from the presence of dealers whose willingness to carry inventories mitigates temporary imbalances in the inflow of buy and sell orders. In line with that discussion, it would seem logical to argue that the price of supplying marketability services should be determined in large measure by factors influencing the inventory policies of dealers.

In this chapter, we analyze the dealership function and the price of marketability services in the NYSE, focusing primarily on inventory management by specialists. We begin with a theoretical discussion of the factors affecting the inventory policies of the specialists and then present the findings of three empirical studies of the determinants of the price of marketability services the NYSE.

Inventory Management: The Theory

For purposes of discussion, the factors affecting the inventory policies of the specialists can be conveniently divided into four broad categories: (1) those affecting the costs of positioning a single issue under conditions of certainty, (2) those determining the extent of uncertainty associated with positioning an individual issue, (3) those affecting the cost structure of specialist units,[1] and (4) those influencing the competitive environment within which specialists operate.

Factors Affecting Inventory Carrying Costs Under Certainty Conditions. If the effects of uncertainty are ignored, the variable costs associated with carrying a position in an individual issue are primarily related to the issue's price, the number of shares positioned, and the length of time they are carried. Beyond this, the specialist incurs certain other costs that do not vary with the volume of inventories carried. Thus, under certainty conditions, the total inventory carrying cost can be expressed algebraically as follows:

$$C_{I_i} = f(P_i, q_i, t_i, G_i) \qquad (6.1)$$

where C_{I_i} is the total cost of carrying inventories in the ith stock, P_i is the price of the ith stock, q_i is the average number of shares of the ith stock held, t_i is the average time period for which q_i shares are held, and G_i is the proportion of fixed costs of the specialist unit allocated to the ith stock. *A priori* reasoning would suggest that the relationships between C_{I_i} and the first three variables ought to be of the following nature:

$$\frac{\partial C_{I_i}}{\partial P_i} > 0; \quad \frac{\partial C_{I_i}}{\partial q_i} > 0; \quad \frac{\partial C_{I_i}}{\partial t_i} > 0 \qquad (6.2)$$

The positive sign of the partial derivative of C_{I_i} with respect to P_i reflects the fact that positions in higher priced stocks tie up a larger portion of the specialist's capital or necessitate the payment of higher interest expenditures on borrowed funds. Similarly, the positive signs of the partials with respect to q_i and t_i indicate that, as the number of shares in inventories increases and/or their turnover rate diminishes, the total cost of financing these positions rises.[2]

The real question, of course, is what determines the size of q_i and t_i, that is, what factors influence the average number of shares positioned in a given issue and average length of time these shares are held? In our judgment, two factors would seem to be of overriding importance in this regard: (1) the time rate of transactions and (2) the size distribution of transactions.

The time rate of transactions. As we have mentioned several times, a specialist unit acts as a residual buyer and seller of securities, whose primary function is to facilitate an orderly market. The Exchange expects the specialists to participate in the market to the extent required by temporal imbalances in the inflow of orders, but only to this extent. Generally speaking, the probability that there will be an imbalance of buy and sell orders varies inversely with the time rate of transactions. In other words, as trading activity increases, the disparities and discontinuities in the inflow of buy and sell orders tend to decline, thus giving the market a "self-equating" quality. Of course, to the extent that active markets tend to self-equate, the need for specialists' inventory participation is reduced, in terms of both the average size of positions and the average holding period. Inactive stocks, on the other hand, require more extensive participation and positioning on the part of the specialist: To make a continuous market and to provide adequate depth of marketability in these issues, the specialist must be prepared, on the average, to hold larger positions for longer periods. As might be expected, then, the *direct* inventory carrying costs associated with dealing in inactive issues are relatively high. Moreover, since the purchasing power locked up in inactive issues reduces the specialist's ability to take on relatively riskless and profitable daylight trading in more active stocks, the *indirect* costs also are substantial.

To the extent that the prices of marketability services reflect the underlying cost of carrying inventories, bid-ask spreads should be expected to vary inversely with the time rate of transactions. Indeed, Demsetz argues:

> The fundamental force working to reduce the spread is the time rate of transactions. The greater the frequency of transacting, the lower will be the cost of waiting in a trading queue of specified length and therefore the lower will be the spreads that traders are willing to submit to pre-empt positions in the trading queue.[3]

In Chapter 2 we presented some empirical evidence on the determinants of the time rate of transactions, noting in particular that common stocks owned by sizable numbers of investors tend to experience greater trading activity. We might hypothesize, then, that bid-ask spreads also ought to vary inversely with the numbers of individuals holding an issue. Here again, of course, the hypothesized relationship depends upon the existence of a tie between the price of marketability services, measured in terms of the bid-ask spread, and the costs of supplying these services.

The size distribution of transactions. We also noted in Chapter 2 that the specialist's ability to smooth out temporary imbalances in the inflow of buy and sell orders is influenced by the size distribution of transactions. More specifically, we pointed out that when the tenders reaching the specialist are of roughly the same size they tend to be self-equating, on the average. On the other hand, the presence of great variability in the size distribution of orders and, particularly, the existence of some transactions that are extremely large relative to the average, tend to reduce the market's self-equating properties, making it necessary for the specialist to position significant amounts of stock for extended periods. Of course, regardless of whether or not they tend to be of equal size, larger average transactions make it necessary for specialists to position more shares, on the average.

Just as the time rate of transactions depends upon the number of individuals holding an issue, the size distribution depends upon the numbers of shares held by various individual owners. When there is a large number of individuals with relatively equal ownership interests, for example, the size distribution tends to possess little diffusion around a relatively low average transaction size. A lack of diffusion in the presence of larger average transaction size indicates the existence of a number of relatively large holders of approximately equal size, while an increase in both diffusion and average transaction size suggests an ownership pattern with a few large holders and many smaller ones.

Among the factors influencing the size distribution of orders in recent years, by far the most significant has been the activity of institutional investors. Over the past three decades, institutions have purchased an increasing percentage of listed common stocks. More important, they have expanded the pace of their trading activity more than in proportion to their increased ownership position. In the first quarter of 1969, institutions accounted for 51 per cent of the share volume and 56 per cent of the dollar value of all transactions executed on the NYSE.[4] Bank trust departments and mutual funds were particularly active traders during that period.[5]

As might be expected, institutional trading activities influence the size distribution of orders in two basic ways. First, since institutions typically make trades that on the average are larger than those of rank-and-file investors, their activities tend to increase the average size of trades consummated. We noted in Chapter 3, for example, that Tiniç finds a positive relationship between the mean of the frequency distribution of transaction size and both the number of institutions holding an issue and the average number of shares held. This relationship may well account for much of the increase in the average size of transaction that has taken place over the last decade. As the data in Table 6–1 indicate, the average size of trades increased by 53 per cent between 1961 and 1968; if anything, this statistic probably understates the true increase in the average size of trades due to the fact that a rising number of block trades have taken place off the Exchange in recent years.

TABLE 6–1
Average Transaction Size in the
New York Stock Exchange

Year	Average Number of Shares per Transaction
1961	197
1962	n.a.
1963	213
1964	n.a.
1965	224
1966	n.a.
1967	257
1968	302

Institutional activity also has an impact on the extent of dispersion in the size distribution of orders. The presence of a few large institutional holders, for example, tends to skew the distribution upward. With a large number of institutions holding relatively comparable positions, on the other hand, the distribution tends to cluster around a higher average size of trade.

To a large extent, then, the impact of institutional trading on the specialist's activities might be expected to depend on the concentration of institutional holding in a particular common stock and the degree to which institutions take parallel activity in trading. Within a certain range, the greater the institutional concentration, the smaller the probability that orders will tend to be offsetting, hence the greater the need for the specialist to take large positions for extended periods. If the number of institutions becomes sufficiently great, on the other hand, their

buy and sell orders will tend to self-equate in the absence of
parallel trading activity, thus requiring less positioning on the
part of the specialists.[6]

Thus far, we have considered factors influencing the inventory policies of specialists assuming no uncertainty about the
future course of stock prices. This is, of course, an unrealistic
assumption: While the information available to specialists puts
them in a position superior to rank-and-file investors, it is by
no means sufficient to eliminate uncertainty concerning future
price movement. Let us turn, therefore, to a discussion of the
impact of uncertainty on the position policies of the specialist
and the behavior of the bid-ask spread.

Risks Associated with Positioning. The primary risk facing a
specialist is the possibility of an adverse change in the equilibrium price of the security during a period when he is holding a
position. Since specialists are registered in more than one issue,
this risk can be somewhat reduced by maintaining diversified
portfolios. However, the risks associated with over-all economic
conditions can be escaped only by maintaining two equally
diversified portfolios of the same size (one long and the other
short); the institutional restrictions of the Exchange and the
high costs of diversified positions effectively preclude specialists
from achieving such positions.

Because the diversification possibilities open to specialists are
limited, the general stability of a stock's price plays an important
role in determining the amount of risk incurred by taking
positions.[7] It can easily be shown that price volatility, measured
in terms of the standard deviation, is directly related to the
probability of losses. Given a purchase price P_B and the probability distribution of prices, the expected revenue of the specialist
from inventory reappraisal is a function of the expected future
price, the purchase price, and the number of shares positioned.
If the probability density function of future prices is represented
by $f_P(P)$ and if the dealer is assumed to purchase q shares of
common stock at P_B, his expected gain is given by the equation:

$$E(\text{Gain}) = \int_0^\infty q(P - P_B)f_P(p)dp = q\left[\int_0^\infty Pf_P(p)dp - P_B \int_0^\infty f_P(p)dp\right]$$

$$= q[E(P) - P_B] \tag{6.3}$$

Given $E(P)$ and P_B, the probability of incurring losses from positioning increases as the standard deviation of the distribution gets larger.

As a residual buyer and seller of securities, the specialist also incurs risks stemming from changes in the over-all conditions of the market. Possibilities of a market break or adverse development in the aggregate economy create opportunities for losses that cannot be avoided by diversification of positions. Moreover, the demand for flexibility, one of the dominant motives for liquidity preference,[8] may well increase in periods of greater over-all economic uncertainty, thus causing the demand for marketability to increase during these periods.

Factors Related to the Structure of the Specialists Units. If the discussion were to terminate at this point, the reader might justifiably conclude that two stocks selling for the same price and having the same level of trading activity, size distribution of transactions, and price volatility ought to have equal bid-ask spreads. This conclusion, however, fails to take account of the impact of differences in the over-all cost structures of specialist units on the bid-ask spreads for individual issues. In particular, it neglects the analysis of differences in the capitalization and portfolios of specialist units.

The capitalization of specialist units. It is widely accepted in the securities industry that the capitalization of specialist units has an impact to the quality of the market. The NYSE explicitly recognizes the significance of capital by requiring that a specialist unit must be able to assume a position of at least 2,000 shares of each 100-share-unit issue in which it is registered.[9] Most specialists, however, utilize more capital than the minimum required by the New York Stock Exchange, and many have additional financing arrangements with other Stock Exchange members or banks.

Under existing laws, the Stock Exchange specialists are exempt from the margin requirements of the Federal Reserve System. They can borrow on any margin acceptable to their clearing organizations and the banks with whom they maintain lines of credit.[10] In general, both clearing firms and banks require lower margins than the Federal Reserve. Therefore, specialists generally enjoy larger leverage capacity than the public investors or other members of the Exchange.

Between specialists, however, there are differences in margin requirements, as well as in the interest paid on borrowed funds.[11] To the extent that the price of marketability services depends on the cost structure of the specialist units, these differences might be expected to show up in the width of bid-ask spreads and the depth of the market. Other things being equal, specialists with substantial borrowing capacity and relatively low debt-servicing costs might be expected to quote narrower spreads and take more extensive positions for longer periods of time. Specialist units with less attractive leverage conditions, on the other hand, might be expected to have wider spreads and to reduce the depth of their marketability services by attempting to maintain even positions at the end of each trading day, that is, by avoiding the difficulties of margining positions overnight. Such attempts, of course, manifest themselves in systematic patterns of specialist participation. According to the *Special Study:*

> During the course of a trading session such a specialist would be careful to assume no position that could not be liquidated by the end of the day, and near the close he might almost totally avoid participation that would increase a position. . . . An analysis of data for the three-week period indicated that 13 of the 110 specialist units showed daylight trading patterns in some stocks, in that they seemed to attempt to even up their positions by the end of the day.[12]

Underfinanced dealers might be expected to be particularly wary of taking long positions overnight in stocks whose market values they expect to depreciate.

The three examples in Figure 19 indicate how a specialist can alter his rate of purchases and sales in the market by varying the bid-ask spread. In (A) the specialist is attempting to liquidate a long position by decreasing his bid prices; in (B) he is increasing his offer prices in order to acquire a larger long position, or possibly to even out an outstanding short position; in (C) he is backing away from the market on both sides.

Effects of the speciality portfolio. The size of a specialist's portfolio and the interrelationships of the securities included in that portfolio might also be expected to influence the costs of supplying marketability services for a given issue. The precise nature of the influence, however, is difficult to characterize, since portfolio considerations can have conflicting effects on the specialist's activities. To the extent that increases in the number

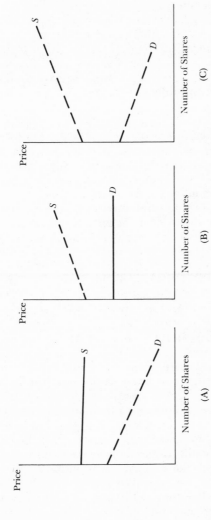

FIGURE 19   Specialist's Reactions to Capital Scarcity.

of stocks carried by the specialist unit provide better opportunities for diversification, they ought to lead to lower costs of supplying marketability services in individual issues. On the other hand, to the extent that such increases reduce the technical efficiency of a specialist, the opposite ought to be the case. The latter effect might be somewhat mitigated by adding more specialists to the units; a potential source of diseconomies, however, lies in the difficulty of coordinating a large number of specialists.

The specialist unit and the cost of positioning. On the basis of the discussion above, it is difficult to make a strong *a priori* case concerning the general behavior of a specialist unit's cost of positioning an individual stock. Demsetz suggests that the presence of economies of scale in trading individual issues gives the specialist units natural monopoly characteristics.[13] Even from a purely theoretical viewpoint, however, it is rather difficult to accept this conclusion. To be sure, the specialist in a given issue may experience some increasing returns to scale in the performance of his centralized brokerage function; but the same need not be the case for his dealership function, where the relevant costs are the marginal costs of carrying inventories. The variable costs incurred in assuming positions include the opportunity cost of capital and/or the interest on borrowed funds and the risks due to the possibility of depreciation in the value of inventories. Because larger positions in a given issue normally require more time to liquidate and involve higher risks for a specialist unit, there is no reason to expect average variable costs to decline continuously with the amount of positioning. Indeed, a case can be made that the loss of diversification associated with a very large position in a given issue should cause the marginal cost of position(s) to begin to increase at some point. Finally, capital scarcity may cause costs to increase even more for very large dealership positions. For all of these reasons, we expect a marginal cost function of the kind presented in Figure 20 rather than a function declining throughout the relevant range of positions in a given issue.

Market Structure and Competition. To complete our analysis of the dealership function in the NYSE, we now consider the competitive environment of the Exchange, identifying sources of competitive pressure and/or monopoly power related to the operation of the specialist system.

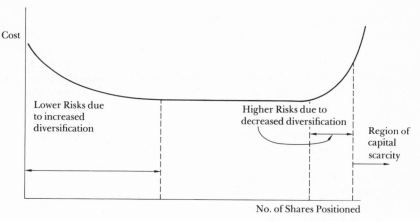

FIGURE 20   Marginal Cost of Positioning an Individual Stock.

As now constituted, the specialist system of the NYSE consists of 110 units, each of which is assigned a number of securities in which it is expected to maintain fair and orderly markets. Although more than one unit may be registered in a common stock, units do not compete. Instead, they participate in joint accounts, with each unit taking a turn at the post and revenues being shared according to some predetermined formula. The prevailing pattern of economic organization of the specialist system, in other words, does not provide for any direct rivalry in the dealership operations. Consequently, from the viewpoint of the Exchange alone, each specialist unit can be classified as a multiproduct monopoly.

There are, however, several forces that restrain the monopoly power of the specialists. These include (1) the surveillance and evaluation of specialists by the NYSE, (2) the competition between specialists in stocks with comparable risk/return characteristics, and (3) the competition provided by other stock exchanges and the over-the-counter market.[14]

Exchange surveillance and evaluation. The NYSE expects specialists to maintain orderly markets in the issues in which they are registered. More specifically, specialist units are expected to participate in the market to insure adequate price stability and continuity. Although the Exchange does not favor rigid rules defining the standards of participation, such activity as cleaning up the book with adverse effects on the stability of prices or participation at prices that would establish new daily highs or lows are generally regarded as undesirable dealership practices that should be avoided.[15] Of course, the empirical evaluation of the Exchange's control over the specialists and of the extent to which this control affects the prices of marketability services presents an extremely difficult problem. Nevertheless, since the allocation of new listings is based in some measure on Exchange judgments concerning appropriate participation, the surveillance of the specialist units may act as something of a deterrent to monopolistic prices for marketability services.

Substitutability and indirect competition. In essence, common stocks are claims on the future earnings of the assets of corporations. Since the operations of firms are subject to varying kinds and degrees of expected returns and risks, the stocks that constitute claims on earnings from operations are differentiated from one another in the eyes of investors largely in terms of their relative return and risk characteristics. In a large population of stocks, nevertheless, there tend to be some issues that are claims on earnings streams having relatively equivalent returns and risks; just as butter and margarine constitute potential substitutes in the marketbaskets of housewives, such issues represent potential substitutes in the portfolios of investors. Of course, how close they come to being substitutable depends in the first instance on their relative prices. If we assume, however, that such issues are priced "right," in the sense that their prices are equal except for a scale factor, the cross-elasticity of *transactions* demand between them should be high. In other words, an increase in the cost of transacting in one such issue should produce an increase in the transactions demand for the others.

The high cross-elasticity of transactions demand between stocks with equivalent risk and return characteristics should constitute a second, indirect deterrent to the exercise of monopoly power on the part of specialists. If a specialist consistently maintains spreads that are wider than spreads on issues that are otherwise substitutable, he should expect to find traders concentrating their activities in the substitutes, and this, in turn, should give him a strong incentive to hold the exercise of his monopoly power somewhat in check. In short, unless specialists systematically possess trading monopolies in issues with similar risk and return parameters, they cannot raise marketability costs indiscriminately without expecting to lose business.

Inter-market competition. As we already have noted, many of the stocks listed on the NYSE can also be traded on one or more of the regional exchanges and in the over-the-counter market. Indeed, they *are* traded in these markets, with increasing frequency. The reasons for the growth of regional and off-board trading in listed stocks will be discussed in some detail in Chapters 8 and 9. For now, it should suffice to note that this trading constitutes still another factor inhibiting the unbridled exercise of the specialists' monopoly power.

Statistical Studies of Marketability Prices

Over the past few years there have been several investigations of the determinants of the prices of marketability services on the NYSE. The earliest study was conducted by the Exchange itself as a part of an analysis of the quality of the markets being made in common stocks. A second study was made by Demsetz and a third by Tiniç. In the remainder of this chapter, we shall discuss the mechanics of all three investigations and compare and contrast their various findings.

The NYSE Study. The results of the NYSE study are based on regression analyses in which bid-ask spreads for two groups of stocks serve as the dependent variable.[16] The first group of stocks includes a sample of 300 common stocks and covers a one-month time period in 1963; the second group includes all common stocks listed on the Exchange and covers the month of May, 1967. For both groups, the Exchange averaged daily data to obtain a single measurement of the bid-ask spread for each issue. It also averaged the data for the independent variables studied.

The Exchange's report states that a large number of independent variables were included in preliminary regression analyses. However, only variables showing statistically significant relationships with spreads are included in the final report. These include (1) trading volume in dollar terms, (2) the average size of transactions, (3) a measure of price variability, and (4) the "average" price for the period studied.

The Exchange's methods of calculating variables and its regression results are presented in Table 6–2. Unfortunately, since the Exchange's report does not contain the standard errors of the estimated coefficients, it is impossible to know the precise significance levels obtained. In general, the results

TABLE 6–2
Regression Results of NYSE Analyses of Bid-Ask Spreads
(Log K)*

		Regression Coefficients				
Year	Intercept	*Log* M†	V‡	T§	*Log* P¶	R^2
1963	1.68878	− 0.246	+ 0.084	+ 0.034	− 0.21	> 0.81
1967	1.76	− 0.164	+ 0.054	+ 0.018	− 0.335	0.86

*K = (average bid-ask spread in a month × 10,000)/average price
†M = dollar value of average daily reported volume/1,000
‡V = (high price–low price) 10/low price
§T = average size of transaction (in shares)/100
¶P = average price in a month

Source: New York Stock Exchange, "Economic Effects of Negotiated Commission Rates on the Brokerage Industry's Practices and the Market for Corporate Securities (unpublished report), (August, 1968), pp. 4, 7.

in Table 6–2 are consistent with a number of hypotheses that derive from the theoretical analysis of inventory management presented above. For example, both equations indicate that spreads are inversely related to trading volume, thus confirming our expectations concerning the relationship between trading activity and the pricing of marketability services. The positive sign of the coefficient for price variability (V) supports another aspect of the theoretical discussion, i.e., the expected relationship between spreads and risk. Similarly, the positive sign of the coefficient for the average size of transaction would seem to confirm the hypothesis that, as transactions become larger, dealers find it more difficult to operate, and thus must increase the width of their spreads.

On the surface, the negative size of the P coefficient would seem to be inconsistent with our earlier statements. The reader should note, however, that the coefficient does not imply a negative relationship between stock prices and the level of bid-ask spreads, but rather a negative relationship between prices and the spread per dollar of price. In other words, the results indicate that the price of marketability services in proportion to the value of a purchase declines as the price of shares increases.[17]

Using the regression equation for the 1967 data, the Exchange attempted to test the effects of competition provided by the regional exchanges. After discarding nine of the stocks, it examined the residuals for signs of a systematic relationship with the percentage of trading volume diverted to the regional exchanges. The coefficient of correlation between the ranked residuals and the ratio of regional volume to the New York Stock Exchange volume was found to be statistically insignificant (below 0.10). Thus, the Exchange's report concludes that the activities of the regional exchanges do not appear to have any systematic impact on the width of spreads in the NYSE.

Demsetz's Study. In his study, Demsetz hypothesizes that the level of bid-ask spreads varies inversely with the time rate of transactions and the number of exchanges on which an issue is listed, and directly with the level of prices. This hypothesis is tested by a multiple regression analysis of data for a sample of 192 randomly selected securities. Observations on price, the time rate of transactions and bid-ask spreads are averaged for two days in 1965. Demsetz reports that he experimented with various functional forms and presents the following two models as having the best "fits":

$$S = \partial_0 + \partial_1 P + \partial_2 \ln T + \partial_3 M \tag{6.4}$$

$$S = \lambda_0 + \lambda_1 P + \lambda_2 \ln N + \lambda_3 M \tag{6.5}$$

where S = average bid-ask spread
P = average price per share
T = average number of transactions
M = the number of markets on which the stock is listed
N = the number of shareowners/100

The results of least-squares estimation of these regression equations are presented in Table 6-3. Demsetz's results are generally consistent with those contained in the NYSE report. Like the Exchange, Demsetz finds a strong negative relationship between the width of spreads and trading activity (measured either in terms of the average activity or on the basis of the number of shareholders). In addition, he too fails to uncover a significant relationship between the number of markets in which a stock is listed and spread behavior. Even Demsetz's findings concerning the relationship between price and spreads are consistent with the Exchange's. Demsetz notes that when spreads are regressed on the log of p rather than the absolute value, the coefficient is highly significant and conforms to the condition $S_{pp} < 0$.[18]

TABLE 6–3
Demsetz' Findings: Regression Coefficients and t-Ratios

Equation	Intercept	P	ln T	ln N	M	R^2	St. error
(6.4)	0.38027 (5.8)	0.0080709 (12.15)	-0.11527 (6.46)	—	-0.022906 (0.97)	0.58	0.28632
(6.5)	0.48411 (5.65)	0.0088554 (13.24)	—	-0.080911 (5.10)	-0.029691 (1.21)	0.54	0.29666

*Adapted from Harold Demsetz, "The Cost of Transacting," *Quarterly Journal of Economics* 82 (February, 1968): 49.

Tiniç's Study. Tiniç's study[19] differs from both the Exchange's and Demsetz's in three important ways. First, it takes into consideration independent variables that are related to the operation of the specialist units as well as those pertaining to individual stocks. Second, it explicitly includes a measure of the impact of institutions on spread behavior, and third, it provides an alternative approach to the measurement of the impact of intermarket competition on spread behavior.

Factors related to the specialist units. Following the reasoning presented in the theoretical section of this chapter, Tiniç concludes that an exhaustive analysis of the determinants of the price of marketability services must include not only factors that influence a specialist's ability to deal in an individual issue but also variables related to the operation of the specialist units. In particular, he argues that the capitalization of specialist units should be included as a measure of the units' positioning capacity. Tiniç also concludes that the number of stocks managed by the specialist units should be included, but he is hesitant to predict the precise nature of the relationship between this variable and the spreads, since the size of a unit's portfolio can have several contradictory influences on its ability to provide marketability services.

The impact of institutions. A second characteristic that distinguishes Tiniç's analysis from earlier studies is its inclusion of a variable to account for the role of institutional investors. Demsetz's study makes virtually no mention of institutions, and the Exchange's only takes account of them indirectly by including the average size of transactions as an independent variable. In contrast, Tiniç adds the number of institutional holders as an independent variable. In discussing the expected relationship between this variable and spreads, Tiniç notes that theoretical considerations suggest a function of the type pictured in Figure 21. The rising portion of the function corresponds to the region in which the addition of institutions adds to the specialist's difficulty in positioning issues. Beyond point M, however, the function declines, because as still more institutions take positions their trading activities begin to develop offsetting qualities. Of course, even when the number of institutional holders becomes extremely large, the level of spreads remains above KP as a result of the increased average size of transactions produced by institutional trading activities.

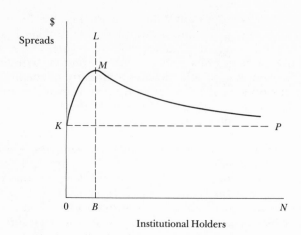

FIGURE 21   Institutional Shareholders and Spreads.

In discussing his empirical studies of spread behavior, Tiniç notes that the functional form pictured in Figure 21 suggests that the number of institutions should enter the analysis in quadratic terms. He notes, however, that for the sample of stocks to be studied, the average number of institutional shareholders exceeds 100. Moreover, he points out that the proportion of issues in the sample owned by five or less institutions is lower than one in six. For both of these reasons, he concludes that, although the underlying relationship between institutional holders and spread behavior ought to resemble Figure 21, the relationship to be expected in the empirical results may more closely resemble only that part of the figure to the right of *BL*. In other words, Tiniç reasons that the most probable empirical relationship between the number of institutions and the behavior of spreads for the stocks in his sample is monotonically decreasing.

The measurement of intermarket competition. The third distinguishing feature of Tiniç's analysis is the method of measuring intermarket competition. Tiniç reasons that the insignificance of the regression coefficient of *M* in Demsetz's study does not necessarily imply the absence of a competitive influence. Although many nationally listed common stocks are also traded in the regional exchanges, they do not all possess the same level of trading volume in these markets. Thus, according to Tiniç, the mere presence of external markets (as measured by the number of multiple listings) need not indicate the degree of effective competitive pressure on the NYSE specialists.[20]

To measure intermarket competition more effectively, Tiniç proposes to use an "index of trading concentration," calculated as follows:[21]

$$M_i = \sum_{h=1}^{n} \left[\frac{m_{ih}}{\sum_{h=i}^{n} m_{ih}} \right]^2 \tag{6.6}$$

where $1/m \le M_i \le 1$, and m_{ih} represents the volume of transactions of the ith stock in the hth market, while n stands for the total number of distinct markets in which the ith security is traded, including the over-the-counter market. As calculated, the higher the level of the index, the less the degree of effective intermarket competition, and the greater the specialists' monopoly power.

Tiniç's Model and Results. The basic model employed by Tiniç is as follows:

$$S = \beta_0 + \beta_1 P + \beta_2 \ln V + \beta_3 C + \beta_4 \sigma_p + \beta_5 I + \beta_6 N + \beta_7 K/T + \beta_8 M \tag{6.7}$$

where S = average bid-ask spread
$\quad P$ = average price of the stock
$\quad V$ = average number of shares traded daily
$\quad C$ = trading continuity of the stock (number of days traded/number of days sampled)
$\quad \sigma_p$ = standard deviation of the price of a security
$\quad I$ = number of institutions holding an issue (includes only investment companies; fire, casualty, and life insurance firms; and common trust funds)
$\quad N$ = total number of specialty stocks carried by the unit registered in the stock
$\quad K$ = total purchasing capacity of the unit
$\quad T$ = average number of daily transactions in a stock (only in NYSE)
$\quad M$ = index of competition for a stock

In view of the extensiveness of the preceding discussion of the studies conducted by the Exchange and Demsetz, and Tiniç's extensions, the methods of measuring most of the independent variables in equation (6.7) and the expected signs of the co-efficients to be estimated are self-evident. An exception, how-ever, is K/T, the variable used to measure the effect of specialists' capitalization on spreads. The total purchasing capacity of a specialist unit need not have an equal influence on the bid-ask spread of each common stock managed. Active stocks can be managed effectively with relatively less capital than inactive issues. Ordinarily, then, the capital requirement per stock should vary directly with the extent of the specialists' participa-tion and inversely with the activity level of the issue. Since information regarding the specialists' rate of participation is not available on an issue-by-issue basis, Tiniç assumes that the amount of capital employed in each issue varies with the level of trading activity. Thus, he uses K/T, purchasing capacity per transaction, as his regressor in equation (6.7).

Tiniç's empirical results are based on multiple regression analysis of data related to specialist units and common stocks drawn from a two-stage stratified random sample. The first stage involves sampling the specialist units; the second, sampling stocks within specialist units. Data for the resulting sample of sixteen specialist units and eighty common stocks reflect trading conditions during the month of March, 1969.

The estimated coefficients of Tiniç's model are presented in Table 6–4.

In general, these results support the hypotheses related to the effects of the trading characteristics of individual stocks on spread behavior: Spreads are found to vary directly with price and inversely with trading volume, continuity, and institutional share ownership. In each case, the regression coefficient is highly significant. The coefficient for the standard deviation of prices, on the other hand, is not statistically different from zero, but it does carry the expected sign.

The coefficient of the concentration index, M, reflects a statistically significant relationship between the activities of dealers in the regional exchanges and over-the-counter markets and the prices of marketability services in the New York Stock Exchange; stocks that are frequently traded in a number of markets tend to have narrower bid-ask spreads on the NYSE.

The significant, positive coefficient of portfolio size, N, would seem to indicate that, for the sample studied, the diseconomies associated with increasing the number of stocks assigned to a

TABLE 6–4
Specialists' Effect and Bid-Ask Spreads

Regressors	Coefficients	Standard Error of Coefficient	t-ratio	β-Coefficient	r^2
β_0	1.139269	0.187706	6.0694†	—	—
P	0.005155	0.000422	12.219†	0.7176	0.6777
$\ln V$	−0.038307	0.006663	−5.7492†	−0.3389	0.3177
C	−0.780223	0.196544	−3.9697†	−0.2104	0.1816
σ_P	0.000176	0.000732	0.24000	0.0116	0.0008
I	−0.000195	0.000086	−2.2808*	−0.1876	0.0683
N	0.001042	0.000515	2.0233*	0.0985	0.0545
K/T	−0.0000015	0.0000029	−0.50564	−0.0242	0.0036
M	0.131399	0.057107	2.3009*	0.1659	0.0694

Standard error of estimate = 0.05978
$R^2 = 0.853097$
R^2 (adjusted) = 0.836545; F-test (8,71) = 51.53917 (significant at 0.001 level)
*Significant at 0.025 level
†Significant at 0.0005 level

specialist unit exert an important influence on the prices of marketability services. Although the effects of capitalization are in the expected direction, the estimated coefficient for K/T is not statistically significant.

A Summary and Some Comparisons. Because they used slightly different functional forms and measured variables in a variety of ways, the three studies just described cannot be compared on the basis of the sizes and significance levels of their estimated coefficients. We can, however, make some comparisons of their general findings concerning the relationships between certain broad factors and the pricing of marketability services in the NYSE. To simplify this task, a summary of the three studies' findings is presented in Table 6–5.

Focusing first at the entries in lines 1 through 4, we see that all three studies find a significant negative relationship between spreads and trading activity. This relationship holds whether trading activity is measured in terms of the number of shares traded, the number of transactions consummated, or the dollar value of trading. Moreover, it is reflected in the coefficient for the number of shareholders, which is highly correlated with

TABLE 6–5
Summary of Findings

		Bid-Ask Spreads		
Variables		*NYSE Study*	*Demsetz*	*Tiniç*
1. Dollar value of daily transactions		—	·	·
2. Number of daily transactions		·	—	·
3. Number of shares traded daily		·	·	—
4. Number of shareowners		·	—	·
5. Volatility of price		+	·	0
6. Effects of competition		0	0	—
7. Transaction size		+	·	·
8. Number of institutional shareowners		·	·	—
9. Number of stocks carried by a specialist unit		·	·	+
10. Trading continuity		·	·	—
11. Capitalization of specialist unit		·	·	0

+, increases spreads; —, decreases spreads; 0, no statistically significant effect; ·, not included in study.

trading activity. In short, no matter how it is measured, trading activity is inversely related to the width of bid-ask spreads in a strong way.

The fifth line indicates that the studies differ somewhat on the relationship between spreads and price volatility. The NYSE study, which measures volatility in terms of the difference between monthly high and low prices, expressed as a percentage of the low price, reports a statistically significant positive relationship. Unfortunately, the failure of the Exchange's study to publish the standard errors of the estimated coefficients means that we do not know the exact level of significance. Tiniç's study also finds a positive relationship between volatility and spreads, but the fact that the standard error is more than four times larger than the estimated coefficient implies that this relationship is not significantly different from zero.

The effects of competition reported in the three studies also differ somewhat. Neither the NYSE study nor Demsetz's study finds a statistically significant relationship between intermarket competition and the behavior of spreads. Tiniç's, in contrast, does. If forced to make a judgment on the basis of these various results, we would tend to place our emphasis on Tiniç's findings on the grounds that his measurement of the impact of intermarket competition is far superior to either of the other two studies; it is the only one of the three that measures actual as opposed to potential competition.

If looked at separately, the results reported in lines 7 and 8 both appear to be consistent with *a priori* reasoning. When considered together, however, they pose something of a dilemma. The positive sign of the coefficient of transaction size in the NYSE's results implies that spreads tend to widen as orders get larger, on the average; yet, according to Tiniç's results, spreads also vary inversely with the number of institutional shareholders, which is positively correlated with average transaction size in his data. Indeed, when Tiniç substitutes the average size of transactions for the number of institutional shareholders in his regression equation, he obtains a negative and significant relationship between spreads and the average size of transactions. While we cannot be certain of the reason for the difference between Tiniç's results and the NYSE's, one possibility is that the empirical relationship between spreads and the size of transaction changed between 1967 and 1969 because of an increase in the number of institutions holding shares in NYSE listed securities. If the number of institutional holders in 1967 was such that the Exchange's data included many companies with few if any institutional owners, we might expect to find a generally positive relationship between spreads and either the average size of transactions or the number of institutions owning an issue. In terms of Figure 21, this situation might be represented by a scatter of data points that include many observations on or near the ordinate, thus giving the plotted relationship a generally positive slope. On the other hand, if institutional ownership increased enough by 1969 to make it difficult to obtain observations on or near the y axis in Figure 21, we might expect to find a generally negative relationship between spreads and the number of institutions owning an issue, corresponding to the portion of the curve to the right of *BL*. Of course, since the average size of transactions is positively correlated with the number of institutional shareholders, we then also expect to find a negative relationship between spreads and average transaction size.

Two pieces of information would seem to support this admittedly *ad hoc* explanation of the difference between Tiniç's results and the NYSE's. The first concerns the change in the distribution of institutions holding shares in the companies included in Tiniç's sample from 1967 to 1969. In 1967, the average number of institutional shareholders per company was slightly above 73; by 1969, it had increased to nearly 102. More important, in 1967 34 per cent of the companies had five or fewer institutional owners; the comparable figure in 1969 was 15 per cent. In short, in the space of only two years, the number of observations near the ordinate in Figure 21 declined by more than 50 per cent. The second piece of evidence concerns the direction and size of the change in the estimated coefficient for the average size of transactions, T, in the NYSE's data between 1963 and 1967. Following the reasoning just presented, we might predict that the size of the coefficient of T would decline from 1963 to 1967. As the data in Table 6–2 indicate, it did just that!

As for the remaining results in Table 6–5, i.e., the results in rows 9 through 11, we have no basis for making any comparisons. The confirmation or contradiction of Tiniç's results concerning the impact of trading continuity and specialists' capitalization and portfolio size on spreads will have to wait for the completion of studies yet to be undertaken.

APPENDIX TO CHAPTER 6

Variability of the Bid-Ask Spread

An additional feature of Tiniç's study is an empirical analysis of the variability of the bid-ask spread. Tiniç hypothesizes that the factors that increase the need for specialists to take large positions also tend to increase the variability of bid-ask spreads in the New York Stock Exchange. Specifically, he argues that specialists might be expected to alter their spreads to avoid excessive positions in relatively inactive stocks with thin trading activity.

The following multiple regression model is employed to test this hypothesis:

$$\sigma_s = \delta_0 + \delta_1 C + \delta_2 T + \delta_3 P + \delta_4 \frac{K}{N} \qquad (6A.1)$$

where σ_s = standard deviation of the spread

C = trading continuity of the stock (number of days traded/number of days sampled)

T = average number of daily transactions in the issue

P = average price of the stock

K = total purchasing capacity of the specialist unit ($1,000)

N = total number of specialty stocks carried by the unit registered in the issue

The results in Table 6a–1 are consistent with the hypothesis concerning the effects of trading continuity and the level of trading activity on the variability of specialists' bid-ask spreads: The bid-ask spreads of issues experiencing large numbers of transactions and continuous trading activity tend to be more stable. Spreads for higher-priced issues, on the other hand, are subject to more variation. Tiniç's findings fail to reveal any effect of specialists' capitalization on the stability of marketability prices.

TABLE 6a–1
Variability of Bid-Ask Spreads

Regressors	Coefficients	Standard Deviation of Coefficients	t-ratio	β-Coefficient	r^2
δ_0	0.135987	0.039841	3.4132†	—	—
C	−0.106687	0.041811	−2.6552†	−0.25615	0.0859
T	−0.000095	0.000044	−2.1692*	−0.21467	0.0590
P	0.000322	0.000077	4.1834‡	0.39856	0.1892
K/N	−0.0000008	0.0000011	−0.7112	−0.06751	0.0067

Standard error of estimate = 0.013681.
R^2 = 0.35586.
R^2 (adjusted) = 0.32150; F-test (4, 75) = 10.3584 (significant at 0.001 level).
*Significant at 0.025 level.
†Significant at 0.005 level.
‡Significant at 0.005 level.

Notes

1. A specialist unit is composed of several specialists who together manage a group of stocks.

2. In the presence of uncertainty, of course, the time element introduces

additional costs associated with the possible depreciation in market value of the security. This point will be considered at length later.

3. Harold Demsetz, "The Cost of Transacting," *Quarterly Journal of Economics* 82 (February, 1968): 41.
4. Albert L. Kraus, "Institutions Do Bulk of Trading," *The New York Times*, September 27, 1969, p. 45.
5. *Ibid.*
6. If parallel action prevails, however, stocks with significant institutional concentration will require even greater specialist activity. The existence of parallel action among institutional investors would seem to depend upon formal or informal agreements and on the sources of information and investment services they utilize. Use of the same market services may cause a certain amount of dependence in trading behavior among institutions. For example, see Robert Ferber, "Short-Run Effects of Stock Market Services on Stock Prices," *Journal of Finance* 13 (March, 1958): 80–95.

   Ferber observes systematic movements in prices of stocks recommended by the stock market services. Systematic behavior of trading volume for recommended issues is more pronounced. However, such movements experience a longer-run pattern rather than day-to-day changes.
7. For a discussion of the determinants of stock price variability, see J. Heins and S. Allison, "Some Factors Affecting Stock Price Variability," *Journal of Business* 14 (January, 1966): at 19.
8. Thomas Marschak and Richard Nelson, "Flexibility, Uncertainty, and Economic Theory," *Metroeconomica* 15 (1962): at 55.
9. New York Stock Exchange, *Now, About the Specialist* (New York: 1969), p. 2.
10. Generally speaking, the purchasing power available to a dealer at any given time consists of his capital and his leverage capacity. Since leverage capacity equals

$$\left[\frac{1}{\text{Percentage Margin}} - 1 \right] X \, [\text{Net Liquid Capital}]$$

the total purchasing power of a specialist can be represented by

$$\left[\frac{1}{\text{Percentage Margin}} \right] \left[\begin{array}{l} (\text{Cash}) + (\text{Value of Securities Held at Cost}) + (\text{Credit} \\ \text{Balance}) - (\text{Value of Short Positions}) - (\text{Debit Balance}) \end{array} \right]$$

11. At present, the average rate of interest charged on lines of credit is about 9.5 per cent per annum.
12. *Report of the Special Study of the Securities Markets of the Securities and Exchange Commission*, U.S., 88th Cong., 1st Sess., House of Representatives Document 95 (Hereafter: *Special Study*) (Washington, D. C.: Government Printing Office, 1965), p. 94.
13. Demsetz, "Cost of Transacting," p. 42.
14. A fourth source of competition is provided by traders who submit limit orders. In comparison with the other three, however, the competition provided by limit orders of public customers is inconsequential.
15. *Special Study*, pp. 80–89.
16. New York Stock Exchange, "Economic Effects of Negotiated Commission Rates on the Brokerage Industry's Practices and the Market for Corporate Securities" (unpublished report, August, 1968), Appendix C.

17. *Ibid.*, p. 5.
18. Demsetz, "Cost of Transacting," p. 48.
19. Seha M. Tiniç, "The Value of Time Preferences, and the Behavior of Liquidity Costs in the New York Stock Exchange" (unpublished doctoral dissertation, Cornell University, 1970), pp. 86–118.
20. Along these same lines, he comments that the Exchange's study of the impact of intermarket competition fails to consider over-the-counter trading, which, for some listed issues, constitutes the major source of competition for NYSE specialists.
21. This index was originally developed by Orris C. Herfindahl, "Concentration in the Steel Industry" (unpublished doctoral dissertation, Columbia University, 1950).

7 Stock Price Behavior and the Exchange Process

This chapter seeks to provide an understanding of the random walk hypothesis of stock price changes, incorporating the results of the foregoing discussion of the exchange process and the analysis of transactions costs. Most treatments of the random walk model of security price changes have neglected the importance of transactions costs, with the unfortunate result that they present a truncated and somewhat artificial perspective. In the section below, we demonstrate that the introduction of these costs, as well as the costs associated with obtaining and processing information relevant to making investment decisions, leads to a version of the random walk model that neatly rationalizes the presence of certain types of nonrandom elements (dependencies). This version, in turn, provides a basis for distinguishing between dependencies that are and are not evidence of "nonrandomness," in the best economic sense of the term. Following this, we consider the types of dependencies that might be expected to result from the presence of transactions costs.

Before proceeding to the body of the chapter, however, let us briefly summarize the basic idea behind the random walk model of stock price behavior. "Adam Smith," in *The Money Game*, states that after a number of conversations with economists who had been studying the random walk hypothesis, it occurred to him "that the whole thing could be defined in one sentence: Prices have no memory and yesterday has nothing to do with tomorrow."[1] In his characteristically colorful way,

"Smith" puts the basic notion quite adequately. James, however, states it somewhat more formally: "The [random walk] hypothesis holds that all price changes are serially independent; that trends are spurious or imaginary manifestations; and that tools of technical analysis such as charts or the Dow Theory are without investment value."[2] In statistical language, a process having the characteristic that the expected value of a random variable is independent of past values of that variable is referred to as a Martingale. This being the case, the random walk hypothesis holds that stock price changes resemble the outcomes of a Martingale process.[3]

The relevant question, of course, is not what is a random walk, but why should stock price changes behave like random walks? Beyond this, is there any reason to believe that the market-making processes discussed in previous chapters might be expected, *per se*, to introduce some types of nonrandom elements? And, if so, do these elements provide a basis for refuting the random walk model, or can it be modified to incorporate them? Let us consider these three questions in order.

The Random Walk Hypothesis and Transaction Costs

In a world without uncertainty or transaction costs, there would be no such thing as random walks in stock prices. On the contrary, all movements would be known in advance on the basis of investors' complete foresight. Moreover, it would be costless for investors to make portfolio adjustments designed to account for these known movements. In essence, then, all asset prices would be determined simply by discounting streams of known future cash flows at "the" rate of interest, and price changes would represent nothing more than adjustments in present values resulting from the passage of time itself.

But what happens when we admit that perfect foresight does not exist in the real world? The answer, of course, is that investors make investment decisions not according to their knowledge of the future, but rather on the basis of probabilistic estimates about the course of stock prices. They make such estimates, presumably, on the basis of information concerning the future prospects of companies, industries and the economy at large. Over time, they reassess their probabilities and alter their estimates of investment value as new pieces of information come to light. Such reassessments, in turn, cause stock prices to change. In other words, under conditions of uncertainty, stock prices may be thought of as changing *primarily* in response to investors' reactions to new information, where the word "information" is used in the broadest possible terms.

If new information is the factor that produces price changes, how can random behavior be rationalized? One not very likely possibility is that as new information becomes available its impact on stock prices is essentially random. Fama comments along these lines:

> Independence of successive price changes for a given security may simply reflect a price mechanism which is totally unrelated to real-world economic and political events. That is, stock prices may be just the accumulation of many bits of randomly generated noise, where by noise in this case we mean psychological and other factors peculiar to different individuals which determine the types of "bets" they are willing to place on different companies.[4]

But in the same article, he notes:

> Even random walk theorists, however, would find such a view of the market unappealing. Although some people may be primarily motivated by whim, there are many individuals and institutions that seem to base their actions in the market on an evaluation (usually extremely painstaking) of economic and political circumstances.[5]

A second approach to rationalizing randomness might involve the assumption of "homogeneous" investor expectations. According to this assumption, all investors begin with the same set of probabilistic estimates of future stock price behavior and react to new information, that is, revise their probabilistic estimates, along identical lines. Lintner eloquently states why this assumption leads to randomness.

> We may observe that under the assumptions of [homogeneous investor expectations] ... one would clearly expect stock prices to to behave as random walks over time .... Such an agreement in assessment is hard to conceive unless everyone had all the information everyone else had — and information that is known to everyone will clearly be reflected in the *current* set of stock prices. In particular any uniformly expected future growth in corporate earnings, etc., would already be "fully discounted" as the saying goes. But new bits of news — whether of a kind which would change judgments of future outcomes or of a kind which would affect assessments of dispersions

of relevant probability distributions—would affect current values. Since by assumption everyone's probability distributions are the same, the "new news" would immediately be reflected in a new set of equilibrium stock prices. And since everything already known will already be discounted, it is entirely reasonable to believe that the timing of the new bit of information, its character, and significance—even whether it will be good or bad—are all random variables contemplated "before-hand through the veil of the unknown." Such are precisely the makings of a random walk.[6]

Of course, the assumption of homogeneous investor expectations isn't much more plausible than the assertion that the impact of new information on stock prices is itself random. To begin with, investors do not all get a new piece of information at the same time; some read the papers in the morning, others at night. Besides, not all investors interpret a given piece of new information in the same way. Indeed, it is the probability that there will be divergences among the investors' discounting of news that makes the stock market a "horse race."

The real problem, then, would seem to be that of rationalizing random behavior in the presence of investors who attempt to calculate the relevance of new information, but who do so in such ways that their calculations often lead to divergences in probabilistic estimates of future behavior. We use the word "problem" because, on the surface, it seems more logical to expect that this set of circumstances would by itself produce decidedly nonrandom behavior. For example, if new information reaches investors with varying lags, is it not reasonable to expect that stock price changes would exhibit short term trends? Similarly, is it not logical, as investors revise their probabilities over time in response to new information, for the growing recognition of the information's "true" significance to cause nonrandom elements to creep into the series of price changes? Lintner observes:

> The very diversity we are now recognizing in the judgments of different investors regarding the relevant probability distributions over different securities means that the "walks" of stock prices do not have to be purely random merely because the securities markets are purely competitive. New information is not in fact instantaneously, uniformly, and costlessly available to all participants in the market. With no trading whatsoever by "insiders" before the news hits the broad tape, some will be in a position to act more

quickly than others and thereby secure differential gains (which would have to cover the cost of having the tape in the office *and* the opportunity cost of not tending to other affairs). More fundamentally, the fact that the diffusion of any new information over the investor population is inevitably a time-consuming and expensive process clearly opens up the possibility of significant nonrandom trends in the changing price quotations on the most purely competitive of markets. Other possibilities of nonrandom trends in price changes are opened up by the fact that some people are quicker to see the significance of new news than others (as a result of more experience or intelligence or better intuition).[7]

To this excellent statement we would only add the following thought: Isn't it also reasonable to expect that under the conditions Lintner describes some traders might become "opinion leaders," in the sense that their actions cause others to revise their expectations? And, if so, would this not represent still another force working toward the creation of dependencies?

The point, of course, is that even if the answers to the questions just posed are in the affirmative, the inherent tendency toward nonrandom behavior might still be overcome by the actions of other traders. Fama suggests that certain "sophisticated traders," for example, might be able to offset the development of nonrandom behavior. He identifies two types of sophisticated traders: (1) those who are "better at predicting the appearance of new information and estimating its effects on intrinsic [stock] values than others," and (2) those who are "better at doing statistical analyses of price behavior."[8] He comments that the two types might be "roughly thought of as [respectively] superior intrinsic value analysts and superior chart readers."[9] Both types would, according to Fama, tend to eliminate the tendencies toward nonrandom behavior described above. Their methods of operation, however, would differ significantly. The superior intrinsic value traders would help to eliminate dependencies by, in effect, anticipating how lags in the information-transmitting process and variations in the assessment of information by less sophisticated investors might be expected to influence price behavior. If, for example, new information consistently affected trading over a lengthy period of time, (as more and more traders became aware of its significance), the superior intrinsic value traders would come to know this and act accordingly, thereby eliminating any dependencies.

The superior chart traders would take a rather different approach. Instead of having above average ability to predict directly the behavior of other traders or the lags in the information transmission process, they would come to know, from their charts, what past price behavior tends to imply about future behavior. More important, they would act on the basis of this knowledge, thereby neutralizing the dependency-generating process.[10]

For the discussion at hand, the important point that follows from the introduction of superior traders is the notion that the elimination of the tendency toward nonrandom behavior is not merely the natural outcome of the assumptions built into the functioning of the market. Rather, it derives from the activities of traders who by their actions thwart the development of dependencies. If we were now to assume that there were no transactions costs or costs associated with reading charts and attempting to determine how investors in general react to new information, the existence of superior traders would be sufficient to permit us to argue that stock price changes could, in theory, be devoid of any nonrandom elements. As we have seen in the preceding chapters, however, transactions costs are not zero in real markets. Dealers, whether they be stock exchange specialists or over-the-counter market-makers, must be paid to provide traders with marketability. In addition, traders must normally pay some form of brokerage commission and, in most cases, transfer taxes. Beyond this, they usually incur costs in obtaining and processing information relevant to making judgments about which stocks to buy or sell. In short, even the superior traders must incur costs in the process of determining their security and portfolio preferences and making trades.

When we recognize the existence of these costs, it quickly becomes apparent that the mere existence of superior traders is not sufficient to insure that no nonrandom elements will surface. To the contrary, any nonrandom elements that are too small to permit superior traders to profit by eliminating them, after paying transactions and other costs, might be expected to persist. This being the case, of course, the random walk hypothesis must now be somewhat modified. No longer is it possible to state that the hypothesis holds that *all* price changes are serially independent. Instead, it must be argued that the hypothesis holds that any dependencies in the series of price changes are too small to provide opportunities for traders to profit from eliminating them after paying transactions costs and other expenses. In other words, the modified version of the hypothesis must recognize the difference between "meaningful" and "meaningless" nonrandom elements in the series of price changes—the difference between the two being that the former imply dependencies large enough for traders to increase expected gains on the basis of past knowledge of price behavior, while the latter do not. According to this version, only meaningful nonrandom elements would violate the random walk hypothesis.

Transactions Costs and Systematic Movements in Stock Price Behavior

Smidt, in an extremely provocative paper on the random walk hypothesis, notes that a significant but largely overlooked implication of the modified version of the random walk hypothesis is that "one should expect to find some systematic dependencies in price changes."[11] According to Smidt, "these dependencies may result from dependencies in the underlying information-generating process, the cost of transactions, the cost of acquiring and processing information, and, in general, all of the frictions and lags that tend to be ignored in abstract discussions of perfectly competitive markets."[12] Because of our preoccupation with the market-making process, let us attempt to provide some insights into this statement by focusing on the analysis of dependencies that might be expected to result from the existence of transactions costs. That is, let us consider why the existence of these costs might be expected to produce nonrandom elements in series of stock price changes.

In the preceding three chapters our analysis has stressed the importance of recognizing that transactions costs are composed of two basic components. The first component, which we have called exchange costs, should not in itself produce dependencies in a series of price changes; it should simply permit a variety of dependencies to exist that would otherwise be eliminated by the actions of traders. Like the costs of processing data, exchange costs make it too expensive to eliminate some of the dependencies resulting from lags in the transmission of new information, etc. *the spread between bid and ask*

A ~~The~~ second component of transactions costs, ~~called market-~~ *gain* ability costs, presents a very different picture. In contrast to ~~exchange costs~~, this component *might* be expected, *per se*, to produce certain forms of dependencies in price series. The

commissions, which simply permit certain types of dependence to remain in a sequence of prices,

logic behind this statement, as well as the nature of the dependencies involved, can be understood in the context of our
earlier discussion of the demand and supply for marketability
services. In Chapter 4 we pointed out that the fundamental
feature of marketability demand is the desire on the part of
some traders to adjust their portfolios rapidly without paying
a substantial cost in the form of a discount or premium price,
that is, to have predictable immediacy in executing a transaction.
We further noted that in the absence of persons who stand
ready to buy or sell at established prices, predictable immediacy
does not automatically exist in markets where buy and sell
orders come in randomly over time. The second point, in turn,
led us into a discussion of the institutions in securities markets
that exist to supply marketability services. In particular, we
discussed the basic characteristics of the dealer who takes on
the task of simultaneously quoting prices on both sides of the
market, thereby giving traders predictable immediacy. Finally,
we presented an analysis of the price of marketability services,
emphasizing the point that in the stock market this price is
represented by the dealer's bid-ask spread.

Why should the interaction of those who demand marketability services and those who supply them tend to produce
dependencies? And what forms of dependencies should this
interaction produce? As far as the second question is concerned,
Niederhoffer and Osborne report that there is a strong tendency
toward series of transactions in which a price change in one
direction is followed by a price change in the opposite direction.[13] They refer to this type of movement as a reversal. According to them, the results of an analysis of the Dow Jones Industrial
Stocks "indicate that after a price rise the odds are approximat-
ly 3 to 1 that the next non-zero change will be a decline, but after a
decline the odds are about 3 to 1 in favor of a rise." Their data
consist of the complete ticker tape record of six of the first seven
stocks in the Industrial Averages for the trading days in the month
of October, 1964. The results of a transaction matrix of consecutive pairs of price changes are reproduced in Table 7–1.

A succint interpretation of the results in the table is presented
by Niederhoffer and Osborne as follows:

Notice how the entries in the diagonal from lower left to upper right
are all, except for the common one, larger than the corresponding
entries in the diagonal from upper left to lower right. If the changes

TABLE 7-1
Transition Matrix of Consecutive Pairs of Price Changes*

ΔY_{t-1} Price Change in Period $t-1$	ΔY_t (Price Change in Period t)							Marginal Probabilities
	$-\frac{3}{8}$	$-\frac{2}{8}$	$-\frac{1}{8}$	$\frac{0}{8}$	$+\frac{1}{8}$	$+\frac{2}{8}$	$+\frac{3}{8}$	
$-\frac{3}{8}$	0.000	0.000	0.143	0.429	0.143	0.190	0.095	0.002
$-\frac{2}{8}$	0.003	0.034	0.110	0.466	0.209	0.175	0.003	0.028
$-\frac{1}{8}$	0.000	0.016	0.106	0.485	0.356	0.037	0.001	0.207
$\frac{0}{8}$	0.001	0.023	0.202	0.563	0.187	0.023	0.001	0.529
$+\frac{1}{8}$	0.004	0.033	0.329	0.512	0.109	0.010	0.002	0.204
$+\frac{2}{8}$	0.017	0.164	0.218	0.440	0.137	0.020	0.003	0.027
$+\frac{3}{8}$	0.143	0.143	0.143	0.429	0.071	0.071	0.000	0.001
Marginal Probabilities	0.002	0.028	0.206	0.525	0.205	0.028	0.001	1.0

*Adapted from Victor Niederhoffer and M. F. M. Osborne, "Market-Making and Reversal on the Stock Exchange," *Journal of the American Statistical Association* 61, No. 316 (December, 1966): 900.

were truly independent—as assumed in the [naive] random walk model—both diagonals should be the same within the limits of the random error. In addition, there should be no significant variation in the conditional distribution of ΔY_t over the tabulated values of ΔY_{t-1}. That is, all those conditional distributions should be the same as the marginal distributions, within the limits of random error.[14]

They further point out that a formal test of the independence of their transition matrix leads to the conclusion that the variations described above "cannot reasonably be attributed to chance."[15]

Turning now to the first question posed above, the reasons for the development of reversals, we find this statement by Smidt informative:

Broadly speaking, the mechanism that produces these reversal tendencies is well known. The tendencies result from the fact that as orders for immediate execution arrive at the market, they tend to be executed at either the bid or asked price.[16]

While technically accurate, this statement lacks something in intuitive appeal. Niederhoffer and Osborne, however, cover that aspect of the argument by discussing the operation of a simulated stock exchange specialist's book, which we reproduce in Table 7-2. As the table indicates, the specialist's book contains considerable buying interest at $33\frac{4}{8}$ bid, $33\frac{5}{8}$ asked. Thus, a buy order specifying immediate action (a market buy order) would be executed at $33\frac{4}{8}$, while a market sell order would be executed at $33\frac{5}{8}$. If we now assume that a stream of buy and sell orders comes in randomly, the process that creates reversals becomes apparent. To quote Niederhoffer and Osborne:

> In the short run, the limit orders on the book will act as a barrier to continued price movement in either direction. Until all limit orders at the highest bid ($33\frac{4}{8}$) and lowest offer ($33\frac{5}{8}$) are executed, transaction prices will fluctuate up and down between the bid and the offer in accordance with the random arrival of market orders. Moreover, the period of oscillation may tend to last longer than a glance at the specialist's book would suggest; additional orders to buy at $33\frac{4}{8}$ and to sell at $33\frac{5}{8}$ are to be expected. Therefore, the

TABLE 7–2

A Page from a Specialist's Book*

	Buy (Limit Orders)		Sell (Limit Orders)	
33	5 Smith	3 Benton		
	3 Abrot	15 Denoff		
	2 Green	1 Fried	33	
	1 Jones			
	1 Elim			
	1 Lakis	*32*		
$\frac{1}{8}$	1 Stahle		$\frac{1}{8}$	
	2 Vied			
		3		
$\frac{2}{8}$	2 James	4 Lurie	$\frac{2}{8}$	
	1 Pratt			
	1 Gelb	*8*		
	1 Ford			
$\frac{3}{8}$	1 Vernon		$\frac{3}{8}$	
		2		
	2 Brown	2 Gross		
	1 White	1 Hand		
$\frac{4}{8}$	7 Dell		$\frac{4}{8}$	
	1 Berger			
	1 Binder			
	1 Shoup	*16*		

TABLE 7–2 (*contd.*)

Buy (Limit Orders)	Sell (Limit Orders)		
		1 Ross	
$\frac{5}{8}$	$\frac{5}{8}$	1 Hunt	
			2
		1 Lee	
$\frac{6}{8}$	$\frac{6}{8}$	2 Block	
		2 Sims	6
		1 Bloom	
		1 Dorf	
$\frac{7}{8}$	$\frac{7}{8}$	1 Mann	
		1 Chan	3

*The simulated page from an imaginary specialist's book which is pictured here contains a record of the highest bids and the lowest offers. In this case it is $33\frac{4}{8}$ bid and $33\frac{5}{8}$ offered. For each order, the name of the broker giving the order, and the number of shares in the order, are entered in the proper location. It should be noted that the bid must be below the offers and offers above the bids, or else they would be executed immediately. This simulated book was constructed by adding the limit and stop orders at the eight fractional prices in each of the five books that have appeared in the literature.

Adapted from Niederhoffer and Osborne, "Market-Making and Reversal," p. 906.

patterns of reversals displayed by the data [for the Dow Jones Industrials] is just what one might expect from the current system of trading on the [New York Stock] Exchange.[17]

We would only add one point to this excellent statement: The willingness of the specialist to quote a bid and ask price of his own, when no limit orders appear, provides still another factor tending to lead to reversals. In the hypothetical case in Table 7–2, for example, the specialist might decide to put his own bid and ask prices at $33\frac{4}{8}$ and $33\frac{5}{8}$, respectively. In this case, the tendency toward reversals would persist even after the limit orders at these two prices were exhausted.

Taken together, the comments of Niederhoffer and Osborne and those of Smidt imply that the extent of reversals should be positively related to the percentage of market orders arriving in the market; that is, the higher the percentage of market, as opposed to limit, orders, the greater the likelihood of reversals. This point can easily be demonstrated through the use of a simple simulation model of the type presented in Chapter 2. Let us simulate a flow of orders with a sequence of three-digit random numbers. The first digit determines whether the order is to buy or sell. Assuming an even probability of orders of either kind, even numbers designate bids and odd numbers indicate asks. The second digit is used to determine the price specified in the case of limit orders, according to the following schedule: $0 = 28\frac{3}{4}$, $1 = 29$, $2 = 29\frac{1}{4}$, etc. (As in the examples in Chapter 2, we assume an equilibrium price between $29\frac{3}{4}$ and 30). The third digit is used to determine whether the order has a price limitation. To investigate the impact of market orders on the behavior of prices, the probability that any order is a market order is varied from zero to 1 at intervals of 20 per cent. In other words, we begin by assuming that all orders are limit orders, then increase the probability of market orders to 0.2, then to 0.4, and so forth. Finally, we assume that a dealer stands ready to buy and sell at $29\frac{1}{2}$ and $30\frac{1}{2}$, respectively.

Some results of carrying out this procedure for thirty series of fifty random numbers are summarized in Figure 22. Specifically, the figure shows the mean of the percentage of reversals at various levels of relative market order importance. As expected, there is a positive relationship between the percentage

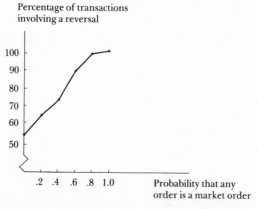

FIGURE 22   Reversals and Market Order Frequency.

of limit orders and the extent of reversals. When all market orders are submitted, the transactions fluctuate up and down between the dealer's bid and ask prices, and we have nothing but reversals. As the percentage of limit orders decreases, however, the dealer is faced with competitors who may submit orders at prices inside his spread. When this occurs, proper sequencing of market orders may trigger a brief run in either direction. Even in these cases, however, the dealer's bid and ask prices serve as effective limits to the size of these runs and insure that a reversal will occur within three or four transactions.

In the introduction to this chapter, we noted that a critical aspect of the dependencies introduced by the market-making process was whether they provide evidence to refute the random walk model. Since the modified form of the model implies that dependencies should not be great enough to provide traders with an opportunity to make above-normal profits, the question would seem to be whether the reversals discussed above provide such opportunities. In addressing himself to this question, Smidt simply concludes that "it is not possible to make a confident statement."[18] Niederhoffer and Osborne, on the other hand, seem to hold out the prospect that they may provide such an opportunity for some traders. In particular, they note that because limit orders tend to cluster at the integer, half integer, quarter integer, and odd eighths, in decending order (see Table 7–2), "reversals are more common at even eighths than at odd eighths, and more common at integers than at half integers."[19] From this observation they conclude that "certain trading rules emerge."

> One is that limit and stop orders should be placed at odd eighths, preferably at $\frac{7}{8}$ for sell orders and at $\frac{1}{8}$ for buy orders. Another is to buy when a stock advances through a barrier, and to sell when it sinks through a barrier.[20]

In the final analysis, of course, whether these rules can be used to improve trading profits, after paying commissions, etc., remains to be seen. To the best of our knowledge, no one has subjected this hypothesis to rigorous empirical testing.[21]

Large Marketability Demands and Stock Price Behavior

Thus far in the discussion, we have said virtually nothing about the relationship between the amount of marketability (predictable immediacy) demanded and the behavior of stock prices. Implicitly, however, we have been focusing on this relationship when the quantity of marketability services demanded by any one trader is relatively small. In the simulation, for example, we assumed that all orders were for one round lot. Similarly, Niederhoffer and Osborne's simulated specialist's book and order flow involves orders for relatively small amounts of stock.

In view of the growing importance of institutional traders and block trading, it seems appropriate to ask whether the conclusions stated above — e.g., that the interaction of the demand and supply for marketability services produces a tendency toward reversals — hold true when the demand for these services increases markedly. Smidt argues that, in principle, the reversal tendency should also result from large marketability demands. He states that "large liquidity [marketability] demands, spread over a period of days, should produce a reversal pattern similar to that observed in transaction data, except that the price moves should be larger, and should be spread over a longer period of time."[22] The logic behind this statement can easily be seen by referring to Figure 23.

In this figure we have depicted a dealer's bid and ask prices, D_b and D_a, respectively, for varying quantities of a security. For reasons that we have already made clear, we have drawn these prices in such a way that they diverge as the quantities involved increase. Imagine now how the pattern of trading (and price changes) might be expected to change if the average size of incoming orders increased from, say, one round lot to ten round lots. In the former case, the dealer's "tight" bid-ask quotes would serve as "reflecting barriers," thus producing

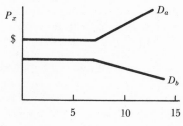

Q_x (in round lots)

FIGURE 23 A Dealer's Demand and Supply Function for a Given Stock.

reversals within a relatively small range. As the order size increased, however, the dealer's spread also would increase, thereby providing for larger reversals. In actuality, of course, matters would be considerably more complex, since at the higher average order size limit orders outside of the dealer's quotes would also be expected to occur. Generally speaking, however, the widening of the dealer's quote, which is to be expected as order size increases, would provide the basis for the kind of price behavior mentioned by Smidt.

What evidence is there to suggest that larger reversals associated with large demands for marketability services can be observed in actual data? Smidt argues that in the case of commodity futures markets, there is considerable evidence of this effect. He notes, however, that the particular institutional characteristics of the stock market make it somewhat more difficult to observe this effect, or to recognize it when it is present. In particular, he points out that the wide range of alternatives open to those who want to buy or sell a large quantity of stock, including the use of off-board trading, the development of secondary issues, and others, means that the true costs of obtaining marketability services "may not appear in the pattern of recorded prices."[23]

Smidt, however, also argues that the results of a study by Fama and Blume *may* indicate the presence of reversals in stock prices that are the results of the demand for large quantities of marketability. Fama and Blume's study is an analysis of the returns from applying filter trading rules to the daily closing prices of the thirty stocks in the Dow Jones Industrial Average. The filter trading rules they test assume that a long position in a stock is taken when its daily closing price is greater than the first day's closing price by the size of the filter (measured in percentage points). This long position is held until a daily closing price is below a subsequent high by the amount of the filter. At this point, the long position is closed and a short position is opened. Filters from 0.5 per cent to 50 per cent are applied to the Dow Jones data by Fama and Blume.[24] Their results, before taking account of brokerage commissions, are summarized in Table 7–3. To illustrate, the entries under the 0.005 filter indicate that the long position for the 0.5 per cent filter yielded a return of approximately 21 per cent, and the short position yielded a return of 1 per cent.

How are these results to be interpreted? Smidt argues that

TABLE 7–3
Before Commissions Annual Rates of Return by
Filter Size: Averaged over All Companies*

Filter	Total Transactions	Long Positions Only (Rounded)	Short Positions Only (Rounded)
0.005	12,514	0.21	0.01
0.010	8,660	0.14	−0.05
0.015	6,270	0.11	−0.08
0.020	4,784	0.09	−0.11
0.025	3,750	0.07	−0.14
0.030	2,994	0.07	−0.14
0.035	2,438	0.07	−0.13
0.040	2,013	0.08	−0.13
0.045	1,720	0.06	−0.15
0.050	1,484	0.06	−0.16
0.060	1,071	0.08	−0.12
0.070	828	0.07	−0.13
0.080	653	0.08	−0.13
0.090	539	0.08	−0.12
0.100	435	0.08	−0.10
0.120	289	0.10	−0.09

*Adapted from E. Fama and M. E. Blume, "Filter Rules
and Stock Market Trading," *Journal of Business* 39, No. 1,
Special Supplement, (January 1966): 237.

since a simple buy and hold strategy applied to the data yields
an annual rate of return of approximately 10 per cent, "one
would expect to earn a return of 10 per cent during the period
when the long positions were open and a return of minus that
amount during the period when the short positions were
open."[25] He then notes that there are four filter levels (0.005,
0.010, 0.045 and 0.050) whose observed returns for both long and
short positions differ in absolute magnitude by 4 per cent or
more from their expected levels. Deviations this large, he
concludes, "cannot reasonably be attributed to chance."[26]
More important, he suggests the hypothesis that these deviations are the result of price concessions by purchasers and
sellers anxious to exchange a large volume of stock quickly. He
then comments

To see why this suggestion is reasonable, first note that for every
filter size . . . the actual returns earned by the long and short positions

are displaced from their expected returns by approximately the same absolute magnitude. This strongly suggests that whatever systematic pattern exists in the stock price sequence is a highly symmetric pattern. The simplest pattern that could account for this characteristic in the data is a wavelike motion around the long-term upward trend in the data. If the waves were all of the same amplitude, then any filter size greater than the amplitude of the wave would produce no transactions. In fact, the data show that the number of transactions decreases as the filter size increases. This suggests a mixture of waves of different amplitudes.... If these wavelike patterns are due to the demands for relatively large amounts of liquidity, the amplitude of the waves presumably results from the number of shares of stock which the anxious buyer or seller has available for exchange, and the intensity of his desire to complete the transaction rapidly.[27]

To be consistent with our earlier format, it seems appropriate to close the discussion by asking whether the types of dependencies associated with large marketability demands constitute evidence that contradicts the random walk hypothesis. Fama and Blume argue quite vigorously that the statistical dependencies contained in their data do not contradict the hypothesis, since after paying transactions costs a trader would be worse off following the rules than employing a simple buy and hold strategy. Indeed, they note that clearing house fees alone are "more than sufficient to push the returns from the simple filter rule below those of a buy and hold policy."[28]

Smidt, however, is not completely persuaded by the logic of Fama and Blume. He points out that their conclusions are based on the assumption that a trader "follows the [filter] rule literally" and adds that a more reasonable assumption might involve having a trader take an average long position (to take advantage of the trend) and use the filter to "trade around" his average position. This policy, utilizing a 5 per cent filter and assuming an investment of temporarily idle funds at a risk-free rate of 5 per cent, produces a return of about 9 per cent. Smidt notes that this is still below the 10 per cent return associated with a buy and hold strategy, but he points out that a valid comparison of the two outcomes should be based on the analysis of relative risks as well as relative returns. Because the policy of trading around the trend involves a more diversified average portfolio, he concludes that it is likely to produce an income stream with less variability. Thus, he concludes that "a member of the

NYSE might well find it attractive to take advantage of the statistical dependencies that Fama and Blume have so well documented."[29]

Of course, the rigorous critic might well argue that Smidt's conclusion is not justified by his data. Technically, a comparison of the outcomes from the buy and hold and filter trading strategies would require that the variability of their relative returns actually be calculated. With these data in hand, it would be possible to compare two strategies, utilizing the models for the analysis of mutual fund performance developed by Treynor, Sharpe, and Jensen.[30] Once again, however, it remains for future researchers to perform this analysis.

Summary

In the introduction to this chapter we stated that it was our objective to analyze the random walk hypothesis, focusing primarily on the role that transaction costs play in influencing the behavior of stock prices. We have now seen that one component of these costs, marketability costs, should be expected to produce certain types of nonrandom elements. The question, then, would seem to be whether or not these elements provide a basis for refuting the random walk hypothesis. In principle, they need not; it all depends on how large they are, that is, on whether or not they provide profit opportunities to investors. This, unfortunately, is an unresolved question for the time being.

Notes

1. "Adam Smith," *The Money Game* (New York: Random House, 1967), p. 148.
2. F. E. James, Jr., "Moving Monthly Averages—An Effective Investment Tool?" *Journal of Financial and Quantitative Analysis*, September, 1968, p. 315.
3. For discussions of this point, see M. G. Jensen, "Risk, the Pricing of Capital Assets, and the Evaluation of Investment Portfolios," *Journal of Business* 42, No. 2 (April, 1969): 167–247, esp. pp. 168–69; B. Mandelbrot, "Forecasts of Future Prices, Unbiased Markets, and 'Martingale' Models," *Journal of Business* 39, No. 1, Part 2 (January, 1966): 242–55; and Paul A. Samuelson, "Proof that Properly Anticipated Prices Fluctuate Randomly," *Industrial Management Review* 6 (Spring, 1965): 41–49.
4. E. Fama, "The Behavior of Stock Market Prices," *Journal of Business* 38, No. 1 (January, 1965): 36.
5. *Ibid.*, p. 36.

6. J. Lintner, "A Model of a Perfectly Functioning Securities Market," in H. Manne, *Economic Policy and the Regulation of Corporate Securities* (Washington, D.C.: American Enterprise Institute, 1969), pp. 143–166.
7. *Ibid.*, p. 164.
8. Fama, "Behavior of Stock Market Prices," p. 37.
9. *Ibid.*, pp. 37–38.
10. Fama correctly notes that the superior chart traders would, by their own activities, eliminate the ability to profit from chart reading. See *ibid.*, pp. 38–39.
11. Seymour Smidt, "A New Look at the Random Walk Hypothesis," *Journal of Financial and Quantitative Analysis* 3 (September, 1968): 237.
12. *Ibid.*
13. V. Niederhoffer and M. F. M. Osborne, "Market-Making and Reversal on the Stock Exchange," *Journal of the American Statistical Association* 61, No. 316 (December, 1966): 897–917.
14. *Ibid.*, p. 901.
15. *Ibid.*
16. Smidt, "New Look at Random Walk," p. 243.
17. Niederhoffer and Osborne, "Market-Making and Reversal," p. 907.
18. Smidt, "New Look at Random Walk," p. 243. He notes, however, that in the commodity future market such dependencies do seem to form a basis for profit opportunities from technical trading.
19. Niederhoffer and Osborne, "Market-Making and Reversal," p. 914.
20. *Ibid.*
21. In another paper, Niederhoffer notes that the empirical analysis of this subject would be extremely difficult. See V. Niederhoffer, "A New Look at Clustering of Stock Prices," *Journal of Business* 39, No. 2 (April, 1966): 313.
22. Smidt, "New Look at Random Walk," p. 245.
23. *Ibid.*, p. 246.
24. E. Fama and M. Blume, "Filter Rules and Stock Market Trading," *Journal of Business* 39, No. 1, Special Supplement (January, 1966): 226–41.
25. Smidt, "New Look at Random Walk," p. 246.
26. *Ibid.*, p. 247.
27. *Ibid.*, pp. 248–49.
28. Fama and Blume, "Filter Rules and Trading," p. 238.
29. Smidt, "New Look at Random Walk," p. 251.
30. J. L. Treynor, "How to Rate the Management of Investment Funds," *Harvard Business Review* 43, No. 1 (January–February, 1965): 63–75; W. Sharpe, "Mutual Fund Performance," *Journal of Business* 39, No. 1, Special Supplement (January, 1966): 119–38; and Jensen, *op. cit.*, note 3 *supra*.

8 The Exchange Industry: Past and Present

In the first seven chapters, our references to the operations of the stock exchanges were made almost exclusively in terms of the analysis of making markets for individual securities. In Chapter 3, for example, we discussed the matter of the allocation of securities between the exchanges and the over-the-counter market primarily in terms of the two markets' approaches to organizing trading in individual issues. Similarly, in the chapters dealing with the determination of the bid-ask spread, we focused on the analysis of factors that influence the specialist's ability to make a market for a particular common stock.

In this chapter and the next, we turn our attention to a discussion of the economics of the stock exchange industry *per se*. Our primary objective in the present chapter is to develop an understanding of the contemporary structure of the industry, the relations among the firms it comprises, and the factors that have produced those relations. Put somewhat differently, this chapter will attempt to provide insight into these questions: (1) What is the relationship between the NYSE and other stock exchanges, including the ASE and the regional exchanges? (2) Why has the NYSE been able to maintain a dominant position in the stock exchange industry for nearly 200 years?

We shall begin by presenting some data on the structure of the stock exchange industry over the past thirty-five years. Next will come a discussion of the historical relationship between the NYSE and other stock exchanges, first the rival stock exchanges established in New York City and then the regional exchanges. The final section is addressed to the question that naturally follows from this discussion: Why has the NYSE been so successful at maintaining its dominant position in the stock exchange industry for such a long time?

The Makeup of the Exchange Industry

Prior to the establishment of the Securities and Exchange Commission in 1934, there was no way to obtain systematic data on the structure of the stock exchange industry. Recognizing the need for such data, the framers of the legislation establishing the SEC specified that one of its duties would be to obtain monthly data on the volume of trading for all of the nation's stock exchanges. Those data, covering the period from 1934 through 1969, are presented in Table 8–1.

From even a cursory glance at this table, a number of rather important aspects of the structure of the exchange industry over the past thirty-five years can be obtained. For example, the data in column 2 indicate that the number of exchanges has been steadily declining during this period. Some exchanges have simply closed their doors for lack of business, the most recent example being the San Francisco Mining Exchange, which ceased operations in August, 1967. In a larger number of cases, however, the declining population in the industry has resulted from merger activities. Mergers were particularly prevalent during the 1940's and 1950's, when the Midwest and Philadelphia-Baltimore-Washington Stock Exchanges were taking shape. Only one new exchange has opened its doors during this entire period; the National Stock Exchange commenced operations in 1964. Its trading volume, while still quite small, has grown steadily in recent years, so that today it is larger than the Detroit Stock Exchange.

A second aspect of the industry's structure that readily becomes apparent, and about which we will have more to say in the next section of this chapter, is the dominant position held by the national exchanges, particularly by the NYSE, during the entire period. It was not until 1968 that the NYSE's share of the total market declined below the 75% level. Furthermore, because of the close ties between the NYSE and the ASE, the more important column (from the viewpoint of the industry's concentration) is No. 6, which shows the volume of trading on the NYSE and ASE as a percentage of total stock exchange volume. As the reader can see, this total, although declining modestly in recent years, has never been below 90%. In other words, the recent decline in the relative position of the NYSE has primarily been the result of an increase in trading on the other national stock exchange.

Within the regional exchange category, the data indicate that there has recently been some modest growth at the expense of the national exchanges. The regionals' total share of the market, while still below 10 per cent, has increased fairly steadily over the last decade. More important, the three largest regionals, the Midwest, Pacific Coast, and Philadelphia-Baltimore-Washington exchanges, have more than held their own with the NYSE and ASE during this period. Other regionals, however, have not been so fortunate. The Detroit Stock Exchange, for example, has suffered a serious drop in its relative position over the past four years.

In summary, the data in Table 8–1 indicate that the stock exchange industry is highly concentrated, with two firms, the NYSE and the ASE, accounting for more than 90 per cent of the industry's volume. Smaller competitors have declined in number over the past thirty-five years, but lately several of the smaller firms have demonstrated an ability to more than hold their relative positions.

The NYSE and Rival Stock Exchanges: Early History

In a recent study of the economic power of the NYSE, Robert Doede concludes that the history of the Exchange reveals it to be an institution conceived from the outset as a cartel arrangement designed to monopolize the business of providing trading facilities for certain classes of securities.[1] According to Doede, the dominant position of the NYSE was achieved not out of happenstance or sheer superiority in providing the public with a product, but rather from a series of maneuvers calculated in advance to reduce and/or eliminate competition in the provision of exchange services. Doede bases this judgment on two aspects of the exchange's history: first, its staunch adherence to a schedule of fixed minimum commission rates to be charged to nonmembers, and second, its aggressive approach to the stifling of competition provided by rival exchanges.

In Chapter 5 we presented a rather lengthy analysis of the structure of the Exchange's commissions. The general thrust of our position was quite similar to Doede's. That is, we too concluded that the fixed minimum commission cannot be justified on the basis of the logic that has been put forward recently by the NYSE, but rather represents an artificial barrier against competitive rate-setting. Let us now consider the second aspect of Doede's argument — the allegation that the NYSE has sought over its history to stifle systematically the competition presented by rival exchanges.

In the early years of the Exchange's development, when it was known as the New York Stock and Exchange Board, or the "Board" for short, its primary source of competition was the "curbstone crowd," composed of brokers who did business on the streets outside of the Exchange's offices. While there are no data to indicate the precise nature or extent of the challenge posed by the curbstone crowd, the Exchange's vigorous attempt to stifle the curb's activities suggests that it was regarded as a real threat. In the fall of 1817, for example, the Exchange passed two resolutions aimed at inhibiting the activities of the curbstone crowd. The first stated that "no member . . . shall either directly or indirectly make, or cause to be made, any purchases or sales whatever . . . for any person or persons acting as a [nonmember] Broker or Brokers without receiving a full commission for the same, and for the faithful performance of which we all mutually pledge our honor."[2] The second resolution, designed, in the words of Doede, "to further enforce the secrecy of transactions at the exchange and to prevent arbitrage with nonmembers trading in the street,"[3] stated that "no member . . . nor any partner of a member, shall hereafter give the prices of any kind of stock, exchange or specie, to any printer for publication and that the secretary . . . only be authorized to give the prices for that purpose."[4]

Despite these resolutions, the curbstone market continued to be a source of concern to the Exchange. Thus, in 1836, a third, more binding resolution was passed. In simple, unvarnished terms, it stated that members were thereafter prohibited from making purchases or sales, either directly or indirectly, in the street. Members contravening the resolution were "subject to suspension at the pleasure of the Board."[5]

In the 1830's and 1840's, two new rivals appeared: the so-called "New Board," founded in 1835, and the Commercial

Exchange Association, started a few years later. Once again, the Exchange reacted by passing a resolution designed to inhibit the growth of its competition. This time, it took the form of a prohibition of members' belonging to any other institution organized for the purpose of exchanging securities.

After varying periods of time, each of the rivals mentioned so far faded into history. However, one rival, the "Open Board of Stockholders" became sufficiently successful to cause the NYSE to merge with it. The Open Board was organized during the Civil War. It grew in part because of the inability of the NYSE, with its small, fixed number of members, to accommodate the growing demand for exchange services resulting from the war-related business boom.[6] Even after the war, however, it continued to flourish, charging lower commissions than the NYSE and being "more innovative in adopting new trading tactics than its older rival."[7] In 1869, the Exchange and the Open Board merged. According to Doede, the real significance of this event was that it "represented the only instance in which a group of outside brokers established a viable rival exchange which could be removed only by merger."

During the latter part of the nineteenth century, still another rival to the NYSE appeared. Called the Consolidated Stock and Petroleum Exchange (CSPE), it resulted from the merger of several small stock exchanges involved in trading in mining and petroleum stocks. To meet the competition of the CSPE, the NYSE both prohibited its members from participating in the activities of the new exchange and established an "unlisted trading department" where CSPE securities not listed on its regular roll could be traded. Since these moves were, according to Doede, "hard but not fatal,"[8] the Exchange subsequently passed a series of resolutions designed to cut off communication between the floors of the two exchanges. Indeed, it went so far as to direct Western Union to stop transmitting quotations to the CSPE. When the courts decreed that this tactic was illegal, the Exchange again attempted to develop a resolution that would "prevent a man who is a member of another exchange from doing any business at all and . . . drive him out of business."[9]

These measures were, according to Doede, only partially successful in destroying the economic power of the CSPE. Its final elimination was the result of the growth of another stock exchange, the New York Curb Market Association (NYCMA).

The NYCMA was an effective competitor for the CSPE for two reasons. First, it provided buyers and sellers with "active trading in an equal or greater number of securities in conjunction with a competitive commission schedule."[10] Second, it offered companies "an avenue to listing on the NYSE, an avenue which was not open to securities traded on the CSPE."[11]

Ironically, the curb, which formed the earliest source of rivalry for the Exchange, was to become in the final analysis its most willing ally. In 1910, its members renounced trading in NYSE listed securities in exchange for an agreement from the NYSE to close the unlisted trading department. Put simply, the 1910 agreement between the NYSE and the NYCMA represented a market-sharing arrangement, whereby the latter would trade in new issues and more risky securities, leaving trading in older, more established firms to the former. Because the two exchanges were no longer rivals, it was possible for brokers to hold memberships in both of them. The pattern established in 1910 persists to this day; since 1953 the NYCMA has been known as the American Stock Exchange.

The NYSE and the Regional Exchanges

Some extremely relevant evidence concerning the attitude of the NYSE toward rival exchanges can be found in the history of its relations with the so-called regional exchanges, i.e., the exchanges located outside of New York. In dealing with these exchanges, the NYSE has varied its attitude in accordance with competitive conditions. When the regional exchanges have not been perceived as a threat, the Exchange has generally pursued a "live and let live" attitude similar to that which characterizes its dealings with the ASE. When the regionals have appeared to pose a significant threat, on the other hand, the NYSE has reacted in much the same way as it has to rival exchanges established in New York.

In a 1957 book, James E. Walter argued that, historically, the primary function of the regional exchanges was to provide a proving ground or primary market for the stocks of regionally known corporations, rather than to offer competition for the secondary markets made by national exchanges. According to Walter:

> Regional exchanges can effectively service regional issues which do not qualify for national listing for one reason or another.

Although able to provide satisfactory markets for nationally distributed issues, regional exchanges are not equipped to take the place of national exchanges.[12]

So long as the logic embodied in this statement was valid, the regional exchanges posed no real economic threat to the NYSE and, thus, were treated as cooperating links in a nationwide market-sharing arrangement. NYSE firms were permitted to own seats on regional exchanges and even to trade NYSE stocks listed on the regionals. Of course, since the commissions on these trades were the same as could be obtained on the Big Board, NYSE members continued to make the vast majority of their trades in New York. Much, if not most, of the trading in NYSE listed securities on the regional exchanges, therefore, was done by regional brokers who were not members of the NYSE. As a percentage of total trading in NYSE listed securities, however, their trading activities were not usually substantial. Moreover, their activities to a large extent represented competition for stocks traded exclusively on the regional exchanges rather than competition for trading conducted on the NYSE. In a statement before the Senate Banking and Currency Committee in 1955, the President of the San Francisco Stock Exchange testified as follows:

Members of our exchange generate orders in [NYSE listed] securities for the very reason that they are traded here. If they were not listed locally, member firms might well recommend to their clients other securities of equal value that were listed locally rather than those traded only in eastern markets.[13]

Along these same lines, an official of the Midwest exchange argued that listings of NYSE listed securities on regional exchanges primarily provide a source of competition for local issues.[14]

While "live and let live" was an appropriate attitude for the NYSE to take under the conditions just described, it did not suffice when the regional exchanges posed a serious threat. On the contrary, the NYSE then reacted in a manner characteristic of its dealing with rival exchanges established in New York. Witness, for example, the NYSE's 1941 attempt to prohibit its members from trading Big Board listed securities on the regionals. At the time, the NYSE's relative hold on the exchange business remained unchallenged, but because of sharply reduced over-all stock trading, its profitability had been cut to an all-time low. In fact, it had suffered deficits for four straight years. In the interest of finding new sources of revenue, it hit on the idea of curtailing the flow of trading in NYSE listed securities on the regional exchanges. Of course, it could not prevent trading by nonmember firms; but, at the very least, it could try to keep its own members from trading NYSE listed stocks outside of New York. Thus, in the Spring of 1941, the Exchange proposed a rule, "under the terms of which members of the NYSE acting as odd lot dealers or specialists of other exchanges, or otherwise publicly dealing 'outside the exchange in securities dealt in on the exchange,' would be subject to proceedings for suspension or expulsion from exchange membership."[15] To anyone familiar with the NYSE's approach to dealing with earlier rivals, such as the "New Board" or the Consolidated Stock and Petroleum Exchange, the thrust of this rule must seem clear.

In contrast to the success of its earlier coups, however, the NYSE's 1941 attempt to stifle competition was challenged by the then relatively new Securities and Exchange Commission. The Commission, "in a unique instance of rapid decision-making,"[16] forced the Exchange to rescind its proposed ruling. Beyond being of overriding importance *per se*, the Multiple Trading Case, as it became known, focused attention on the growing importance of trading in NYSE listed securities on the regional exchanges. To quote the *Special Study*:

> The Commission pointed out that many securities traded on the NYSE were also traded on one or more of the seventeen regional exchanges in existence at the time, that nine exchanges had facilities for executing odd-lot transactions in dually traded securities at NYSE prices, and that on six of these exchanges NYSE members who were also members of the regional exchange (i.e., dual members) either handled or financed the odd-lot or specialist function.[17]

In other words, by 1941 the role of the regional stock exchange was no longer primarily that of providing trading activity in local issues. Instead, for a variety of reasons, it had become that of providing multiple markets for securities listed on the national exchanges.

For the next two decades, the developments that led to a change in the status of the regional exchanges from primary markets in local issues to multiple markets in NYSE listed securities resulted in a significant decline in their importance.

As the *Special Study* noted in 1962:

> The regionals, as occupants of the difficult middle ground between the major exchanges and the over-the-counter markets, have had the unhappy experience of generally feeling the adverse impacts and never the favorable impacts of these various developments. The noticeable decline in their role as a primary markets [for local securities] has been accompanied by a very substantial increase in their role as "dual" markets for securities traded on the New York Stock Exchange and, to a limited extent, the American Exchange. Not the least of the factors, of course, accounting for this change has been the sheer struggle for survival in the face of their declining function as primary markets.[18]

Paradoxically, at the time the *Special Study* was being prepared, the regional exchanges found themselves in the early stages of a growth period the likes of which they had not experienced in several decades. Even more paradoxically, the source of that growth was not the resurgence in the significance of regional trading of local issues but, instead, the expansion in regional trading of NYSE listed securities. The NYSE's reactions to this resurgence provide the most recent evidence concerning the attitude of the Big Board toward rival exchanges. A detailed account of these reactions and the complex circumstances surrounding them would therefore seem in order. To put the discussion in the proper context, however, we begin with a few comments on the reasons for the resurgence in regional exchanges.

In large measure, the growth in the regional trading of NYSE listed securities during the early 1960's resulted from special variations of the so-called give-up arrangements that were fostered by the regional exchanges. The give-up was a technique originally developed by the NYSE to provide institutional investors with the opportunity to split commissions among members of the exchange. A mutual fund, for example, could use the give-up to reward a brokerage firm that had been doing research or selling shares for it but did not actually make its trades. Under the system, the fund would direct a broker with whom it placed commission business to give up a portion of its commission to the firm providing research or selling services.

The regional exchanges, hungry for institutional business, adopted the give-up techniques and added a twist of their own: They not only permitted members to share commissions among themselves but also permitted them to share them with non-members as well. In other words, they provided the institutions with an opportunity to reward brokers who were not members of *any* exchange for services they might have rendered. With the aid of this "augmented" give-up system, the regional exchanges prospered; even New York Stock Exchange member firms sought seats on the regionals as a means of giving up a portion of their commissions to nonmembers. In the words of a *Business Week* writer, the give-up system became "if not quite the life blood of the regional exchanges, at least the cream that made them fat."[19]

In the fall of 1966, the give-up came under serious attack in a lengthy SEC report on the mutual fund industry. The SEC proposed that give-ups be abolished in favor of direct commission reductions, arguing that give-ups "have potentially adverse effects on mutual funds shareholders . . . because the technique encourages fund managers to direct their brokerage in such a way as to produce the greatest sale of fund shares, without regard to best or most economic execution of portfolio transactions."[20] In addition, it concluded that give-ups may encourage dealers to recommend funds to their customers on the basis of the expectation of receiving commission business rather than on the basis of the suitability of the fund to the investor's needs.

Although it might have been able to argue against these claims, the NYSE reacted by proposing that the give-up practice be "reformed" so that only exchange members who actually participated in the processing of a customer's order could obtain or be eligible for them. The *Wall Street Journal*, with other segments of the financial and business press, was quick to note that the Exchange's proposal "was seen as a method of curtailing the diversion of business away from the Big Board to regional exchanges." Noting, in particular, that the Pacific Coast Exchange had pioneered in the development of give-ups to nonmembers, the *Journal* commented as follows:

> It's no secret that the Pacific Coast exchange has been the most aggressive in draining Big Board business away from the New York Market. . . . As the Big Board sees it, it's unlikely that these Pacific Coast nonmembers would be allowed by that exchange's rules to handle an order, perhaps to the limited extent of "introducing" an account; thus it's conceivable if the Big Board's reciprocity rule were adopted by the SEC for the Pacific exchange, its nonmembers would be pretty much barred from further commission sharing.[21]

Finally, it commented that the proposal also was aimed "directly at institutional customers":

> The reasoning is that if institutions can no longer order transactions in dually listed stocks on regional exchanges to reward firms affiliated with (but not members of) these exchanges, much of the diverted business would be restored to New York.[22]

In the weeks following this "trial balloon," the Big Board discovered, no doubt to its surprise, that many of its own smaller members were vehemently opposed to the elimination of give-ups except among firms actually executing an order. In reaction to this development, the NYSE took a somewhat different approach. According to the *Wall Street Journal,*

> Rebuffed by a significant block of its members in an attempt to resolve the thorny "give-up" problem, the NYSE is said to be approaching the question from a different angle. Wall Street sources say the exchange is readying a new proposal for the granting by member firms of discounts for large volume securities transactions.... This would replace a tentatively advanced proposal that would have restricted fee-splitting among member firms.[23]

For the next several months, there was little mention of the NYSE's development of a volume discount proposal. Then, in the fall of 1967, reports began to circulate that the plan would not even be made public until the early part of 1969. According to one account, the reason for the delay was the initiation of a study of the volume discount question by an outside consulting firm.[24]

Much to the surprise of the financial community, the NYSE presented the SEC with a proposed volume discount package less than two months later. In addition to containing a suggested approach to the development of a volume discount for commissions on large trades, the Exchange's proposal, in something of a turnabout from the previous year, espoused the general practice of give-ups, but suggested that they be limited in amount. More important, the proposal also (1) "urged the SEC to join the Exchange in prohibiting certain give-up practices which have resulted in brokerage business being diverted to the regional stock exchanges" and (2) proposed that the Commission "limit both membership on any stock exchange and broker dealer allowances to 'bona fide' broker dealers."[25] The *Wall Street Journal* noted that this last provision "would conceivably bar any further arrangements whereby some mutual funds have set up brokerage-firm subsidiaries on the Pacific Coast Exchange as a cost saving technique for their holders."[26] It also added that "these three proposals were viewed by some industry sources as an attempt by the Big Board to consolidate its position as the nation's foremost securities marketplace in the face of rising competition by regional exchanges."[27] A West Coast investment official put matters somewhat more bluntly by way of analogy: "Do you suppose that General Motors could get a rule through that would prohibit everyone from buying anything other than GM cars? That is what the Big Board seems to be asking!"[28]

In the next few months, the already complex scenario concerning the give-up issue and the relationship between the NYSE and the regional exchanges became even more complicated. The first complicating factor was an announcement by the SEC that it was putting forth its own plan to eliminate give-ups.[29] The SEC's plan, in contrast to the NYSE's, was designed to ban all give-ups that did not result in a direct return to the institutional investor. In others words, its intention was to eliminate give-ups unless their benefits went to the institutional investor placing the commission business in the first place.

Almost before the NYSE could react to the SEC's proposal, the Department of Justice, in an unparalleled move, announced that it was prepared to challenge the entire legal and economic basis of the Big Board's minimum commission policy. As a part of its argument, the Department of Justice pointed out that to the extent give-ups represented commission reductions, they were *prima facie* evidence that the minimum commission system was not vital to the continued existence of the Exchange.[30]

At this stage in the proceedings, the NYSE found itself between a rock and a whirlpool; if it argued too vigorously for some form of give-up for itself while advocating the elimination of the type of give-up pioneered by the regional exchanges, it would be giving the Justice Department ammunition to use against it. Moreover, that ammunition would not sit idle for long, because the entire matter of minimum commissions and give-ups was about to be aired in a series of hearings to be conducted by the SEC.

In the weeks preceding the start of the hearings, reports began to circulate that the NYSE was prepared to "give up on give-ups" to bolster its case in defense of minimum commissions. According to a story in the *Wall Street Journal*, the Exchange's President, Robert Haack, had sent a letter to the members in which he stated: "The question the Exchange must face is whether the continuance of give-up practices will weaken the economic basis for minimum commissions."[31] When asked what this statement meant, Mr. Haack said: "All I did was ask the question about give-ups. I want some people to think about it."[32]

Less than three weeks later, on the eve of the SEC hearings, the thinking was complete: The Exchange announced that it would henceforth oppose all forms of customer-directed give-ups. In a statement to member firms, President Haack noted that "at a time when the principle of minimum commissions is being questioned, it may be difficult to defend the economic basis of [minimum commissions] if members are able to give-up or give away a substantial portion of the minimum commission."[33]

As the hearings progressed during the next several months, the SEC and the NYSE negotiated about an "acceptable" procedure for developing a volume discount for large trades. The SEC at first unveiled a discount plan that was found unacceptable by the NYSE. The Exchange reacted by putting forth a plan of its own, calling for the maintenance of the fixed minimum commission concept, combined with a volume discount on large trades. Its other key provision was the elimination of most give-ups.[34] Unfortunately, as originally worded, this provision did not seem to specify precisely what kinds of reciprocal arrangements would be outlawed and what kinds sanctioned. The regional exchanges, fearing that it might be interpreted broadly to exclude reciprocal orders as well as give-ups, petitioned the SEC to clarify matters. In particular, they argued that reciprocal orders, whereby a regional member directs stock business to the NYSE and receives a reciprocal order at a later date, were not intended to be (and should not be) prohibited.[35] As accepted by the SEC in early September, the NYSE's proposal was not interpreted to eliminate reciprocal business of this nature. In a *Wall Street Journal* article, SEC Chairman Manual Cohen was quoted as follows: "We understand that this change is intended to prohibit all forms of customer directed give-ups, but isn't meant to preclude or intervene with certain other types of reciprocal business arrangements." He mentioned that these arrangements included "noncustomer directed interdealer reciprocal business of regional exchanges."[36]

Even before the new system was to take effect on December 5, 1968, it became apparent to the NYSE that the elimination of give-ups without a ban on reciprocal arrangements would not be sufficient to stifle the competition presented by the regional exchanges. In a letter sent to exchange members about the end of November, President Haack declared that "instances are coming to light where some members and their institutional customers seek to violate the spirit if not the letter of the ban on give-ups by means of reciprocal and clearing arrangements."[37] He then went on to make this statement:

> It cannot be emphasized too strongly that the ban on give-ups was adopted as one means of strengthening and preserving the minimum commission structure, and it mustn't be circumvented through the misuse of traditional arrangements between members of this exchange and the regional exchanges.[38]

And he concluded that, although the prohibition of give-ups was not intended to abolish such arrangements, the NYSE might have to consider abolishing them "if it becomes apparent that the integrity of the minimum commission schedule is violated."[39] To obtain data on the use of "recip," as reciprocal business is called, Mr. Haack announced that the Exchange was drafting a rule that would require all member firms to file written reports of all reciprocal dealings, listing the names of the participants and the dollar amounts involved. The rule, number 382, took effect before the year was out.

Mr. Haack's concern about the use of recip was quite valid. Reports at the time stated that some mutual funds were suggesting to nonmember firms that they join a regional exchange in order to participate in reciprocal arrangements. To accommodate the additional demand for seats created thereby, several of the regional exchanges increased the number of seats authorized. The Philadelphia-Baltimore-Washington Exchange, for example, doubled the number of seats by issuing to each seat holder an additional seat.

To anyone familiar with the NYSE's traditional approach to dealing with rivals, the next step in the proceedings must have been completely predictable: On May 2, 1969, almost five months to the day following its initiation of the volume discount and the plan to eliminate give-ups, the Exchange informed the

SEC that it was considering the banning of reciprocal business arrangements between its members and those of regional stock exchanges. In a statement before the Commission, President Haack testified that nonmembers who used to thrive on give-ups had begun to join the regional exchanges to take advantage of reciprocal arrangements. The regional exchanges, he stated, were "in a way tending to become rebative mechanisms."[40]

Mr. Haack's statements about the possibility of banning reciprocal arrangements met with a cold reception from regional exchange officials. In sharply worded letters to the SEC, the presidents of the Midwest, Pacific Coast and Philadelphia-Baltimore-Washington Exchanges assailed the NYSE's proposals as an attempt to stifle competition from the regionals. Thomas Phelan, the Pacific Coast Exchange president, charged that "at a minimum it is certain that they will have a profound effect on other stock exchanges and, undoubtedly, were designed with the express intent of completely eliminating any and all competition provided by exchanges in dealing in securities also traded on the NYSE."[41] Mr. Phelan added that, if the Exchange promulgated its proposed ban on reciprocity, the Pacific Exchange would be forced to take whatever action was necessary to insure its continuing existence as a "viable institution." Among other things, he mentioned the possibility of offering memberships directly to institutions.

As of this writing, the NYSE has not banned reciprocal business. Nor have the regionals, other than Philadelphia-Baltimore-Washington, offered institutions the opportunity to become members. The NYSE, for its part, has steadfastly opposed institutional memberships. Its recent granting of permission for member firms to sell their stock publicly expressly forbids any firm not primarily engaged in the brokerage business to own a controlling share in an NYSE member firm. All this may change at any time, but for now the national and regional exchanges seem to hold a common notion that institutional memberships are not in their best interest. We shall have more to say about this matter later.

For now, however, let us close this section of the discussion by briefly mentioning two additional aspects of the NYSE's recent behavior toward potential competitors. The first concerns the NYSE's behavior toward the so-called third market, that is, the over-the-counter market in listed stocks. Like the regional exchanges, the third market has become an increasing source of competition for the NYSE. In contrast to the regional situation, however, the traditional relationship between the Exchange and the third market has been one of open antagonism rather than cooperation. There have been no reciprocal arrangements with the third market. To the contrary, the long-standing rules of the NYSE have expressly prohibited members from trading listed stocks off of the board. This prohibition, however, was challenged in the mid 1960's by M. A. Shapiro & Co., an over-the-counter dealer in bank stocks. Threatening to take legal action against the Exchange, Shapiro led a successful fight for the granting of permission to exchange members to trade with nonmembers. This permission, embodied in Exchange Rule 394, was given with admitted reluctance. According to knowledgeable Exchange members, the procedures for its application were deliberately designed to make it difficult for Exchange members to take advantage of it in practice. Quite recently, however, the Exchange moved to simplify these procedures, but only after the Justice Department submitted a memorandum to the SEC stating that its original procedure for administering Rule 394 constituted "an effective boycott in antitrust terms."[42] In other words, just as it *reluctantly* established Rule 394, it has now *reluctantly* made it more workable.

The other aspect of the NYSE's recent behavior toward competitors concerns its reactions to the appearance of automated information and trading systems, such as AutEx and Instinet. As these systems have appeared, the Exchange has consistently urged the SEC to subject them to considerable regulatory control. Last year, for example, it argued that Instinet should be classified as a national stock exchange for regulatory purposes.[43] Of course, if this classification were to be made, Instinet would, in effect, be "regulated out of business"!

The Basis for NYSE Dominance

As both a sequel to our discussion of the past relationships between the NYSE and other stock exchanges and a prelude to our comments on the future of the exchanges in the equities market, we turn now to the following question: Why has the NYSE been so pre-eminent in the stock exchange industry for such a long time? Or, put somewhat differently, what economic factors account for the NYSE's dominance of the exchange business? Doede, in his analysis of the NYSE's power base, notes that "it seems implausible, especially in a competitive economy, that not one effective competitor [of the NYSE] has been able to survive during the entire history of the United States.... It is even more puzzling when one recognizes that there have been no scarce resources, legal edicts, or technological capabilities upon which the Exchange might base its monopoly power."[44]

On the basis of the discussion in the previous section, one is inclined to conclude that the reason for the NYSE's prolonged success has been its willingness to attack its rivals vigorously at every turn. As Doede notes, however, "the restrictive business practices implemented by the NYSE were readily available to other exchanges as well."[45] The answer, therefore, must lie elsewhere.

According to Doede, the NYSE's long-standing dominance has been based on three aspects of the economics of the securities exchange business that result in increasing economies of scale, i.e., natural monopoly. One of these relates to "cost reductions associated with the geographical localization of the securities trading industry in lower Manhattan and the concomitant gains to specialization."[46] Doede argues that such reductions, "though they may have been contributory... certainly are not the mainstay of the NYSE's monopoly power."[47] We would concur in this judgment and simply add that, if anything, their value to the NYSE has declined over the years with advances in telecommunications.

The second factor Doede cites is of greater importance. It relates to Harold Demsetz's finding that "there are increasing returns associated with some aspects of individual member participation in the activity on the floor of the exchange."[48] Doede is referring, of course, to Demsetz's conclusion that "trading is subject to scale economies on the NYSE, where scale refers to trading in a particular security and not necessarily to trading in a heterogeneous bundle of securities."[49] When we reported earlier the results of empirical tests confirming Demsetz's finding that the cost of transacting declines as trading activity increases, we also argued that it is extremely difficult to accept the hypothesis that the specialists' dealership activities (as opposed to their brokerage activities) are subject to scale economies over a wide range. Moreover, we would point out that historical evidence from the bond markets suggests that increases in the pace of trading activity need not imply that trading activities are more efficiently organized on a centralized, auction basis. We shall have more to say on this point when the time comes to discuss the future role of the stock exchanges in the equities market. In any event, it should suffice to note that even Doede regards scale economies in trading an individual security as "an indirect rather than a direct source of [the Exchange's] monopoly power (where monopoly power is defined as a monopoly in the trading of many *different* securities)."[50]

This brings us to Doede's third factor, which concerns "the organization and maintenance of the exchanges themselves."[51] According to Doede, "there are economies of scale in the costs of establishing and operating securities exchanges which provide direct support for the NYSE's monopolization of the industry." These economies imply "that the optimal number of firms in the industry [in terms of private costs] is one."[52]

In support of the "natural monopoly" hypothesis, Doede presents two basic types of evidence: the first involves the ability of the NYSE to "survive and prosper"; the second is related to the behavior of costs in the stock exchange industry. The evidence related to the NYSE's ability to survive is analyzed in terms of Stigler's survivorship test, which maintains that "competition of different sizes of firms sifts out the more efficient enterprises."[53] Dividing the history of the NYSE into two periods, separated by the year 1935, Doede first demonstrates that the Exchange was able to outlast virtually all of its competitors during the earlier period. In the case of exchanges located in New York, for example, it survived all but the ASE, which, as Doede points out, was not a source of competition to the NYSE. The continued existence of the regional exchanges during the earlier period is rationalized by Doede with the observation that they were not competing with the NYSE but rather operating as providers of markets for the stocks of local companies. In the later period, when increases in multipally listed securities made the regional exchanges competitors for the NYSE and ASE, the evidence, according to Doede, also supports the survivor hypothesis. As he points out, the NYSE and ASE together "have always controlled at least 91 per cent of the total dollar volume of securities traded in the United States."[54] While we would not quarrel with the general thrust of this remark, we would make two points: First, the percentage of

trading done on the NYSE and ASE had begun to decline somewhat in the last few years of the period studied by Doede, and
it has continued to decline in recent years; second, the figures
cited by Doede do not include *all* stock-trading activities, but
only trading that took place on an exchange. This latter point
seems to us of critical significance, since an important source of
competition for the NYSE in recent years has been over-the-
counter trading in listed stocks.

Reasoning that the evidence from the survival test indicates
natural monopoly, but not the source of that monopoly, Doede
next presents an analysis of exchange cost data that provides
support for the argument that one such source is the behavior
of the costs of operating exchanges. To avoid biasing his parameters, Doede conducts the analysis in terms of total costs and
derives implications for the behavior of average costs from his
findings. In particular, he notes that because $N_{ac} = N_{tc} - 1$,
where N_{ac} is the elasticity of average costs with respect to output
and N_{tc} is the elasticity of total costs, the results for total cost
data have "direct implications for both the slope and elasticity
of the average cost function."[55]

Doede assumes that the total cost elasticity is constant throughout the output range of the firms in the industry, thus giving
him the equation

$$TC = Aq^B \qquad (8.1)$$

where q represents output and A and B are the parameters to
be estimated. Since this relationship implies that $N_{tc} = B$, the
elasticity of total cost is estimated with the following simple
linear regression:

$$\log_e TC = \log_e A + B \log_e q + u \qquad (8.2)$$

To estimate this relationship, Doede uses paired observations
of cost and volume for the five largest stock exchanges for the
period 1955–65. Because of the problem of developing a sample
size sufficient to permit meaningful estimation, he pools the
resulting fifty observations. His results are presented in Table
8–2. The over-all fit of the equation is excellent, and the coefficient for the output variable is highly significant. More important,
the fact that the coefficient is less than one leads Doede to
conclude that the elasticity of average costs, $N_{tc} - 1$, is negative,
i.e., that the long-run average cost is negatively sloped. He
concludes, therefore, that the results of this test lent "further

TABLE 8–2

Estimation of Total Cost Elasticity For Five Largest Stock Exchanges 1955–65*

Regression Coefficients, Standard Errors and t Statistics	R^2	N	t
$\log_e TC = -2.15 + 0.752 \log_e q$ (0.493) (0.021) -4.36 34.50	0.961	50	-11.27

KEY: R^2 = Coefficients of multiple determinants; N = number of observations; t = value of the t test to determine if the regression coefficient of $\log_e q$ is significantly different from one.

*Adapted from Robert W. Doede, "The Monopoly Power of the New York Stock Exchange" (unpublished doctoral thesis, University of Chicago, 1967), p. 41.

support to the general hypothesis that the monopoly power of the NYSE is due to economies of scale."[56]

As an added feature, Doede presents a graphical analysis of the cost data underlying his regression results. These data are reproduced in Figure 24. According to Doede, "the main point brought out by the graph, which was hidden in the regression

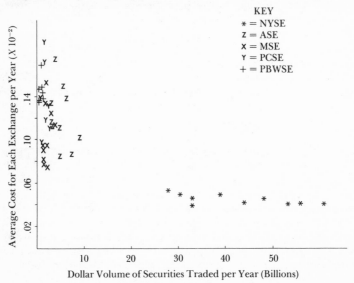

FIGURE 24 Average Costs of the Five Largest Stock Exchanges (1955–65).

analysis, is that over the ten year period none of the four smaller exchanges were [*sic*] ever able to operate as efficiently as the NYSE."[57]

Summary

In the introduction to this chapter we stated that our purpose was to explore two related questions: (1) What is the relationship between the NYSE and other stock exchanges, and (2) why has the NYSE been able to maintain a dominant position in the exchange industry for nearly 200 years? The answer to the first question that emerges from our analysis of the NYSE's dealings with other stock exchanges is that its relationships have been friendly and helpful so long as these exchanges were not viewed as competitors. In the case of the ASE, for example, the relationship has clearly been of this nature. When a stock exchange has appeared to represent a threat to the NYSE, on the other hand, the Exchange has consistently taken steps to eliminate this threat. In general, its activities in this regard have been extremely successful.

As far as the second question is concerned, the answer given by Doede, and subscribed to by us, is that the Exchange's basic monopoly power derives from economies of scale in exchange operations. It is also dependent, however, on the presence of some economies of scale in making a market for a particular stock; for in the absence of those economies the *raison d'être* of the exchange approach to market-making would cease to exist. This latter point is of extreme importance, as we shall see in the next chapter, which speculates about future developments in the structure of the exchange industry.

Notes

1. R. W. Doede, "The Monopoly Power of the New York Stock Exchange" (unpublished doctoral dissertation, University of Chicago, 1967), p. 6.
2. Edmund C. Stedman, ed., *The New York Stock Exchange* 1 (New York: New York Stock Exchange Historical Company, 1905): 65.
3. Doede, "Monopoly Power of NYSE," p. 9.
4. Stedman, ed., *New York Stock Exchange*, 1: 66.
5. H. B. Neil, *The Inside Story of the Stock Exchange* (New York: B. C. Forbes, 1950), p. 56.
6. Doede, "Monopoly Power of NYSE," p. 10.
7. *Ibid.*, p. 11.
8. *Ibid.*, p. 13.

9. U.S., Congress, House of Representatives, Subcommittee of the Committee on Banking and Currency, *Report of the Committee Appointed to Investigate the Concentration of Control of Money and Credit* (Washington, D.C., 1913) I: 387.
10. Doede, "Monopoly Power of NYSE," p. 16.
11. *Ibid.*
12. James E. Walter, *The Role of the Regional Security Exchange* (Berkeley and Los Angeles: University of California Press, 1957), p. 25.
13. U.S., 84th Congress, 1st Sess., Senate Committee on Banking and Currency, *Stock Market Study: Hearings on Factors Affecting Buying and Selling of Equity Securities* (Washington, D.C.: Government Printing Office, 1955), p. 241.
14. Walter, *Role of Regional Security Exchange*, p. 31.
15. *Report of the Special Study of the Securities Markets of the Securities and Exchange Commission*, U.S., 88th Cong., 1st Sess., House of Representatives Document 95 (hereafter: *Special Study*) (Washington, D.C.: Government Printing Office, 1965), p. 923.
16. Doede, "Monopoly Power of NYSE," p. 18.
17. *Special Study*, p. 923.
18. *Ibid.*, p. 937.
19. "Are 'Give-ups' on the Way Out?" *Business Week*, January 14, 1967, p. 125.
20. *Wall Street Journal*, January 5, 1967, p. 3.
21. *Wall Street Journal*, February 6, 1967, p. 6.
22. *Ibid.*
23. *Wall Street Journal*, May 5, 1967, p. 28.
24. *Wall Street Journal*, November 22, 1967, p. 4.
25. *Wall Street Journal*, January 3, 1968, p. 3.
26. *Ibid.*
27. *Ibid.*
28. *Ibid.*
29. *Wall Street Journal*, January 26, 1968, p. 26.
30. SEC Release No. 8239: "Inquiry into Proposal to Modify the Commission Rate Structure of the New York Stock Exchange: Comments of the United States Department of Justice."
31. *Wall Street Journal*, June 11, 1968, p. 3.
32. *Ibid.*
33. *Wall Street Journal*, June 28, 1968, p. 28.
34. *Wall Street Journal*, August 9, 1968, p. 11.
35. *Wall Street Journal*, August 26, 1968, p. 4.
36. *Wall Street Journal*, September 5, 1968, p. 21.
37. *Wall Street Journal*, January 26, 1969, p. 27.
38. *Ibid.*
39. *Ibid.*
40. *Wall Street Journal*, May 5, 1969, p. 6.
41. *Wall Street Journal*, June 10, 1969, p. 7.
42. *The New York Times*, May 13, 1970, p. 36.
43. *Wall Street Journal*, September 24, 1969, p. 38.
44. Doede, "Monopoly Power of NYSE," p. 21.
45. *Ibid.*
46. *Ibid.*, p. 22.
47. *Ibid.*, p. 23.
48. *Ibid.*

49. *Ibid.*
50. *Ibid.*
51. *Ibid.*
52. *Ibid.*
53. George J. Stigler, "The Economies of Scale," *Journal of Law and Economics* 1 (October, 1958): at 55.
54. Doede, "Monopoly Power of NYSE," p. 35.
55. *Ibid.*, p. 38.
56. *Ibid.*, p. 42.
57. *Ibid.*, p. 44.

9 The Future Structure of the Equities Market: Some Tentative Conclusions

At one point in his analysis of the NYSE's monopoly position, Doede comments that in spite of the absence of legal edicts, scarce resources, or technological capabilities, the Exchange's power was greater in 1965 than it had been 100 years earlier. Indeed, Doede concludes that the NYSE has represented "one of the most resilient and effective long-run monopolies in the history of the United States."[1] In view of the fact that these observations are hardly more than three years old, the reader might easily anticipate that the theme of this, the final chapter, would be a prediction of even greater success for the NYSE in years to come. The tone of current discussions of the future structure of the stock market, however, suggests that a very different theme may be more appropriate. Consider, for example, the following passage from a recent article, provocatively entitled "Can the New York Stock Exchange Survive?":

> For many years, the New York Stock Exchange was able to prosper, secure in the knowledge that its high walls and wide moats protected the privileges of the members and kept the customers at arm's length. But suddenly, the walls began to crumble and the moats to dry up, posing an awesome *threat to the very existence of the Exchange itself.*[2]

Why should the NYSE, having survived through war and peace, prosperity, and depression for a period approaching 200 years, now find its future existence threatened? Beyond this, what would become of the regional exchanges if the NYSE were to fall on hard times? Would they become the Big Board's beneficiaries, or would they too suffer? And, if the latter, where would trading in equities take place? In the pages that follow we shall try to provide some tentative answers to these questions, leaving it to historians to write the definitive ones.

Why the NYSE Is Not Threatened

After having just finished the discussion in Chapter 8 of Doede's analysis of the NYSE's power base, the astute reader might conclude that the most obvious threat to the Exchange's future existence would come from an erosion of the economies of scale associated with operating a stock exchange. While such a development would, no doubt, present a grave threat to the NYSE, there is little evidence to support the argument that the relative cost positions of the various major exchanges have changed materially in recent years. As the data in Figure 25 indicate, neither the ASE nor any of the three largest regional exchanges has been able to reduce its average cost of operations to the level achieved by the NYSE in the last four years. In short,

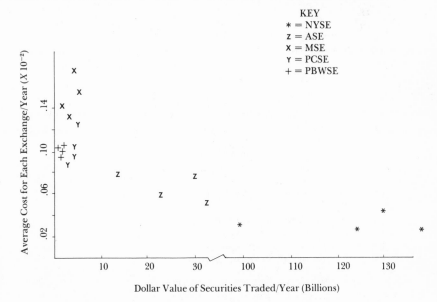

FIGURE 25 Average Costs of Five Largest Stock Exchanges (1966–69).

whatever the cause of the NYSE's current problems, it has not been a sudden shift in the cost structure of providing exchange services!

A somewhat more plausible argument is that the Exchange has recently lost its ability to turn its inherent cost advantages into monopoly profits. The major premise behind this argument is that institutional investors, supported in some measure by the SEC and the Department of Justice, have made it increasingly difficult for the Exchange to maintain a commission structure that can yield profits of the kind it earned when the market was dominated by small investors. According to this argument, the "high walls and wide moats protected the privileges of the members and kept the customers at arm's length" only so long as the "customers" did not have sufficient power to challenge the minimum commission system. Once the institutions achieved the power to challenge the system, however, "the walls began to crumble and the moats started to dry up."

If the threat facing the NYSE were as simple and straight-forward as this argument implies, the real question would appear to be: Will the NYSE *permit* itself to survive? Or, put somewhat differently: Will the Exchange reduce commissions on block trades to the point where the institutions no longer view them as exorbitant? Presumably, if it did so, the threat posed by the institutions would disappear, thus assuring the Exchange of a long, if somewhat less profitable, life. As one partner of a member firm recently stated:

> All this [talk] about disaster is a myth. It really is. . . . I just can't imagine that all these institutions will all rush out and set up broker-age houses and provide themselves with all the services we are giving them, like research, clearing, execution, a feeling for the market, and block positioning. The only reason some of them are doing a little of this now is because our rates for their trades are too high. But if the rates were reasonable, why should the [Prudential Life Insurance Company] or anyone else bother. Companies don't go out and place their own ads, do they? They hire ad agencies who have the expertise, and they pay them a fair, reasonable fee. I mean, why does anyone go to a professional. . . . Look, I am a professional market-maker, and I'm a good one, and no matter what happens, the institutions are going to need me.[3]

Indeed, following this logic just one step further, it might even be argued that lower commissions would strengthen the NYSE's relative position in the equities market by stemming the flow of business to the regional exchanges. Doede, for example, suggests that if the NYSE were to lower its rates to the "competitive" level, "the other exchanges would probably be forced out of business, since they would not be able to operate profitably. . ."[4]

The Real Threat

Unfortunately for the NYSE, the problems created by the growth of institutional investors go well beyond those concerned with the level of commission rates. At the risk of oversimplifying matters, we would argue that the continuous auction process, the backbone of the exchange method of market-making, is simply not well suited to the trading needs of the institutions. What is more, innovations having to do with commissions cannot eliminate its deficiencies in this regard.

At the heart of the continuous auction system is the stock exchange specialist who performs the dual functions of broker and dealer. As a broker, he holds and executes public orders forwarded to him; as a dealer, he stands ready to take positions to iron out temporary imbalances in the inflow of orders. As we have already demonstrated, the specialist can perform his dealer role more effectively when there is a steady flow of well-balanced buy and sell orders. When the flow of orders begins to dry up, when it becomes one-sided, or when it entails a significant amount of "lumpiness" (block trading), the specialist's task is soon complicated. The problems posed by thin markets are well understood, and the Exchange attempts to deal with them by excluding issues with insufficient trading volume. The problems posed by block trading, however, have not been dealt with adequately by the Exchange. Moreover, there appears to be little that it can really do to deal with the problems: The history of the bond market and the government securities market would seem to suggest that in the presence of blocks, the over-the-counter market simply has inherent advantages over the exchange system—the most important one being its negotiated character. Donald Weeden, a prominent over-the-counter dealer, recently told the SEC:

> The hard truth is that the economic interests of the institutional investor are better served by a negotiated market than by an auction market. The institutional investor prefers to control his own order;

he wants direct access to the market-makers. ... The increase in block business has drastically reduced the effectiveness of the specialist, *not so much because the specialist lacks capital*, but because he has lost contact with the market.[5]

We have italicized the phrase, "not so much because the specialist lacks capital," because it highlights an important point concerning the long run prospects of the NYSE in the age of block trading. In some quarters it has become fashionable to argue that the Exchange's difficulty in dealing with blocks would be solved if only the specialists were better capitalized. The inadequacy of specialists' capital is a particularly popular subject among advocates of public ownership of stock exchange member firms. Consider, for example, the following statement from a recent issue of *Fortune*:

> The proponents of public ownership have argued that the street needs public capital. ... The huge increase in institutional trading has created a situation in which many specialists are undercapitalized. They simply cannot in all cases absorb the stock that is available for sale.[6]

There is a real question, however, whether the addition of more capital to the specialist system would make it possible for the Exchange to prosper. As Donald Weeden put it, it is not just that the specialist lacks capital, he has "lost touch with the market." Mr. Weeden's point is that the only real source of marketability for an institutional seller is an institutional buyer. Yet the specialist, being forbidden to solicit orders and lacking a line of communication to the institutions, is not in touch with potential buyers. And, under the circumstances, it would be foolish for him to take on some block positions, even if he had the capital to do so.

In recent years a growing number of stock exchange member firms have come to sense, if not to understand fully, the difficulty of accommodating block trading within the continuous auction market. In response, they have developed block-trading capacities similar to those possessed by over-the-counter dealers in listed securities and dealers in governments.[7] Not being constrained by the rules governing the specialist's activities, and possessing direct communications with institutions, they can attempt to develop demand or supply where it does not appear to exist. Of course, when offsetting orders cannot be found, they must commit their own capital; even in these instances, however, they can continue to "shop" a block aggressively, while the specialist must wait for the incoming flow of orders to "bail him out."

There are some signs that the major stock exchanges are attempting to remedy the deficiencies of the auction market by attempting to enlist the support of member firms that make markets off the floor of the Exchange. Ralph Saul, President of the ASE, recently made the following comments concerning this development:

> To better serve the needs of large investors and to help guard against diminishing the value of the small investors' holdings by the actions of a few portfolio managers, the [American Stock] Exchange is attracting more capital into its specialist system. One method we have used is to link specialists on our floor with large member firms having capital and market-making capability. Several well-known "block" positioning firms with large capital resources are now specializing on the floor of the American Stock Exchange.[8]

It is doubtful, however, that this approach to solving the Exchange's problems will work in the long run. Why, after all, should firms having "capital and market-making capability" be interested in becoming specialists when they can make just as good a market, perhaps even a better one, in the over-the-counter market? Put somewhat differently, why should they bring their negotiated trading techniques into the auction market when these techniques work best in an over-the-counter environment? What, in short, does the Exchange have to offer them?

Along these same lines, we might well ask why these firms even continue to maintain memberships in the major exchanges at the present time? One argument is that they stay with the Exchange in order to make use of the specialist system to work out positions that are taken when crosses cannot be found. This argument would make sense if members were the only dealers who could make use of the specialists' services in this regard; nonmembers, however, can also use the floor of the Exchange in working out positions taken in the process of servicing institutional customers. The argument's thrust, then, must be based not on members' ability to use the specialist system, but rather on their ability to use it without having to pay nonmember commissions. In other words, it must be that it is the prohibitive cost of the system to nonmembers that encourages block traders to stay with the Exchange at this time.

Staying with the Exchange on these terms, however, represents a far different situation from the one that existed when firms held seats in order to funnel all of their business to the floor for servicing. In the "old days" the member firm valued its seat because it gave it access to "the" marketplace. Today, in contrast, the block positioning firm values a membership primarily because a seat provides it with cheap access to an ancillary source of marketability. More and more, then, the floor is becoming an adjunct to the block positioning firm, rather than vice versa.

In terms of Doede's framework of analysis, the point we are making is that the NYSE's problem results from a decline in the importance of the economies associated with centralizing trading in individual common stocks. As we noted in the preceding chapter, one of Doede's premises is that the economies associated with centralizing trading represent a necessary but not sufficient basis for the NYSE's dominance in the exchange industry. In the days when most trades were for a few round lots there was little question that such economies contributed to the Exchange's power base. In the age of block trades, however, the inherent advantages of the central auction market for an individual stock are more questionable. Without these advantages, however, the economies of operating an exchange become relatively unimportant: the threat to the NYSE is not other exchanges but rather the over-the-counter market.

From an historical perspective, it can readily be seen that the major threat to the NYSE's economic power has always come from the over-the-counter market rather than rival stock exchanges. In his study of the NYSE, Doede notes that the Exchange's original "constitution," the Buttonwood Tree Agreement, "represented a successful move by a group of brokers to monopolize dealing in Federal securities created by the funding of the debt by the Continental Congress."[9] Today, however, the Exchange does almost none of the trading in U.S. Government obligations. It lost this business several decades ago, not to the regional exchanges or the American Exchange, but to the over-the-counter market. As we saw in Chapter 3, it lost the business in governments because the over-the-counter market was better suited to the trading conditions created by heavy institutional interest. In the words of the

Treasury–Federal Reserve study of the government securities, the movement of trading from the Exchange represented a "natural evolution."[10]

Thus far the thrust of our argument has been that the primary threat to the major exchanges comes from the over-the-counter market. We might then ask where this leaves the regional exchanges? The answer would appear to depend on the NYSE's policy in regard to commissions. If it were to move the commission structure to the competitive level, it would almost certainly "monopolize" the trading that does not take place in the over-the-counter market. This would include the trading done by rank-and-file investors as well as the transactions made by the over-the-counter firms in the process of evening out their positions. On the other hand, if the Exchange were to attempt to maintain a price somewhat higher than the competitive level, it would provide an umbrella under which the regional exchanges could, perhaps, survive. In either event, however, the future of the regional exchanges, like that of the major exchanges, seems destined to be somewhat less than rosy.

As far as the institutional investors are concerned, there seems to be little reason to expect them to find membership in stock exchanges particularly worthwhile in the long run. The point is not that they will find memberships unrewarding because commissions will eventually fall to the competitive level; rather, it is that the exchanges will not be able to do their trades as effectively as the block trading over-the-counter firms. The recent growth in the third market and the "fourth market" indicates this is already the case in many circumstances. One writer recently noted:

> Often unable to find liquidity on the exchange floor, the institutional trader goes to the [over-the-counter] block house. [If] the block house [is] a member, it dutifully brings the trade to the floor [for execution], but its ability to do business depends not so much on its access to the floor as its ability and willingness to provide liquidity. Exchange membership, from the institution's standpoint, thus becomes progressively more irrelevant in making a decision on where to take a block.[11]

Confirming this argument, a recent survey of twenty-five major institutional investors showed that fewer than 20 per cent were "anxious" to "moderately interested" in the question of becoming a member of the NYSE.

A Concluding Comment

In sum, regardless of the particular form it takes, the stock market of the future will probably be a refined version of the type of market now being made by third market dealers and block trading Exchange members. The essential feature of this market is its emphasis on negotiated dealings between institutional investors and broker-dealers who possess the capital and information systems to put together "instant secondaries." In such a market, the specialist, or someone very much like him, can continue to make an auction market for rank-and-file investors, much as is now done for the small investor in corporate bonds.[12] In addition, he can assist the block positioning firms in working out their positions. But he is no longer "the" market-maker, as he was prior to the age of block trading.

Notes

1. R. W. Doede, "The Monopoly Power of the New York Stock Exchange" (unpublished doctoral dissertation, University of Chicago, 1967), p. 20.
2. Chris Welles, "Can the New York Stock Exchange Survive?" *Institutional Investor,* June, 1970, p. 25. Emphasis added.
3. *Ibid.*, p. 82.
4. Doede, "Monopoly Power of NYSE," p. 97.
5. Letter of Donald Weeden to the Securities and Exchange Commission, December 19, 1969. Emphasis added.
6. Carol J. Loomis, "They're Tearing Up Wall Street," *Fortune,* August 1, 1969, pp. 88–91 ff.
7. For an interesting discussion of block trading, see "The Toughest Kid in Block Trading," *Business Week,* October 4, 1969, pp. 114–116.
8. Ralph Saul, "New Perspectives in the Securities," *Financial Executive,* January 1970, p. 40.
9. Doede, "Monopoly Power of NYSE," p. 6.
10. *Treasury-Federal Reserve Study of the Government Securities Market* (Washington, D.C.: n.p., 1959), p. 26.
11. Welles, "Can the NYSE Survive?," p. 29.
12. It may well be that this type of trading would lend itself to computerization similar to that which is now being used for trade in odd lots on the Pacific Coast Stock Exchange.